Karl Popper

UNENDED QUEST
An Intellectual Autobiography

FONTANA/COLLINS

First published as 'Autobiography of Karl Popper' in *The Philosophy of Karl Popper* in *The Library of Living Philosophers*, ed. Paul Arthur Schilpp, by the Open Court Publishing Co., Illinois, 1974
First published in this revised edition by Fontana 1976
Second Impression October 1976
Third Impression June 1977

Made and printed in Great Britain by
William Collins Sons & Co Ltd Glasgow

The photograph of Sir Karl Popper on the back cover is by Lotte Meitner-Graf, and is reproduced by permission

Contents

Contents

Acknowledgements

This Autobiography was originally written to form a part of the two volume work *The Philosophy of Karl Popper*, edited by Paul Arthur Schilpp, and published as volumes 14/I and 14/II of *The Library of Living Philosophers* (La Salle, Illinois: The Open Court Publishing Company, 1974). Like all the contributions to this Library, the autobiography is due to the initiative of Professor Schilpp, the founder of the Library. I am most grateful to him for everything he did in this connection and for his infinite patience in waiting for my autobiography from 1963 to 1969.

I am deeply grateful to Ernst Gombrich, Bryan Magee, Arne Petersen, Jeremy Shearmur, Mrs Pamela Watts, and most of all to David Miller and to my wife, for their patience in reading and improving my manuscript.

Many problems arose in the course of the production of the original edition. It was only after the galley proofs had been corrected that, for technical reasons, the decision had to be made to collect the notes at the end of each contribution. (This is not unimportant because the manuscript was prepared on the understanding that the notes would be printed as footnotes on the bottom of the relevant pages.)

The work done during the production of the original volumes in *The Library of Living Philosophers* by Professor Eugene Freeman, Mrs Ann Freeman and by their editorial staff was immense, and I wish to thank them again at this place for their help and their care.

The text of the present edition has been revised. A few small additions have been made, and one passage has been removed from the text, and has been incorporated in note 20.

Penn, Buckinghamshire
May, 1975

K.R.P.

> What to leave out and what to put in? That's the problem.
>
> HUGH LOFTING, *Doctor Dolittle's Zoo.*

1. Omniscience and Fallibility

When I was twenty I became apprenticed to an old master cabinetmaker in Vienna whose name was Adalbert Pösch, and I worked with him from 1922 to 1924, not long after the First World War. He looked exactly like Georges Clemenceau, but he was a very mild and kind man. After I had gained his confidence he would often, when we were alone in his workshop, give me the benefit of his inexhaustible store of knowledge. Once he told me that he had worked for many years on various models of a perpetual motion machine, adding musingly: "They say you can't make it; but once it's been made they'll talk different!" ("Da sag'n s' dass ma' so was net mach'n kann; aber wann amal eina ein's g'macht hat, dann wer'n s' schon anders red'n!") A favourite practice of his was to ask me a historical question and to answer it himself when it turned out that I did not know the answer (although I, his pupil, was a University student—a fact of which he was very proud). "And do you know", he would ask, "who invented topboots? You don't? It was Wallenstein, the Duke of Friedland, during the Thirty Years War." After one or two even more difficult questions, posed by himself and triumphantly answered by himself, my master would say with modest pride: "There, you can ask me whatever you like: *I know everything.*" ("Da können S' mi' frag'n was Sie woll'n: *ich weiss alles.*")

I believe I learned more about the theory of knowledge from my dear omniscient master Adalbert Pösch than from any other of my teachers. None did so much to turn me into a disciple of Socrates. For it was my master who taught me not only how very little I knew but also that any wisdom to which I might ever aspire could consist only in realizing more fully the infinity of my ignorance.

These and other thoughts which belonged to the field of epistemology were occupying my mind while I was working on a writing desk. We had at that time a large order for thirty mahogany kneehole desks, with many, many drawers. I fear that the quality of some of these desks, and especially their French polish, suffered badly from my preoccupation with epistemology. This suggested to my master and also brought home to me that I was too ignorant and too fallible for this kind of work. So I made up my mind that on completing my apprenticeship in October, 1924, I should look for something easier than making mahogany writing desks. For a year I took up social work with neglected children, which I had done before and found very difficult. Then, after five more years spent mainly in studying and writing, I married and settled down happily as a schoolteacher. This was in 1930.

At that time I had no professional ambitions beyond schoolteaching, though I got a little tired of it after I had published my *Logik der Forschung*, late in 1934. I therefore felt myself very fortunate when in 1937 I had an opportunity to give up schoolteaching and to become a professional philosopher. I was almost thirty-five and I thought that I had now finally solved the problem of how to work on a writing desk and yet be preoccupied with epistemology.

2. Childhood Memories

Although most of us know the date and the place of our birth—mine is July 28, 1902, at a place called Himmelhof in the Ober St Veit district of Vienna—few know when and how their intellectual life began. So far as my philosophical development goes, I do remember some of its early stages. But it certainly started later than my emotional and moral development.

As a child I was, I suspect, somewhat puritanical, even priggish, though this attitude was perhaps tempered by the feeling that I had no right to sit in judgement on anybody except myself. Among my earliest memories are feelings of admiration for my elders and betters, for example for my cousin Eric Schiff, whom I greatly admired for being one year older than I, for his tidiness and, especially, for his good looks: gifts which I always regarded as important and unattainable.

One often hears it said nowadays that children are cruel by nature. I do not believe it. I was, as a child, what Americans might call a "softy", and compassion is one of the strongest emotions I remember. It was the main component of my first experience of falling in love, which happened when I was four or five years old. I was taken to a kindergarten, and there was a beautiful little girl who was blind. My heart was torn, both by the charm of her smile and by the tragedy of her blindness. It was love at first sight. I have never forgotten her, though I saw her only once, and only for an hour or two. I was not sent to the kindergarten again; perhaps my mother noticed how much I was upset.

The sight of abject poverty in Vienna was one of the main problems which agitated me when I was still a small child—so much so that it was almost always at the back of my mind. Few people now living in one of the Western democracies know what poverty meant at the beginning of this century: men, women, and children suffering from hunger, cold and hopelessness. But we children could not help. We could do no more than ask for a few coppers to give to some poor people.

It was only after many years that I found that my father had worked hard and long to do something about this situation, although he had never talked about these activities. He worked on two committees which were running homes for the homeless: a freemasons' lodge of which he was for many years the Master ran a home for orphans, while the other committee (not masonic) built and administered a large institution for homeless adults and families. (An inmate of the latter institution—the *"Asyl für Obdachlose"*—was Adolf Hitler during his early stay in Vienna.)

This work of my father's received unexpected recognition when the old Emperor made him a knight of the Order of Francis Joseph (*Ritter des Franz Josef Ordens*), which must have been not only a surprise but a problem. For although my father—like most Austrians—respected the Emperor, he was a radical liberal of the school of John Stuart Mill, and not at all a supporter of the government.

As a freemason he was even a member of a society which at that time was declared illegal by the Austrian government, though not by the Hungarian government of Francis Joseph. Thus the freemasons often met beyond the Hungarian border, in Pressburg (now Bratislava in Czechoslovakia). The Austro-Hungarian Empire, though a constitutional monarchy, was not ruled by its two Parliaments: they had no power to dismiss the two Prime Ministers or the two Cabinets, not even by a vote of censure. The Austrian Parliament, it would seem, was even weaker than the English Parliament under William and Mary, if such a comparison can be made at all. There were few checks and balances, and there was severe political censorship; for example, a brilliant political satire, *Anno 1903,* which my father had written under the pen name Siegmund Karl Pflug, was seized by the police on its publication in 1904 and remained on the Index of prohibited books until 1918.

Nevertheless, in those days before 1914 there was an atmosphere of liberalism in Europe west of Czarist Russia; an atmosphere which also pervaded Austria and which was destroyed, for ever it now seems, by the First World War. The University of Vienna, with its many teachers of real eminence, had a great degree of freedom and autonomy. So had the theatres, which were important in the life of Vienna—almost as important as music. The Emperor kept aloof from all political parties and did not identify himself with any of his governments. Indeed he followed, almost to the letter, the precept given by Søren Kierkegaard to Christian VIII of Denmark.[1]

3. Early Influences

The atmosphere in which I was brought up was decidedly bookish. My father Dr Simon Siegmund Carl Popper, like his two brothers, was a doctor of law of the University of Vienna. He had a large library, and there were books everywhere—with the exception of the dining room, in which there was a Bösendorfer concert grand and many volumes of Bach, Haydn, Mozart, Beethoven, Schubert, and Brahms. My father, who was the same age as Sigmund Freud—whose works he possessed, and had read on publication—was a barrister and solicitor. About my mother Jenny Popper, *née* Schiff, I shall say more when I come to speak about music. My father was an accomplished speaker. I heard him plead in court only once, in 1924 or 1925, when I myself was the defendant. The case was, in my opinion, clear-cut.[2] I had therefore not asked my father to defend me, and was embarassed when he insisted. But the utter simplicity, clarity, and sincerity of his speech impressed me greatly.

My father worked hard in his profession. He had been a

friend and partner of the last liberal Burgomaster of Vienna, Dr Carl Grübl, and had taken over his law office. This office was part of the large apartment in which we lived, in the very heart of Vienna, opposite the central door of the cathedral (*Stephanskirche*). He worked long hours in this office, but he was really more of a scholar than a lawyer. He was a historian (the historical part of his library was considerable) and was interested especially in the Hellenistic period, and in the eighteenth and nineteenth centuries. He wrote poetry, and translated Greek and Latin verse into German. (He rarely spoke of these matters. It was by sheer accident that I found one day some light-hearted verse translations of Horace. His special gifts were a light touch and a strong sense of humour.) He was greatly interested in philosophy. I still possess his Plato, Bacon, Descartes, Spinoza, Locke, Kant, Schopenhauer, and Eduard von Hartmann; J. S. Mill's collected works, in a German translation edited by Theodor Gomperz (whose *Greek Thinkers* he valued highly); most of Kierkegaard's, Nietzche's, and Eucken's works, and those of Ernst Mach; Fritz Mauthner's *Critique of Language* and Otto Weininger's *Geschlecht und Charakter* (both of which seem to have had some influence on Wittgenstein);[3] and translations of most of Darwin's books. (Pictures of Darwin and of Schopenhauer hung in his study.) There were, of course, the standard authors of German, French, English, Russian, and Scandinavian literature. But one of his main interests was in social problems. He not only possessed the chief works of Marx and Engels, of Lassalle, Karl Kautsky, and Eduard Bernstein, but also those of the critics of Marx: Böhm-Bawerk, Carl Menger, Anton Menger, P. A. Kropotkin, and Josef Popper-Lynkeus (apparently a distant relative of mine, since he was born in Kolin, the little town from which my paternal grandfather came). The library had also a pacifist section, with books by Bertha von Suttner, Friedrich Wilhelm Förster, and Norman Angell.

Thus books were part of my life long before I could read them. The first book which made a big and lasting impression on me was read by my mother to my two sisters and to me, shortly before I learned to read. (I was the youngest of three children.) It was a book for children by the great Swedish writer Selma Lagerlöf, in a beautiful German translation (*Wunderbare Reise des kleinen Nils Holgersson mit den Wildgänsen;* the English translation is entitled *The Wonderful*

Adventures of Nils). For many, many, years I reread this book at least once a year; and in the course of time I probably read everything by Selma Lagerlöf more than once. I do not like her first novel, *Gösta Berling*, though it is no doubt very remarkable. But every single one of her other books remains, for me, a masterpiece.

Learning to read, and to a lesser degree, to write, are of course *the* major events in one's intellectual development. There is nothing to compare with it, since very few people (Helen Keller is the great exception) can remember what it meant for them to learn to speak. I shall be for ever grateful to my first teacher, Emma Goldberger, who taught me the three R's. They are, I think, the only essentials a child has to be taught; and some children do not even need to be taught in order to learn these. Everything else is atmosphere, and learning through reading and thinking.

Apart from my parents, my first schoolteacher, and Selma Lagerlöf, the greatest influence on my early intellectual development was, I suppose, my lifelong friend Arthur Arndt, a relative of Ernst Moritz von Arndt who had been one of the famous founding fathers of German nationalism in the period of the Napoleonic wars.[4] Arthur Arndt was an ardent anti-nationalist. Though of German descent, he was born in Moscow, where he also spent his youth. He was my senior by about twenty years—he was near thirty when first I met him in 1912. He had studied engineering at the University of Riga, and had been one of the student leaders during the abortive Russian revolution of 1905. He was a socialist and at the same time a strong opponent of the Bolsheviks, some of whose leaders he knew personally from 1905. He described them as the Jesuits of socialism, that is, capable of sacrificing innocent men, even of their own persuasion, because great ends justified all means. Arndt was not a convinced Marxist, yet he thought that Marx had been the most important theorist of socialism so far. He found me very willing to listen to socialist ideas; nothing, I felt, could be more important than to end poverty.

Arndt was also deeply interested (much more so than my father was) in the movement which had been started by the pupils of Ernst Mach and of Wilhelm Ostwald, a society whose members called themselves "The Monists". (There was a connection with the famous American journal, *The Monist*, to which Mach was a contributor.) They were interested in science, epistemology, and in what nowadays would be called the philosophy of science. Among the Monists of Vienna the "half-socialist" Popper-Lynkeus had a considerable following, which included Otto Neurath.

The first book on socialism I read (probably under the influence of my friend Arndt—my father was reluctant to influence me) was Edward Bellamy's *Looking Backward*. I must have read it when I was about twelve, and it made a great impression on me. Arndt took me on Sunday excursions, arranged by the Monists, to the Vienna Woods, and on these occasions he explained and discussed Marxism and Darwinism. No doubt most of this was far beyond my grasp. But it was interesting and exciting.

One of these Sunday excursions by the Monists was on June 28, 1914. Towards evening, as we approached the outskirts of Vienna, we heard that the Archduke Franz Ferdinand, heir apparent of Austria, had been assassinated in Sarajevo. A week or so after this my mother took me and my two sisters for our summer holidays to Alt-Aussee, a village not far from Salzburg. And there, on my twelfth birthday, I received a letter from my father in which he said that he was sorry not to be able to come for my birthday, as he had intended, "because, unfortunately, there is war" ("*denn es ist leider Krieg*"). Since this letter arrived on the day of the actual declaration of war between Austria-Hungary and Serbia, it seems that my father realized that it was coming.

4. The First World War

I was twelve, then, when the First World War broke out; and the war years, and their aftermath, were in every respect decisive for my intellectual development. They made me critical of accepted opinions, especially political opinions.

Of course, few people knew at that time what war meant. There was a deafening clamour of patriotism throughout the country in which even some of the members of our previously far from warmongering circle participated. My father was sad and depressed. Yet even Arndt could see something hopeful. He hoped for a democratic revolution in Russia.

Afterwards I often remembered these days. Before the war, many members of our circle had discussed political theories which were decidedly pacifist, and at least highly critical of the existing order, and had been critical of the alliance between Austria and Germany, and of the expansionist policy of Austria in the Balkans, especially in Serbia. I was staggered by the fact that they could suddenly become supporters of that very policy.

Today I understand these things a little better. It was not only the pressure of public opinion; it was the problem of divided loyalties. And there was also fear—the fear of violent measures which, in war, have to be taken by the authorities against dissenters, since no sharp line can be drawn between dissent and treason. But at the time I was greatly puzzled. I knew, of course, nothing about what had happened to the socialist parties of Germany and France: how their internationalism disintegrated. (A marvellous description of these events can be found in the last volumes of Roger Martin du Gard's *Les Thibaults*.)[5]

For a few weeks, under the influence of war propaganda in my school, I became a little infected by the general mood. In the autumn of 1914 I wrote a silly poem "Celebrating the Peace", in which the assumption was expressed that the Austrians and the Germans had successfully resisted the attack (I then believed that "we" had been attacked) and which described, and celebrated, the restoration of peace. Though it was not a very warlike poem I soon became thoroughly ashamed of the assumption that "we" had been attacked. I realized that the Austrian attack on Serbia and the German attack on Belgium were terrible things and that a huge apparatus of propaganda was trying to persuade us that they had been justified. In the winter of 1915-16 I became convinced—under the influence, no doubt, of prewar socialist propaganda—that the cause of Austria and Germany was a bad cause and that we deserved to lose the war (and therefore that we should lose it, as I naively argued).

One day, I think it must have been in 1916, I approached my father with a reasonably well-prepared statement of this position, but found him less responsive than I expected. He was more doubtful than I about the rights and wrongs of the war, and also about its outcome. In both respects he was, of course, correct, and obviously I had seen these things in an oversimplified manner. Yet he took my views very seriously, and after a lengthy discussion he expressed an inclination to agree with them. So did my friend Arndt. After this I had few doubts.

Meanwhile all of my cousins who were old enough were fighting as officers in the Austrian army, and so were many of our friends. My mother still took us for our summer vacation to the Alps, and in 1916 we were again in the Salzkammergut —this time in Ischl, where we rented a little house high up on a wooded slope. With us was Freud's sister, Rosa Graf, who was a friend of my parents. Her son Hermann, only five years my senior, came for a visit in uniform on his final leave before going to the front. Soon after came the news of his death. The grief of his mother—and of his sister, Freud's favourite niece —was terrible. It made me realize the meaning of those frightful long lists of people killed, wounded and missing.

Soon afterwards political issues made themselves felt again. The old Austria had been a multilingual state: there were Czechs, Slovaks, Poles, southern Slavs (Yugoslavs), and Italian-speaking people. Now rumour began to leak through of the defection of Czechs, Slavs, and Italians from the Austrian army. The dissolution had begun. A friend of our family who was acting as judge advocate told us about the Pan-Slavic movement, which he had to study professionally, and about Masaryk, a philosopher from the Universities of Vienna and Prague who was the leader of the Czechs. We heard about the Czech army formed in Russia by Czech-speaking Austrian prisoners of war. And then we heard rumours about death sentences for treason, and the terror directed by the Austrian authorities against people suspected of disloyalty.

5. *An Early Philosophical Problem: Infinity*

I have long believed that there are genuine philosophical problems which are not mere puzzles arising out of the misuse of language. Some of these problems are childishly obvious. It so happened that I stumbled upon one of them when I was still a child, probably about eight.

Somehow I had heard about the solar system and the infinity of space (no doubt of Newtonian space) and I was worried: I could neither imagine that space was finite (for what, then, was outside it?) nor that it was infinite. My father suggested that I ask one of his brothers who, he told me, was very good at explaining such things. This uncle asked me first whether I had any trouble about a sequence of numbers going on and on. I had not. Then he asked me to imagine a stack of bricks, and to add to it one brick, and again one brick, and so on without end; it would never fill the space of the universe. I agreed, somewhat reluctantly, that this was a very helpful answer, though I was not completely happy about it. Of course, I was unable to formulate the misgivings I still felt: it was the difference between potential and actual infinity, and the impossibility of reducing the actual infinity to the potential. The problem is, of course, part (the spatial part) of Kant's first antinomy, and it is (especially if the temporal part is added) a serious and still unsolved[6] philosophical problem—especially since Einstein's hopes of solving it by showing that the universe is a closed Riemannian space of finite radius have been more or less abandoned. It did not, of course, occur to me that what was worrying me might be an open problem. Rather, I thought that this was a question which an intelligent adult like my uncle must understand, while I was still too ignorant, or perhaps too young, or too stupid, to grasp it completely.

I remember a number of similar problems—serious problems, not puzzles—from later, when I was twelve or thirteen; for example, the problems of the origin of life, left open by Darwinian theory, and whether life is simply a chemical process (I opted for the theory that organisms are flames).

These, I think, are almost unavoidable problems for anybody who has ever heard about Darwin, whether child or adult. The fact that experimental work is done in connection with them does not make them nonphilosophical. Least of all should we decree in a high-handed manner that philosophical problems do not exist, or that they are insoluble (though perhaps dissoluble).

My own attitude towards such problems remained the same for a long time. I never thought it possible that any of those which bothered me had not been solved long ago; even less that any of them could be new. I had no doubt that people like the great Wilhelm Ostwald, editor of the journal *Das monistische Jahrhundert* (i.e. The Century of Monism), would know all the answers. My difficulties, I thought, were entirely due to my limited understanding.

6. My First Philosophical Failure: The Problem of Essentialism

I remember the first discussion of the first philosophical issue to become decisive for my intellectual development. The issue arose from my rejection of the attitude of attributing importance to *words and their meaning (or their "true meaning")*.

I must have been about fifteen. My father had suggested that I should read some of the volumes of Strindberg's autobiography. I do not remember which of its passages prompted me, in a conversation with my father, to criticize what I felt was an obscurantist attitude of Strindberg's: his attempt to extract something important from the "true" meanings of certain words. But I remember that when I tried to press my objections I was disturbed, indeed shocked, to find that my father did not see my point. The issue seemed obvious to me, and the more so the longer our discussion continued. When we broke it off late at night I realized that I had failed to make much impact. There was a real gulf between us on an issue of importance. I remember how, after this discussion, I tried strongly to impress on myself that I must always remember *the principle of never arguing about words and their meanings,* because such arguments are specious and insignificant. Moreover, I remember that I did not doubt that this simple principle must be well known and widely accepted; I suspected that both Strindberg and my father must be behind the times in these matters.

Years later I was to find that I had done them an injustice, and that the belief in the importance of the meanings of words, especially definitions, was almost universal. The attitude which I later came to call "essentialism"[7] is still widespread, and the sense of failure which I felt as a schoolboy has often come back to me in later years.

The first repetition of this sense of failure came when I tried to read some of the philosophical books in my father's library. I soon found that Strindberg's and my father's attitude was quite general. This created very great difficulties for me, and a dislike of philosophy. My father had suggested that I should try Spinoza (perhaps as a cure). Unfortunately I did not try his

Letters, but the *Ethics* and the *Principles According to Descartes,* both of them full of definitions which seemed to me arbitrary, pointless, and question-begging, so far as there was any question at all. It gave me a lifetime's dislike of theorizing about God. (Theology, I still think, is due to lack of faith.) I also felt that the similarity between the ways of geometry, the most fascinating subject to me at school, and Spinoza's *more geometrico* was quite superficial. Kant was different. Though I found the *Critique* much too difficult I could see that it was about real problems. I remember that after trying to read (I do not suppose with much understanding, but certainly with fascination) the Preface to the second edition of the *Critique* (in the edition by Benno Erdmann), I turned the pages and was struck and puzzled by that queer arrangement of the Antinomies. I did not get the point. I could not understand what Kant (or anybody) might mean by saying that reason can contradict itself. Yet I saw from the table of the First Antinomy that real problems were being argued; and also, from the Preface, that mathematics and physics were needed to understand these things.

But here I feel I must turn to the issue underlying that discussion, whose impact on me I remember so well. It is an issue that still divides me from most of my contemporaries, and since it has turned out to be so crucial for my later life as a philosopher I feel I must examine it in some detail, at the cost even of a long digression.

7. A Long Digression Concerning Essentialism: What Still Divides Me from Most Contemporary Philosophers

I call this a digression for two reasons. First, the formulation of my anti-essentialism in the third paragraph of the present section is undoubtedly biased by hindsight. Secondly, because the later parts of the present section are devoted not so much to carrying on the story of my intellectual development (though this is not neglected) as to discussing an issue which it has taken me a lifetime to clarify.

I do not wish to suggest that the following formulation was in my mind when I was fifteen, yet I cannot now state better than in this way the attitude I reached in that discussion with my father which I mentioned in the previous section:

Never let yourself be goaded into taking seriously problems about words and their meanings. What must be taken seriously are questions of fact, and assertions about facts: theories and hypotheses; the problems they solve; and the problems they raise.

In the sequel I shall refer to this piece of self-advice as my *anti-essentialist exhortation*. Apart from the reference to theories and hypotheses which is likely to be of a much later date, this exhortation cannot be very far from an articulation of the feelings I harboured when I first became conscious of the trap set by worries or quarrels about words and their meanings. This, I still think, is the surest path to intellectual perdition: the abandonment of real problems for the sake of verbal problems.

However, my own thoughts on this issue were for a long time bedevilled by my naive yet confident belief that all this must be well known, especially to philosophers, provided they were sufficiently up to date. This belief led me later, when I began more seriously to read philosophical books, to try to identify my problem—the relative unimportance of words—with one of the standard problems of philosophy. Thus I decided that it was very closely related to the classical problem of universals. And although I realized fairly soon that my problem was not identical with that classical problem, I tried hard to see it as a variant of the classical problem. This was a mistake. But in consequence I became greatly interested in the problem of universals and its history; and I soon came to the conclusion that behind the classical problem of universal words and their meaning (or sense, or denotation) there loomed a deeper and more important problem: the problem of universal laws and their truth; that is, the problem of regularities.

The problem of universals is even today treated as if it were a problem of words or of language usages; or of similarities in situations, and how they are matched by similarities in our linguistic symbolism. It seemed to me quite obvious, however, that it was much more general; that it was fundamentally a problem of *reacting similarly*, to biologically similar situations. Since all (or almost all) reactions have, biologically, an anticipatory value, we are led to the problem of anticipation or expectation, and so to that of adaptation to regularities.

Now throughout my life I have not only believed in the

existence of what philosophers call an "external world" but I have also regarded the opposite view as one not worth taking seriously. This does not mean that I never argued the issue with myself, or that I never experimented with, for example, "neutral monism" and similar idealistic positions. Yet I was always an adherent of *realism*; and this made me sensitive to the fact that within the context of the problem of universals this term *"realism"* was used in a quite different sense; that is, to denote positions opposed to *nominalism*. In order to avoid this somewhat misleading use I invented, when working on *The Poverty of Historicism* (probably in 1935; see the "Historical Note" to the book edition), the term *"essentialism"* as a name for any (classical) position which is opposed to *nominalism*, and especially for the theories of Plato and Aristotle (and, among the moderns, for Husserl's "intuition of essences").

At least ten years before I chose this name I had become aware of the fact that my own problem, as opposed to the classical problem of universals (and its biological variant), was *a problem of method*. After all, what I had originally impressed on my mind was an exhortation to think, to proceed, in one way rather than in another. This is why, long before I invented the terms *"essentialism"* and *"anti-essentialism"*, I had qualified the term "nominalism" by the term "methodological", using the name "methodological nominalism" for the attitude characteristic of my exhortation. (I now think this name a little misleading. The choice of the word "nominalism" was the result of my attempt to identify my attitude with some well-known position, or at least to find similarities between it and some such position. Classical "nominalism", however, was a position which I never accepted.)

In the early 1920s I had two discussions which had some influence on these ideas. The first was a discussion with Karl Polanyi, the economist and political theorist. Polanyi thought that what I described as "methodological nominalism" was characteristic of the natural sciences but not of the social sciences. The second discussion, somewhat later, was with Heinrich Gomperz, a thinker of great originality and immense erudition, who shocked me by describing my position as "realist" in *both* senses of the word.

I now believe that Polanyi and Gomperz were both right. Polanyi was right because the natural sciences are largely free from verbal discussion, while verbalism was, and still is, rampant in many forms in the social sciences. But there is more to it. I should now say[7a] that social relations belong, in many ways, to what I have more recently called "the third world" or better "world 3", the world of theories, of books, of ideas, of problems; a world which, ever since Plato—who saw it as a world of concepts—has been studied mainly by essentialists. Gomperz was right because a realist who believes in an "external world" necessarily believes in the existence of a cosmos rather than a chaos; that is, in regularities. And though I felt more opposed to classical essentialism than to nominalism, I did not then realize that, in substituting the problem of biological adaptation to regularities for the problem of the existence of similarities, I stood closer to "realism" than to nominalism.

In order to explain these matters as I see them at present, I will make use of a table of ideas which I first published in "On the Sources of Knowledge and of Ignorance".[8]

IDEAS	
that is	
DESIGNATIONS or TERMS or CONCEPTS	STATEMENTS or PROPOSITIONS or THEORIES
may be formulated in	
WORDS	ASSERTIONS
which may be	
MEANINGFUL	TRUE
and their	
MEANING	TRUTH
may be reduced, by way of	
DEFINITIONS	DERIVATIONS
to that of	
UNDEFINED CONCEPTS	PRIMITIVE PROPOSITIONS
the attempt to establish (rather than reduce) by these means their	
MEANING	TRUTH
leads to an infinite regress	

This table is in itself quite trivial: the logical analogy between the *left* and *right* sides is well established. However, it can be used to bring home my exhortation, which may now be reformulated as follows.

In spite of the perfect logical analogy between the left and the right sides of this table, the left-hand side is philosophically unimportant, while the right-hand side is philosophically all-important.[9]

This implies the view that meaning philosophies and language philosophies (so far as they are concerned with words) are on the wrong track. *In matters of the intellect, the only things worth striving for are true theories, or theories which come near to the truth*—at any rate nearer than some other (competing) theory, for example an older one.

This, I suppose, most people will admit; but they will be inclined to argue as follows. Whether a theory is true, or new, or intellectually significant, depends on its meaning; and *the meaning of a theory* (provided it is grammatically unambiguously formulated) *is a function of the meanings of the words in which the theory is formulated.* (Here, as in mathematics, a "function" is intended to take account of the order of the arguments.)

This view of the meaning of a theory seems almost obvious; it is widely held, and often unconsciously taken for granted.[10] Nevertheless, there is hardly any truth in it. I would counter it with the following rough formulation.

The relationship between a theory (or a statement) and the words used in its formulation is in several ways analogous to that between written words and the letters used in writing them down.

Obviously the letters have no "meaning" in the sense in which the words have "meaning"; although we must know the letters (that is, their "meaning" in some other sense) if we are to recognize the words, and so discern their meaning. Approximately the same may be said about words and statements or theories.

Letters play a merely technical or pragmatic role in the formulation of words. In my opinion, words also play a merely technical or pragmatic role in the formulation of theories. Thus both letters and words are mere means to ends (different ends). And the only intellectually important ends are: the formulation of problems; the tentative proposing of theories to solve them; and the critical discussion of the competing theories. The critical discussion assesses the submitted theories in terms of their rational or intellectual value as solutions to the problem under consideration; and as regards their truth, or nearness to truth. Truth is the main regulative principle in the criticism of theories; their power to raise new problems and to solve them is another. (See my *Conjectures and Refutations,* Chapter 10.)

There are some excellent examples showing that two theories, T_1 and T_2, which are formulated in entirely different terms (terms which are not one-to-one translatable) may nevertheless be logically equivalent, so that we may say that T_1 and T_2 are merely different formulations of one and the same theory. This shows that it is a mistake to look on the logical "meaning" of a theory as a function of the "meanings" of the words. (In order to establish the equivalence of T_1 and T_2 it may be necessary to construct a richer theory T_3 into which both T_1 and T_2 can be translated. Examples are various axiomatizations of projective geometry; and also the particle and the wave formalisms of quantum mechanics, whose equivalence can be established by translating them both into an operator language.)[11]

Of course, it is quite obvious that a change of one word can radically change the meaning of a statement; just as a change of one letter can radically change the meaning of a word, and with it, of a theory—as anybody interested in the interpretation of, say, Parmenides, will realize. Yet the mistakes of copyists or printers, though they may be fatally misleading, can more often than not be corrected by reflecting on the context.

Everybody who has done some translating, and who has thought about it, knows that there is no such thing as a grammatically correct and also almost literal translation of any interesting text. Every good translation is an *interpretation* of the original text; and I would even go so far as to say that every good translation of a nontrivial text must be a theoretical reconstruction. Thus it will even incorporate bits of a commentary. Every good translation must be, at the same time, close *and* free. Incidentally, it is a mistake to think that in an attempt to translate a piece of purely theoretical writing, aesthetic considerations are not important. One need only think of a theory like Newton's or Einstein's to see that a translation which gives the content of a theory but fails to bring out certain internal symmetries may be quite unsatisfactory; so much so that if somebody were given only this translation he would, if he discovered those symmetries, rightly feel he had himself made an original contribution, that he had discovered a theorem, even if the theorem was interesting chiefly for aesthetic reasons. (Somewhat similarly, a verse translation of Xenophanes, Parmenides, Empedocles, or Lucretius, is, other things being equal, preferable to a prose translation.)[12]

In any case, although a translation may be bad because it is not *sufficiently* precise, a *precise* translation of a difficult text simply does not exist. And if the two languages have a different structure, some theories may be almost untranslatable (as Benjamin Lee Whorf has shown so beautifully). Of course, if the languages are as closely related as, say, Latin and Greek, the introduction of a few newly coined words may suffice to make a translation possible. But in other cases an elaborate commentary may have to take the place of a translation.[13]

In view of all this, the idea of a precise language, or of precision in language, seems to be altogether misconceived. If we were to enter "Precision" in the *Table of Ideas* (see above), it would stand on the left-hand side (because the linguistic precision of a statement would indeed depend entirely on the precision of the words used); its analogue on the right-hand side might be "Certainty". I did not enter these two ideas, however, because my table is so constructed that the ideas on the right-hand side are all valuable; yet both precision and certainty are false ideals. They are impossible to attain, and therefore dangerously misleading if they are *uncritically* accepted as guides. *The quest for precision is analogous to the quest for certainty, and both should be abandoned.*

I do not suggest, of course, that an increase in the precision of, say, a prediction, or even a formulation, may not sometimes be highly desirable. What I do suggest is that *it is always undesirable to make an effort to increase precision for its own sake—especially linguistic precision—since this usually leads to loss of clarity,* and to a waste of time and effort on preliminaries which often turn out to be useless, because they are bypassed by the real advance of the subject: *one should never try to be more precise than the problem situation demands.*

I might perhaps state my position as follows. *Every increase in clarity is of intellectual value in itself; an increase in precision or exactness has only a pragmatic value as a means to some definite end*—where the end is usually an increase in testability or criticizability demanded by the problem situation (which for example may demand that we distinguish between two competing theories which lead to predictions that can be distinguished only if we increase the precision of our measurements).[14]

It will be clear that these views differ greatly from those implicitly held by many contemporary philosophers of science. Their attitude towards precision dates, I think, from the days when mathematics and physics were regarded as the Exact Sciences. Scientists, and also scientifically inclined philosophers, were greatly impressed. They felt it to be almost a duty to live up to, or to emulate, this "exactness", perhaps hoping that fertility would emerge from exactness as a kind of by-product. But fertility is the result not of exactness but of seeing new problems where none have been seen before, and of finding new ways of solving them.

However, I will postpone my remarks on the history of contemporary philosophy to the end of this digression, and turn again to the question of the meaning or significance of a statement or a theory.

Having in mind my own exhortation never to quarrel about words, I am very ready to admit (with a shrug, as it were) that there may be meanings of the word "meaning" such that the meaning of a theory depends entirely on that of the words used in a very explicit formulation of the theory. (Perhaps Frege's "sense" is one of them, though much that he says speaks against this.) Nor do I deny that, as a rule, we must understand the words in order to understand a theory (although this is by no means true in general, as the existence of implicit definition suggests). But what makes a theory interesting or significant— what we try to understand, if we wish to understand a theory —is something different. To put the idea first in a way which is merely intuitive, and perhaps a bit woolly, it is its logical relation to the prevailing problem situation which makes a theory interesting: its relation to preceding and competing theories: its power to solve existing problems, and to suggest new ones. In other words, the meaning or significance of a theory in this sense depends on very comprehensive contexts, although of course the significance of these contexts in their turn depends on the various theories, problems, and problem situations of which they are composed.

It is interesting that this apparently vague (and one might say "holistic") idea of the significance of a theory can be analysed and clarified to a considerable extent in purely logical terms—with the help of the idea of the *content* of a statement or a theory.

There are in use, in the main, two intuitively very different but logically almost identical ideas of content, which I have sometimes called *"logical content"* and *"informative content"*; a special case of the latter I have also called "empirical content".

The logical content of a statement or theory may be identified with what Tarski has called its "consequence class"; that is, the class of all the (nontautological) consequences which can be derived from the statement of theory.

For the *informative content* (as I have called it) we must consider the intuitive idea that statements or theories tell us the more "the more they prohibit" or exclude.[15] This intuitive idea leads to a definition of informative content which, to some people, has seemed absurd: *the informative content of a theory is the set of statements which are incompatible with the theory.*[16]

It may be seen at once, however, that the elements of this set and the elements of the logical content stand in a one-one correspondence: to every element which is in one of the sets, there is in the other set a corresponding element, namely its *negation.*

We therefore find that whenever the logical strength, or the power, or the amount of information in a theory increases or decreases, its logical content and its informative content must both likewise increase or decrease. This shows that the two ideas are very similar: there is a one-one correspondence between what can be said about the one, and what can be said about the other. This shows that my definition of informative content is not entirely absurd.

But there are also differences. For example, for the *logical* content the following *rule of transitivity* holds: if *b* is an element of the content of *a*, and *c* an element of the content of *b*, then *c* is also an element of the content of *a*. Although there of course exists a corresponding rule for *informative* content, it is not a simple transitivity rule like this.[17]

Moreover, the content of any (nontautological) statement —say a theory *t*—is *infinite.* For let there be an *infinite* list of statements *a, b, c, . . . ,* which are pairwise contradictory, and which individually do not entail *t.* (For most *t*'s, something like *a*: "the number of planets is 0", *b*: "the number of planets is 1", and so on, would be adequate.) Then the statement "*t or a or both*" is deducible from *t*, and therefore belongs to the logical content of *t*; and the same holds for *b* and any other statement in the list. From our assumptions about *a, b, c, . . .* , it can now be shown simply that no pair of statements of the sequence "*t or a or both*", "*t or b or both*", . . . , are interdeducible; that is, none of these statements entails any other. Thus the logical content of *t* must be infinite.

This elementary result concerning the logical content of any nontautological theory is of course well known. The argument is trivial since it is based on a trivial operation with the logical (nonexclusive) "*or*";[18] and so one may doubt, perhaps, whether the infinity of the content is not altogether a trivial affair, depending merely on those statements like "*t or a or both*" which are the results of a trivial method of weakening *t*. However, in terms of *informative content* it immediately becomes clear that the matter is not quite as trivial as it looks.

For let the theory under consideration be Newton's theory of gravitation; call it *N*. Then any statement or any theory which is incompatible with *N* will belong to the informative content of *N*. Let us call Einstein's theory of gravitation *E*. Since the two theories are incompatible, each belongs to the informative content of the other; each excludes, or forbids, or prohibits the other.

This shows in a very intuitive way that the informative content of a theory *t* is infinite in a far from trivial way: any theory which is incompatible with *t*, and thus *any future theory which one day may supersede t* (say, after some crucial experiment has decided against *t*) *obviously belongs to the informative content of t*. But just as obviously, we cannot know, or construct, these theories in advance: Newton could not foresee Einstein or Einstein's successors.

Of course, it is now easy to find a precisely similar, though slightly less intuitive, situation concerning the logical content: since *E* belongs to the *informative* content of *N*, *non-E* belongs to the *logical* content of *N*: *non-E* is entailed by *N*, a fact which, obviously, could also not have been known to Newton, or anybody else, before *E* was discovered.

I have in lectures often described this interesting situation by saying: *we never know what we are talking about*. For when we propose a theory, or try to understand a theory, we also propose, or try to understand, its logical implications; that is, all those statements which follow from it. But this, as we have just seen, is a hopeless task: there is *an infinity of unforeseeable nontrivial statements belonging to the informative content of any theory,* and an exactly corresponding infinity of statements belonging to its logical content. We can therefore never know or understand all the implications of any theory, or its full significance.

This, I think, is a surprising result as far as it concerns logical content; though for informative content it turns out to be rather natural. (I have only once seen it stated in print,[19] although I have referred to it in lectures for many years.) It shows, among other things, that understanding a theory is always an infinite task, and that theories can in principle be understood better and better. It also shows that, if we wish to understand a theory better, what we have to do *first* is to discover its logical relation to those existing problems and existing theories which constitute what we may call the *"problem situation" at the particular moment of time.*

Admittedly, we also *try* to look ahead: we try to discover new problems raised by our theory. But the task is infinite, and can never be completed.

Thus it turns out that the formulation which I have said earlier was "merely intuitive, and perhaps a bit woolly" can now be clarified. The nontrivial infinity of a theory's content, as I have described it here, turns the significance of the theory into a partly logical and partly historical matter. The latter depends on what has been discovered, *at a certain time,* in the light of the prevailing problem situation, about the theory's content; it is, as it were, a projection of this historical problem situation upon the logical content of the theory.[20]

To sum up, there is at least one meaning of the "meaning" (or "significance") of a theory which makes it dependent upon its content and thus more dependent on its relations with other theories than on the meaning of any set of words.

These, I think, are some of the more important results which, during a lifetime, emerged from my anti-essentialist exhortation—which, in its turn, was the result of the discussion described in section 6. One further result is, quite simply, the realization that the quest for precision, in words or concepts or meanings, is a wild-goose chase. There simply is no such thing as a precise concept (say, in Frege's sense), though concepts like "price of this kettle" and "thirty pence" are usually precise enough for the problem context in which they are used. (But note the fact that "thirty pence" is, as a social or economic concept, highly variable: it had a different significance a few years ago from what it has today.)

Frege's opinion is different; for he writes: "A definition of a concept . . . must determine unambiguously of any object whether or not it falls under the concept . . . Using a metaphor, we may say: the concept must have a sharp boundary."[21] But it is clear that for this kind of absolute precision to be demanded of a *defined* concept, it must first be demanded of the *defining* concepts, and ultimately of our *undefined,* or *primitive,* terms. Yet this is impossible. For either our undefined or primitive terms have a traditional meaning (which is never very precise) or they are introduced by so-called "implicit definitions"—that is, through the way they are used in the context of a theory. This last way of introducing them—if they have to be "introduced"—seems to be the best. But it makes the meaning of the concepts depend on that of the theory, and most theories can be interpreted in more than one way. As a result, implicitly defined concepts, and thus all concepts which are defined explicitly with their help, become not merely "vague" but *systematically ambiguous.* And the various systematically ambiguous interpretations (such as the points and straight lines of projective geometry) may be *completely distinct.*

This should be sufficient to establish the fact that "unambiguous" concepts, or concepts with "sharp boundary lines", do not exist. Thus we need not be surprised at a remark like that by Clifford A. Truesdell about the laws of thermodynamics: "Every physicist knows exactly what the first and the second law mean, but . . . no two physicists agree about them."[22]

We know now that the choice of undefined terms is largely arbitrary, as is the choice of the axioms of a theory. Frege was, I think, mistaken on this point, at least in 1892: he believed that there were terms which were intrinsically undefinable because "what is logically simple cannot have a proper definition".[23] However, what he thought of as an example of a simple concept—the concept of "concept"—turned out to be quite unlike what he thought it was. It has since developed into that of "set", and few would now call it either unambiguous or simple.

At any rate, the wild-goose chase (I mean the interest in the left-hand side of the *Table of Ideas*) did go on. When I wrote my *Logik der Forschung* I thought that the quest for the meanings of words was about to end. I was an optimist: it was gaining momentum.[24] The task of philosophy was more and more widely described as concerned with meaning, and this meant, mainly, the meanings of words. And nobody seriously questioned the implicitly accepted dogma that the meaning of a statement, at least in its most explicit and unambiguous formulation, depends on (or is a function of) that of its words. This is true equally of the British language analysts and of those who follow Carnap in upholding the view that the task of philosophy is the "explication of concepts", that is, making concepts precise. Yet *there simply is no such thing as an "explication", or an "explicated" or "precise" concept.*

However, the problem still remains: what should we do in order to make our meaning clearer, if greater clarity is needed, or to make it more precise, if greater precision is needed? In the light of my exhortation the main answer to this question is: any move to increase clarity or precision must be *ad hoc* or "piecemeal". If because of lack of clarity a misunderstanding arises, do not try to lay new and more solid foundations on which to build a more precise "conceptual framework", but reformulate your formulations *ad hoc,* with a view to avoiding those misunderstandings which have arisen or which you can foresee. And always remember that *it is impossible to speak in such a way that you cannot be misunderstood*: there will always be some who misunderstand you. If greater precision is needed, it is needed because *the problem to be solved* demands it. Simply try your best to solve your problems and do not try in advance to make your concepts or formulations more precise in the fond hope that this will provide you with an arsenal for future use in tackling problems which have not yet arisen. *They may never arise;* the evolution of the theory may bypass all your efforts. The intellectual weapons which will be needed at a later date may be very different from those which anyone has in store. For example, it is almost certain that nobody trying to make the concept of simultaneity more precise would, before the discovery of Einstein's problem (the asymmetries in the electro-

dynamics of moving bodies), have hit on Einstein's "analysis".
(It should not be thought that I subscribe to the still popular
view that Einstein's achievement was one of "operational
analysis". It was not. See page 20 of my *Open Society*,
[1957(h)]* and later editions, Volume II.)

The *ad hoc* method of dealing with problems of clarity or
precision as the need arises might be called *"dialysis"*, in order
to distinguish it from *analysis*: from the idea that language
analysis as such may solve problems, or create an armoury
for future use. Dialysis cannot solve problems. It cannot do so
any more than definition or explication or language analysis
can: problems can only be solved with the help of new ideas.
But our problems may sometimes demand that we make new
distinctions—*ad hoc*, for the purpose in hand.

This long digression[25] has led me away from my main
story, to which I will now return.

8. *A Crucial Year: Marxism; Science and Pseudoscience*

It was during the last terrible years of the war, probably
in 1917, at a time when I was suffering from a long illness, that
I realized very clearly what I had felt in my bones for a considerable time: that in our famous Austrian secondary schools
(called *"Gymnasium"* and — *horribile dictu* — *"Realgym-
nasium"*) we were wasting our time shockingly, even though
our teachers were well educated and tried hard to make the
schools the best in the world. That much of their teaching was
boring in the extreme—hours and hours of hopeless torture—
was not new to me. (They immunized me: never since have I
suffered from boredom. In school one was liable to be found
out if one thought of something unconnected with the lesson:
one was compelled to attend. Later on, when a lecturer was
boring, one could entertain oneself with one's own thoughts.)
There was just one subject in which we had an interesting and
truly inspiring teacher. The subject was mathematics, and the
name of the teacher was Philipp Freud (I do not know whether
he was a relative of Sigmund Freud's). Yet when I returned
to school after an illness of over two months I found that my

* References in square brackets such as [1957(h)] are to the
Select Bibliography, pp. 240-7.

class had made hardly any progress, not even in mathematics. This was an eye-opener: it made me eager to leave school.

The breakdown of the Austrian Empire and the aftermath of the First World War, the famine, the hunger riots in Vienna, and the runaway inflation, have often been described. They destroyed the world in which I had grown up; and there began a period of cold and hot civil war which ended with Hitler's invasion of Austria, and which led to the Second World War. I was over sixteen when the war ended, and the revolution incited me to stage my own private revolution. I decided to leave school, late in 1918, to study on my own. I enrolled at the University of Vienna where I was, at first, a non-matriculated student, since I did not take the entrance examination (*"Matura"*) until 1922, when I became a matriculated student. There were no scholarships, but the cost of enrolling at the University was nominal. And every student could attend any lecture course.

It was a time of upheavals, though not only political ones. I was close enough to hear the bullets whistle when, on the occasion of the Declaration of the Austrian Republic, soldiers started shooting at the members of the Provisional Government assembled at the top of the steps leading to the Parliament building. (This experience led me to write a paper on freedom.) There was little to eat; and as for clothing, most of us could afford only discarded army uniforms, adapted for civilian use. Few of us thought seriously of careers—there were none (except perhaps in a bank; but the thought of a career in commerce never entered my head). We studied not for a career but for the sake of studying. We studied; and we discussed politics.

There were three main political parties: the social democrats, and the two antisocialist parties, the German nationalists (then the smallest of the three main parties, and later to be absorbed by the Nazis), and what was in effect the party of the Roman Church (Austria had a vast Roman Catholic majority) which called itself "Christian" and "social" (*christlich-sozial*) although it was antisocialist. Then there was the small communist party. I became a member of the association of socialist pupils of secondary schools (*sozialistische Mittelschüler*) and went to their meetings. I went also to meetings of the socialist university students. The speakers at these meetings belonged sometimes to the social democratic and sometimes to the communist parties. Their Marxist beliefs were at that time very similar. And they all dwelt, rightly, on the horrors of war. The communists claimed that they had proved their pacifism in Russia, by ending the war, at Brest-Litovsk. Peace, they said, was what they primarily stood for. At that particular time they were not only for peace but, in their propaganda at least, against all "unnecessary" violence.[26] For a time I was suspicious of the communists, mainly because of what my friend Arndt had told me about them. But in the spring of 1919 I, together with a few friends, was converted by their propaganda. For about two or three months I regarded myself as a communist.

I was soon to be disenchanted. The incident that turned me against communism, and that soon led me away from Marxism altogether, was one of the most important incidents in my life. It happened shortly before my seventeenth birthday. In Vienna, shooting broke out during a demonstration by un-armed young socialists who, instigated by the communists, tried to help some communists to escape who were under arrest in the central police station in Vienna. Several young socialist and communist workers were killed. I was horrified and shocked by the brutality of the police, but also by myself. For I felt that as a Marxist I bore part of the responsibility for the tragedy—at least in principle. Marxist theory demands that the class struggle be intensified, in order to speed up the coming of socialism. Its thesis is that although the revolution may claim some victims, capitalism is claiming more victims than the whole socialist revolution.

That was the Marxist theory—part of so-called "scientific socialism". I now asked myself whether such a calculation could ever be supported by "science". The whole experience, and especially this question, produced in me a life-long revulsion of feeling.

Communism is a creed which promises to bring about a better world. It claims to be based on knowledge: knowledge of the laws of historical development. I still hoped for a better world, a less violent and more just world, but I questioned whether I really *knew*—whether what I had thought was knowledge was not perhaps mere pretence. I had, of course, read some Marx and Engels—but had I really understood it? Had I examined it *critically*, as anybody should do before he accepts a creed which justifies its means by a somewhat distant end?

I was shocked to have to admit to myself that not only had I accepted a complex theory somewhat uncritically, but that I had also actually noticed quite a bit of what was wrong, in the theory as well as in the practice of communism. But I had repressed this—partly out of loyalty to my friends, partly out of loyalty to "the cause", and partly because there is a mechanism of getting oneself more and more deeply involved: once one has sacrificed one's intellectual conscience over a minor point one does not wish to give in too easily; one wishes to justify the self-sacrifice by convincing oneself of the fundamental goodness of the cause, which is seen to outweigh any little moral or intellectual compromise that may be required. With every such moral or intellectual sacrifice one gets more deeply involved. One becomes ready to back one's moral or intellectual investments in the cause with further investments. It is like being eager to throw good money after bad.

I saw how this mechanism had been working in my case, and I was horrified. I also saw it at work in others, especially in my communist friends. And the experience enabled me to understand later many things which otherwise I would not have understood.

I had accepted a dangerous creed uncritically, dogmatically. The reaction made me first a sceptic; then it led me, though only for a very short time, to react against all rationalism. (As I found later, this is a typical reaction of a disappointed Marxist.)

By the time I was seventeen I had become an anti-Marxist. I realized the dogmatic character of the creed, and its incredible intellectual arrogance. It was a terrible thing to arrogate to oneself a kind of knowledge which made it a duty to risk the lives of other people for an uncritically accepted dogma, or for a dream which might turn out not to be realizable. It was particularly bad for an intellectual, for one who could read and think. It was awfully depressing to have fallen into such a trap.

Once I had looked at it critically, the gaps and loopholes and inconsistencies in the Marxist theory became obvious. Take its central point with respect to violence, the dictatorship of the proletariat: who were the proletariat? Lenin, Trotsky, and the other leaders? The communists had never formed a majority. They did not hold a majority even among the workers in the factories. In Austria, certainly, they were a very small minority, and apparently it was the same elsewhere.

It took me some years of study before I felt with any confidence that I had grasped the heart of the Marxian argument. It consists of a historical prophecy, combined with an implicit appeal to the following moral law: *Help to bring about the inevitable!* Even then I had no intention of publishing my criticism of Marx, for anti-Marxism in Austria was a worse thing than Marxism: since the social democrats were Marxists, anti-Marxism was very nearly identical with those authoritarian movements which were later called fascist. Of course, I talked about it to my friends. But it was not till sixteen years later, in 1935, that I began to write about Marxism with the intention of publishing what I wrote. As a consequence, two books emerged between 1935 and 1943—*The Poverty of Historicism* and *The Open Society and Its Enemies.*

Yet at the time I am now speaking about (it must have been in 1919 or 1920) one of the things which revolted me was the intellectual presumption of some of my Marxist friends and fellow students, who almost took it for granted that they were the future leaders of the working class. They had, I knew, no special intellectual qualifications. All they could claim was some acquaintance with Marxist literature—though not even a thorough one, and certainly not a critical one. Of the life of a manual worker most of them knew less than I did. (I had at least worked for some months during the war in a factory.) I reacted strongly to this attitude. I felt that we were greatly privileged in being able to study—indeed, undeservedly so— and I decided to try to become a manual worker. I also decided never to seek any influence in party politics.

I did in fact make several attempts to become a manual worker. My second attempt broke down because I did not have the physical stamina needed for digging concrete-hard road surfaces with a pickaxe for days and days on end. My last attempt was to become a cabinetmaker. Physically this was not demanding, but the trouble was that certain speculative ideas which interested me interfered with my work.

Perhaps this is the place to say how much I admired the workers of Vienna and their great movement—led by the social democratic party—even though I regarded the Marxist historicism of their social democratic leaders as fatally mistaken.[27] Their leaders were able to inspire them with a marvellous faith in their mission, which was nothing less, they

believed, than the liberation of mankind. Although the social
democratic movement was largely atheistic (despite a small and
admirable group who described themselves as religious socialists), the whole movement was inspired by what can only be
described as an ardent religious and humanitarian faith. It was
a movement of the workers to educate themselves in order to
fulfil their "historic mission"; to emancipate themselves, and
thus to help liberate mankind; and above all, to end war. In
their restricted spare time many workers, young and old, went
to extension courses, or to one of the "People's Universities"
(*Volkshochschulen*). They took a great interest not only in self-
education but in the education of their children, and in improving housing conditions. It was an admirable programme. In
their lives, showing on occasion, perhaps, a touch of priggish-
ness, they substituted mountaineering for alcohol, classical
music for swing, serious reading for thrillers. These activities
were all peaceful, and they were carried on in an atmosphere
poisoned by fascism and latent civil war; and also, most unfortunately, by repeated and confused threats from the workers' leaders that they would give up democratic methods and
take recourse to violence—a legacy of the ambiguous attitude
of Marx and Engels. This great movement and its tragic
destruction by fascism made a deep impression on some
English and American observers (for example, G. E. R.
Gedye).[28]

I remained a socialist for several years, even after my rejection of Marxism; and if there could be such a thing as
socialism combined with individual liberty, I would be a
socialist still. For nothing could be better than living a modest,
simple, and free life in an egalitarian society. It took some time
before I recognized this as no more than a beautiful dream;
that freedom is more important than equality; that the attempt
to realize equality endangers freedom; and that, if freedom
is lost, there will not even be equality among the unfree.

The encounter with Marxism was one of the main events
in my intellectual development. It taught me a number of
lessons which I have never forgotten. It taught me the wisdom
of the Socratic saying, "I know that I do not know". It made
me a fallibilist, and impressed on me the value of intellectual
modesty. And it made me most conscious of the differences
between dogmatic and critical thinking.

Compared with this encounter, the somewhat similar pattern of my encounters with Alfred Adler's "individual psychology" and with Freudian psychoanalysis—which were more or less contemporaneous (it all happened in 1919)—were of minor importance.[29]

Looking back at that year I am amazed that so much can happen to one's intellectual development in so short a spell. For at the same time I learned about Einstein; and this became a dominant influence on my thinking—in the long run perhaps the most important influence of all. In May, 1919, Einstein's eclipse predictions were successfully tested by two British expeditions. With these tests a new theory of gravitation and a new cosmology suddenly appeared, not just as a mere possibility, but as a real improvement on Newton—a better approximation to the truth.

Einstein gave a lecture in Vienna, to which I went; but I remember only that I was dazed. This thing was quite beyond my understanding. I had been brought up in an atmosphere in which Newton's mechanics and Maxwell's electrodynamics were accepted side by side as unquestionable truths. Even Mach in *The Science of Mechanics,* in which he criticized Newton's theory of absolute space and absolute time, had retained Newton's laws—including the law of inertia, for which he had offered a new and fascinating interpretation. And although he did consider the possibility of a non-Newtonian theory he thought that before we could start on it we would have to await new experiences, which might come, perhaps, from new physical or astronomical knowledge about regions of space containing faster and more complex movements than could be found in our own solar system.[30] Hertz's mechanics too did not deviate from Newton's, except in its presentation.

The general assumption of the truth of Newton's theory was of course the result of its incredible success, culminating in the discovery of the planet Neptune. The success was so impressive because (as I later put it) Newton's theory repeatedly *corrected the empirical material which it set out to explain.*[31] Yet in spite of all this, Einstein had managed to produce a real alternative and, it appeared, a better theory, without waiting for new experiences. Like Newton himself, he predicted new effects within (and also without) our solar system. And some of these predictions, when tested, had now proved successful.

I was fortunate in being introduced to these ideas by a brilliant young student of mathematics, Max Elstein, a friend who died in 1922 at the age of twenty-one. He was not a positivist (as Einstein was in those days, and for years to come), and he therefore stressed the objective aspects of Einstein's theory: the field-theoretical approach; the electro-dynamics and mechanics and their new link; and the marvellous idea of a new cosmology—a finite but unbounded universe. He drew my attention to the fact that Einstein himself regarded it as one of the main arguments in favour of his theory that it yielded Newton's theory as a very good approximation; also, that Einstein, though convinced that his theory was a better approximation than Newton's, regarded his own theory merely as a step towards a still more general theory; and further that Hermann Weyl had already published, even before the eclipse observations, a book (*Raum, Zeit, Materie*, 1918) in which was offered a more general and comprehensive theory than Einstein's.

No doubt Einstein had all this in mind, and especially his own theory, when he wrote in another context: "There could be no fairer destiny for any physical theory than that it should point the way to a more comprehensive theory, in which it lives on as a limiting case."[32] But what impressed me most was Einstein's own clear statement that he would regard his theory as untenable if it should fail in certain tests. Thus he wrote, for example: "If the redshift of spectral lines due to the gravitational potential should not exist, then the general theory of relativity will be untenable."[33]

Here was an attitude utterly different from the dogmatic attitude of Marx, Freud, Adler, and even more so that of their followers. Einstein was looking for crucial experiments whose agreement with his predictions would by no means establish his theory; while a disagreement, as he was the first to stress, would show his theory to be untenable.

This, I felt, was the true scientific attitude. It was utterly different from the dogmatic attitude which constantly claimed to find "verifications" for its favourite theories.

Thus I arrived, by the end of 1919, at the conclusion that the scientific attitude was the critical attitude, which did not look for verifications but for crucial tests; tests which could *refute* the theory tested, though they could never establish it.

9. Early Studies

Although the years after the First World War were grim for most of my friends and also for myself, it was an exhilarating time. Not that we were happy. Most of us had no prospects and no plans. We lived in a very poor country in which civil war was endemic, flaring up in earnest from time to time. We were often depressed, discouraged, disgusted. But we were learning, our minds were active and growing. We were reading ravenously, omnivorously; debating, changing our opinions, studying, sifting critically, thinking. We listened to music, went tramping in the beautiful Austrian mountains, and dreamt of a better, healthier, simpler, and more honest world.

During the winter of 1919-20 I left home to live in a disused part of a former military hospital converted by students into an extremely primitive students' home. I wanted to be independent, and I tried not to be a burden to my father, who was well over sixty and had lost all his savings in the runaway inflation after the war. My parents would have preferred me to stay at home.

I had been doing some unpaid work in Alfred Adler's child guidance clinics, and I was now doing other occasional work with hardly any pay at all. Some of it was hard (road making). But I also coached some American university students, who were very generous. I needed very little: there was not much to eat, and I did not smoke or drink. The only necessities which were sometimes hard to come by were tickets for concerts. Though the tickets were cheap (if one stood), they were for a number of years almost a daily expenditure.

At the University I sampled lecture courses in various subjects: history, literature, psychology, philosophy, and even lectures at the medical school. But I soon gave up going to lectures, with the exception of those in mathematics and theoretical physics. The University had, at that time, most eminent teachers, but reading their books was an incomparably greater experience than listening to their lectures. (Seminars were for advanced students only.) I also started fighting my way through the *Critique of Pure Reason* and the *Prolegomena*.

Only the department of mathematics offered really fascinating lectures. The professors at the time were Wirtinger,

Furtwängler, and Hans Hahn. All three were creative mathematicians of world reputation. Wirtinger, whom departmental rumour rated as the greatest genius of the three, I found difficult to follow. Furtwängler was amazing in his clarity and the mastery of his subjects (algebra, number theory). But I learned most from Hans Hahn. His lectures attained a degree of perfection which I have never encountered again. Each lecture was a work of art: dramatic in logical structure; not a word too much; of perfect clarity; and delivered in beautiful and civilized language. The subject, and sometimes the problems discussed, were introduced by an exciting historical sketch. Everything was alive, though due to its very perfection a bit aloof.

There was also Dozent Helly, who lectured on probability theory and from whom I first heard the name of Richard von Mises. Later there came for a short time a very young and charming professor from Germany, Kurt Reidemeister; I went to his lectures on tensor algebra. All these men—except perhaps Reidemeister, who was not averse to interruptions—were demigods. They were infinitely beyond our reach. There was no contact between professors and students who had not qualified for a Ph.D. dissertation. I had neither the slightest ambition to make, nor the prospect of making, their acquaintance. I never expected that I should later become personally acquainted with Hahn, Helly, von Mises, and Hans Thirring, who taught theoretical physics.

I studied mathematics because I simply wanted to learn, and I thought that in mathematics I would learn something about standards of truth; and also because I was interested in theoretical physics. Mathematics was a huge and difficult subject, and had I ever thought of becoming a professional mathematician I might soon have been discouraged. But I had no such ambition. If I thought of a future, I dreamt of one day founding a school in which young people could learn without boredom, and would be stimulated to pose problems and discuss them; a school in which no unwanted answers to unasked questions would have to be listened to; in which one did not study for the sake of passing examinations.

I passed my *"Matura"* as a private pupil in 1922, one year later than I should have, had I continued at school. But the experiment had been worth the year I "lost". I now became a fully matriculated university student. Two years later I passed a second *"Matura"* at a teachers' training college, which qualified me to teach in primary schools. I took this examination while learning to be a cabinetmaker. (Later I added qualifications to teach mathematics, physics, and chemistry in secondary schools.) However, there were no posts available for teachers, and after concluding my apprenticeship as a cabinetmaker I became, as I have mentioned, a social worker (*Horterzieher*) with neglected children.

Early during this period I developed further my ideas about the *demarcation between scientific theories* (like Einstein's) *and pseudoscientific theories* (like Marx's, Freud's, and Adler's). It became clear to me that what made a theory, or a statement, scientific was its power to rule out, or exclude, the occurrence of some possible events—to prohibit, or forbid, the occurrence of these events. Thus *the more a theory forbids, the more it tells us.*[34]

Although this idea is closely related to that of the "informative content" of a theory, and contains the latter idea in a nutshell, I did not, at the time, develop it beyond this point. I was, however, much concerned with the problem of *dogmatic thinking and its relation to critical thinking.* What especially interested me was the idea that dogmatic thinking, which I regarded as prescientific, was a stage that was needed if critical thinking was to be possible. Critical thinking must have before it something to criticize, and this, I thought, must be the result of dogmatic thinking.

I shall say here a few more words on the *problem of demarcation* and my solution.

(1) As it occurred to me first, the problem of demarcation was not the problem of demarcating science from metaphysics but rather the problem of demarcating science from pseudoscience. At the time I was not at all interested in metaphysics. It was only later that I extended my *"criterion of demarcation"* to metaphysics.

(2) My main idea in 1919 was this. If somebody proposed a scientific theory he should answer, as Einstein did, the question: "Under what conditions would I admit that my theory is untenable?" In other words, what conceivable facts would I accept as refutations, or falsifications, of my theory?

(3) I had been shocked by the fact that the Marxists (whose central claim was that they were social scientists) and the

psychoanalysts of all schools were able to interpret any conceivable event as a verification of their theories. This, together with my criterion of demarcation, led me to the view that only attempted refutations which did not succeed *qua* refutations should count as "verifications".

(4) I still uphold (2). But when a little later I tentatively introduced the idea of *falsifiability (or testability or refutability) of a theory as a criterion of demarcation*, I very soon found that every theory can be "immunized" (this excellent term is due to Hans Albert)[35] against criticism. If we allow such immunization, then every theory becomes unfalsifiable. Thus we must exclude at least some immunizations.

On the other hand, I also realized that we must not exclude all immunizations, not even all which introduced *ad hoc* auxiliary hypotheses. For example the observed motion of Uranus might have been regarded as a falsification of Newton's theory. Instead the auxiliary hypothesis of an outer planet was introduced *ad hoc*, thus immunizing the theory. This turned out to be fortunate; for the auxiliary hypothesis was a testable one, even if difficult to test, and it stood up to tests successfully.

All this shows not only that some degree of dogmatism is fruitful, even in science, but also that logically speaking falsifiability, or testability, cannot be regarded as a very sharp criterion. Later, in my *Logik der Forschung*, I dealt with this problem very fully. I introduced *degrees of testability*, and these turned out to be closely related to (degrees of) *content*, and surprisingly fertile: increase of content became the criterion for whether we should, or should not, tentatively adopt an auxiliary hypothesis.

In spite of the fact that all this was clearly stated in my *Logik der Forschung* of 1934, a number of legends were propagated about my views.[36] First, that I had introduced falsifiability as a meaning criterion rather than as a criterion of demarcation. Secondly, that I had not seen that immunization was always possible, and had therefore overlooked the fact that since all theories could be rescued from falsification none could simply be described as "falsifiable". In other words my own results were, in these legends, turned into reasons for rejecting my approach.[37]

(5) As a kind of summary it may be useful to show, with the help of examples, how various types of theoretical systems

are related to testability (or falsifiability) and to immunization procedures.

(a) There are metaphysical theories of a *purely existential* character (discussed especially in *Conjectures and Refutations*).[38]

(b) There are theories like the psychoanalytic theories of Freud, Adler, and Jung, or like (sufficiently vague) astrological lore.[39]

(c) There are what one might call "unsophisticated" theories like "All swans are white" or the geocentric "All stars other than the planets move in circles". Kepler's laws may be included (though they are in many senses highly sophisticated). These theories are falsifiable, though falsifications can, of course, be evaded: immunization is *always* possible. But the evasion would usually be dishonest: it would consist, say, in denying that a black swan was a swan, or that it was black; or that a non-Keplerian planet was a planet.

(d) The case of Marxism is interesting. As I pointed out in my *Open Society*,[40] one may regard Marx's theory as refuted by events that occurred during the Russian Revolution. According to Marx the revolutionary changes start at the bottom, as it were: means of production change first, then social conditions of production, then political power, and ultimately ideological beliefs, which change last. But in the Russian Revolution the political power changed first, and then the ideology (Dictatorship plus Electrification) began to change the social conditions and the means of production from the top. The reinterpretation of Marx's theory of revolution to evade this falsification immunized it against further attacks, transforming it into the vulgar-Marxist (or socioanalytic) theory which tells us that the "economic motive" and the class struggle pervade social life.

(e) There are more abstract theories, like Newton's or Einstein's theories of gravitation. They are falsifiable—say, by not finding predicted perturbations, or perhaps by a negative outcome of radar tests replacing solar eclipse observations. But in their case a prima facie falsification *may* be evaded, not only by uninteresting immunizations but also, as in the Uranus-Neptune kind of case, by the introduction of testable auxiliary hypotheses, so that the empirical content of the system—consisting of the original theory plus the auxiliary hypothesis

—is greater than that of the original system. We may regard this as an increase of informative content—as a case of *growth* in our knowledge. There are, of course, also auxiliary hypotheses which are merely evasive immunizing moves. They decrease the content. All this suggests the *methodological rule* not to put up with any content-decreasing manoeuvres (or with "degenerating problem shifts", in the terminology of Imre Lakatos[41]).

10. A Second Digression: Dogmatic and Critical Thinking; Learning without Induction

Konrad Lorenz is the author of a marvellous theory in the field of animal psychology, which he calls "imprinting". It implies that young animals have an inborn mechanism for jumping to unshakable conclusions. For example, a newly hatched gosling adopts as its "mother" the first moving thing it sets eyes on. This mechanism is well adapted to normal circumstances, though a bit risky for the gosling. (It may also be risky for the chosen foster parent, as we learn from Lorenz.) But it is a successful mechanism under normal circumstances; and also under some which are not quite normal.

The following points about Lorenz's "imprinting" are important:

(1) It is a process—not the only one—of learning by observation.

(2) The problem solved under the stimulus of the observation is inborn; that is, the gosling is genetically conditioned to look out for its mother: it expects to see its mother.

(3) The theory or expectation which solves the problem is also to some extent inborn, or genetically conditioned: it goes far beyond the actual observation, which merely (so to speak) releases or triggers the adoption of a theory which is largely preformed in the organism.

(4) The learning process is *nonrepetitive,* though it may take a certain amount of time (a short time),[42] and involve often some activity or "effort" on the part of the organism; it therefore may involve a situation not too far removed from that normally encountered. I shall say of such nonrepetitive learning processes that they are "noninductive", taking repetition as the characteristic of "induction". (The theory of nonrepetitive learning may be described as *selective* or Darwinian,

while the theory of inductive or repetitive learning is a theory of *instructive* learning; it is Lamarckian.) Of course, this is purely terminological: should anybody insist on calling imprinting an inductive process I should just have to change my terminology.

(5) The observation itself works only like the turning of a key in a lock. Its role is important, but the highly complex result is almost completely preformed.

(6) Imprinting is an irreversible process of learning; that is, it is not subject to correction or revision.

Of course I knew nothing in 1922 of Konrad Lorenz's theories (though I had known him as a boy in Altenberg, where we had close friends in common). I shall here use the theory of imprinting merely as a means of explaining my own conjecture, which was similar yet different. My conjecture was not about animals (though I was influenced by C. Lloyd Morgan and even more by H. S. Jennings[43]) but about human beings, especially young children. It was this.

Most (or perhaps all) learning processes consist in theory formation; that is, in the formation of expectations. The formation of a theory or conjecture has always a "dogmatic", and often a "critical", phase. This dogmatic phase shares, with imprinting, the characteristics (2) to (4), and sometimes also (1) and (5), but not normally (6). The critical phase consists in giving up the dogmatic theory under the pressure of disappointed expectations or refutations, and in trying out other dogmas. I noticed that sometimes the dogma was so strongly entrenched that no disappointment could shake it. It is clear that in this case—though only in this case— dogmatic theory formation comes very close to imprinting, of which (6) is characteristic.[44] However, I was inclined to look on (6) as a kind of neurotic aberration (even though neuroses did not really interest me: it was the psychology of discovery I was trying to get at). This attitude towards (6) shows that what I had in mind was different from imprinting, though perhaps related to it.

I looked on this method of theory formation as a method of learning by trial and error. But when I called the formation of a theoretical dogma a "trial", *I did not mean a random trial.*

It is of some interest to consider the problem of the randomness (or otherwise) of trials in a trial-and-error procedure.

Take a simple arithmetical example: division by a number (say, 74856) whose multiplication table we do not know by heart is usually done by trial and error; but this does not mean that the trials are random, for we do know the multiplication tables for 7 and 8.[44] Of course we could programme a computer to divide by a method of selecting *at random* one of the ten digits 0, 1, . . . 9, as a trial and, in case of error, one of the remaining nine (the erroneous digit having been excluded) by the same random procedure. But this would obviously be inferior to a more systematic procedure: at the very least we should make the computer notice whether its first trial was in error because the selected digit was too small or because it was too big, thus reducing the range of digits for the second selection.

To this example the idea of randomness is in principle applicable, because in every step in long division there is a selection to be made from a well-defined set of possibilities (the digits). But in most zoological examples of learning by trial and error the range or set of possible reactions (movements of any degree of complexity) is not given in advance; and since we do not know the elements of this range we cannot attribute probabilities to them, which we should have to do in order to speak of randomness in any clear sense.

Thus we have to reject the idea that the method of trial and error operates in general, or normally, with trials which are *random*, even though we may, with some ingenuity, construct highly artificial conditions (such as a maze for rats) to which the idea of randomness may be applicable. But its mere applicability does not, of course, establish that the trials are in fact random: our computer may adopt with advantage a more systematic method of selecting the digits; and a rat running a maze may also operate on principles which are not random.

On the other hand, in any case in which the method of trial and error is applied to the solution of such a problem as the problem of adaptation (to a maze, say), the trials are as a rule not determined, or not completely determined, by the problem; nor can they anticipate its (unknown) solution otherwise than by a fortunate accident. In the terminology of D. T. Campbell, we may say that the trials must be "blind" (I should perhaps prefer to say they must be "blind to the solution of the problem").[46] It is not from the trial but only from the critical method, the method of error elimination, that we find, *after* the trial—which corresponds to the dogma—whether or not it was a lucky guess; that is, whether it was sufficiently successful in solving the problem in hand to avoid being eliminated for the time being.

Yet the trials are not always quite blind to the demands of the problem: the problem often determines the range from which the trials are selected (such as the range of the digits). This is well described by David Katz: "A hungry animal divides the environment into edible and inedible things. An animal in flight sees roads of escape and hiding places."[47] Moreover, the problem may change somewhat with the successive trials; for example, the range may narrow. But there may also be quite different cases, especially on the human level; cases in which everything depends upon an ability to break through the limits of the assumed range. These cases show that the selection of the range itself may be a trial (an unconscious conjecture), and that critical thinking may consist not only in a rejection of any particular trial or conjecture, but also in a rejection of what may be described as a deeper conjecture—the assumption of the range of "all possible trials". This, I suggest, is what happens in many cases of "creative" thinking.

What characterizes creative thinking, apart from the intensity of the interest in the problem, seems to me often the ability to break through the limits of the range—or to vary the range—from which a less creative thinker selects his trials. This ability, which clearly is a critical ability, may be described as *critical imagination*. It is often the result of culture clash, that is, a clash between ideas, or frameworks of ideas. Such a clash may help us to break through the ordinary bounds of our imagination.

Remarks like this, however, would hardly satisfy those who seek for a psychological theory of creative thinking, and especially of scientific discovery. For what they are after is a theory of *successful* thinking.

I think that the demand for a theory of successful thinking cannot be satisfied, and that it is not the same as the demand for a theory of creative thinking. Success depends on many things—for example on luck. It may depend on meeting with a promising problem. It depends on not being anticipated. It depends on such things as a fortunate division of one's time between trying to keep up-to-date and concentrating on working out one's own ideas.

But it seems to me that what is essential to "creative" or "inventive" thinking is a combination of intense interest in some problem (and thus a readiness to try again and again) with highly critical thinking; with a readiness to attack even those presuppositions which for less critical thought determine the limits of the range from which trials (conjectures) are selected; with an imaginative freedom that allows us to see so far unsuspected sources of error: possible prejudices in need of critical examination.

(It is my opinion that most investigations into the psychology of creative thought are pretty barren—or else more logical than psychological. For critical thought, or error elimination, can be better characterized in logical terms than in psychological terms.)

A "trial" or a newly formed "dogma" or a new "expectation" is largely the result of inborn *needs* that give rise to specific *problems*. But it is also the result of the inborn need to form expectations (in certain specific fields, which in their turn are related to some other needs); and it may also be partly the result of disappointed earlier expectations. I do not of course deny that there may also be an element of personal ingenuity present in the formation of trials or dogmas, but I think that ingenuity and imagination play their main part in the *critical process of error elimination*. Most of the great theories which are among the supreme achievements of the human mind are the offspring of earlier dogmas, plus criticism.

What became clear to me first, in connection with dogma-formation, was that children—especially small children—urgently need discoverable regularities around them; there was an inborn need not only for food and for being loved but also for discoverable structural invariants of the environment ("things" are such discoverable invariants), for a settled routine, for settled expectations. This infantile dogmatism has been observed by Jane Austen: "Henry and John were still asking every day for the story of Harriet and the gipsies, and still tenaciously setting [Emma] . . . right if she varied in the slightest particular from the original recital."[48] There was, especially in older children, enjoyment in variation, but mainly within a limited range or framework of expectations. Games, for example, were of this kind; and the rules (the invariants) of the game were often almost impossible to learn by mere observation."[49]

My main point was that the dogmatic way of thinking was due to an inborn need for regularities, and to inborn mechanisms of discovery; mechanisms which make us search for regularities. And one of my theses was that if we speak glibly of "heredity and environment" we are liable to underrate the overwhelming role of heredity—which, among other things, largely determines what aspects of its objective environment (the ecological niche) do or do not belong to an animal's subjective, or biologically significant, environment.

I distinguished three main types of learning process, of which the first was the fundamental one:

(1) Learning in the sense of discovery: (dogmatic) formation of theories or expectations, or regular behaviour, checked by (critical) error elimination.

(2) Learning by imitation. This can be shown to be a special case of (1).

(3) Learning by "repetition" or "practising", as in learning to play an instrument or to drive a car. Here my thesis is that (a) there is no genuine "repetition"[50] but rather (b) change through error elimination (following theory formation) and (c) a process which helps to make certain actions or reactions automatic, thereby allowing them to sink to a merely physiological level, and to be performed without attention.

The significance of inborn dispositions or needs for discovering regularities and rules may be seen in the child's learning to speak a language, a process that has been much studied. It is, of course, a kind of learning by imitation; and the most astonishing thing is that this very early process is one of trial and critical error elimination, in which the critical error elimination plays a very important role. The power of innate dispositions and needs in this development can best be seen in children who, owing to their deafness, do not participate in the speech situations of their social environment in the normal way. The most convincing cases are perhaps children who are deaf *and* blind like Laura Bridgman—or Helen Keller, of whom I heard only at a later date. Admittedly, even in these cases we find social contacts—Helen Keller's contact with her teacher—and we also find imitation. But Helen Keller's imitation of her teacher's spelling into her hand is far removed from the ordinary child's imitation of sounds heard over a long period, sounds whose communicative function can be understood, and responded to, even by a dog.

The great differences between human languages show that there must be an important environmental component in language learning. Moreover, the child's learning of a language is almost entirely an instance of learning by imitation. Yet reflection on various biological aspects of language shows that the genetic factors are much more important. Thus I agree with the statement of Joseph Church: "While some part of the change that occurs in infancy can be accounted for in terms of physical maturation, we know that maturation stands in a circular, feedback relationship to experience—the things the organism does, feels, and has done to it. This is not to disparage the role of maturation; it is only to insist that we cannot view it as a simple blossoming of predestined biological characteristics."[51] Yet I differ from Church in contending that the genetically founded maturation process is much more complex and has much greater influence than the releasing signals and the experience of receiving them, though no doubt a certain minimum of this is needed to stimulate the "blossoming". Helen Keller's grasping that the spelled word "water" meant the thing which she could feel with her hand and which she knew so well had, I think, some similarity with "imprinting"; but there are also many dissimilarities. The similarity was the ineradicable impression made on her, and the way in which a single experience released pent-up dispositions and needs. An obvious dissimilarity was the tremendous range of variation which the experience opened up for her, and which led in time to her mastery of language.

In the light of this I doubt the aptness of Church's comment: "The baby does not walk because his 'walking mechanisms' have come into flower, but because he has achieved a kind of orientation to space whereby walking becomes a possible mode of action."[52] It seems to me that in Helen Keller's case there was no orientation in linguistic space or, at any rate, extremely little, prior to her discovery that the touch of her teacher's fingers denoted water, and her jumping to the conclusion that certain touches may have denotational or referential significance. What must have been there was a readiness, a disposition, a need, to interpret signals; and a need, a readiness, to learn to use these signals by imitation, by the method of trial and error (by nonrandom trials and the critical elimination of spelling errors).

It appears that there must be inborn dispositions of great

variety and complexity which cooperate in this field: the disposition to love, to sympathize, to emulate movements, to control and correct the emulated movements; the disposition to use them, and to communicate with their help; the disposition to use language for receiving commands, requests, admonitions, warnings; the disposition to interpret descriptive statements, and to produce descriptive statements. In Helen Keller's case (as opposed to that of normal children) most of her information about reality came through language. As a consequence she was unable for a time to distinguish clearly between what we might call "hearsay" and experience, and even her own imagination: all three came to her in terms of the same symbolic code.[53]

The example of language learning showed me that my schema of a natural sequence consisting of a dogmatic phase followed by a critical phase was too simple. In language learning there is clearly an inborn disposition to correct (that is, to be flexible and critical, to eliminate errors) which after a time peters out. When a child, having learned to say "mice" uses "hice" for the plural of "house", then a disposition to find regularities is at work. The child will soon correct himself, perhaps under the influence of adult criticism. But there seems to be a phase in language learning when the language structure becomes rigid—perhaps under the influence of "automatization", as explained in 3 (c) above.

I have used language learning merely as an example from which we can see that imitation is a special case of the method of trial and error-elimination.[54] It is also an example of the cooperation between phases of dogmatic theory formation, expectation formation, or the formation of behavioural regularities, on the one hand, and phases of criticism on the other.

But although the theory of a dogmatic phase followed by a critical phase is too simple, it is true that *there can be no critical phase without a preceding dogmatic phase, a phase in which something—an expectation, a regularity of behaviour— is formed, so that error elimination can begin to work on it.*

This view made me reject the psychological theory of learning by induction, a theory to which Hume adhered even after he had rejected induction on logical grounds. (I do not wish to repeat what I have said in *Conjectures and Refutations* about Hume's views on habit.)[55] It also led me to see that there is no such thing as an unprejudiced observation. All observation is an activity with an aim (to find, or to check, some regularity which is *at least* vaguely conjectured); an activity guided by problems, and by the context of expectations (the "horizon of expectations" as I later called it). There is no such thing as passive experience; no passively impressed association of impressed ideas. Experience is the result of active exploration by the organism, of the search for regularities or invariants. There is no such thing as a perception except in the context of interests and expectations, and hence of regularities or "laws".

All this led me to the view that conjecture or hypothesis must come before observation or perception: we have inborn expectations; we have latent inborn knowledge, in the form of latent expectations, to be activated by stimuli to which we react as a rule while engaged in active exploration. All learning is a modification (it may be a refutation) of some prior knowledge and thus, in the last analysis, of some inborn knowledge.[56]

It was this psychological theory which I elaborated, tentatively and in a clumsy terminology, between 1921 and 1926. It was this theory of the formation of our knowledge which engaged and distracted me during my apprenticeship as a cabinetmaker.

One of the strange things about my intellectual history is this. Although I was at the time interested in the contrast between dogmatic and critical thinking, and although I looked upon dogmatic thinking as prescientific (and, where it pretends to be scientific, as "unscientific"), and although I realized the link with the falsifiability criterion of demarcation between science and pseudoscience, I did not appreciate that there was a connection between all this and the problem of induction. For years these two problems lived in different (and it appears almost watertight) compartments of my mind, even though I believed that I had solved the problem of induction by the simple discovery that induction by repetition did not exist (any more than did learning something new by repetition): the alleged inductive method of science had to be replaced by the method of (dogmatic) trial and (critical) error elimination, which was the mode of discovery of all organisms from the amoeba to Einstein.

Of course I was aware that my solutions to both these problems—the problem of demarcation, the problem of induction—made use of the same idea: that of the separation of dogmatic and critical thinking. Nevertheless the two problems seemed to me quite different; demarcation had no similarity with Darwinian selection. Only after some years did I realize that there was a close link, and that the problem of induction arose essentially from a mistaken solution of the problem of demarcation—from the mistaken belief that what elevated science over pseudoscience was the "scientific method" of finding true, secure, and justifiable knowledge, and that this method was the method of induction: a belief that erred in more ways than one.

11. Music

In all this, speculations about music played a considerable part, especially during my apprenticeship.

Music has been a dominant theme in my life. My mother was very musical: she played the piano beautifully. It seems that music is a thing that runs in families, though why this should be so is very puzzling indeed. European music seems much too recent an invention to be genetically based, and primitive music is a thing which many very musical people dislike as much as they love the music written since Dunstable, Dufay, Josquin des Prés, Palestrina, Lassus, and Byrd.

However this may be, my mother's family was "musical". It may have come down through my maternal grandmother, *née* Schlesinger. (Bruno Walter was a member of the Schlesinger family. I was not, in fact, an admirer of his, especially after singing under his direction in Bach's *St Matthew Passion*.) My grandparents Schiff were both founder-members of the famous *Gesellschaft der Musikfreunde*, which built the beautiful *Musikvereinssaal* in Vienna. Both my mother's sisters played the piano very well. The elder sister was a professional pianist, whose three children were also gifted musicians—as were three other cousins of mine on my mother's side. One of her brothers played, for many years, first violin in an excellent quartet.

As a child I had a few violin lessons, but I did not get far. I had no piano lessons, and even though I liked to play the piano, I played it (and still play it) very badly. When I was seventeen I met Rudolf Serkin. We became friends and throughout my life I have remained an ardent admirer of his incomparable way of playing, completely absorbed in the work he plays, and forgetful of self.

For a time—between the autumn of 1920 and perhaps 1922—I myself thought quite seriously of becoming a musician. But as with so many other things—mathematics, physics, cabinetmaking—I felt in the end that I was not really good enough. I have done a little composing throughout my life, taking pieces of Bach as my Platonic model, but I have never deceived myself about the merits of my compositions.

I was always conservative in the field of music. I felt that Schubert was the last of the really great composers, though I liked and admired Bruckner (especially his last three symphonies) and *some* Brahms (the *Requiem*). I disliked Richard Wagner even more as the author of the words of the *Ring* (words which, frankly, I could only regard as ludicrous) than as a composer, and I also greatly disliked the music of Richard Strauss, even though I fully appreciated that both of them were full-blooded musicians. (Anybody can see at a glance that *Der Rosenkavalier* was intended to be a *Figaro* rewritten for the modern age; but leaving aside the fact that this historicist intention is misconceived, how could a musician like Strauss be so unperceptive as to think even for a minute that this intention was realized?) However, under the influence of some of Mahler's music (an influence that did not last), and of the fact that Mahler had defended Schönberg, I felt that I ought to make a real effort to get to know and to like contemporary music. So I became a member of the Society for Private Performances (*"Verein für musikalische Privataufführungen"*) presided over by Arnold Schönberg. The Society was dedicated to performing compositions by Schönberg, Alban Berg, Anton von Webern, and other contemporary "advanced" composers like Ravel, Bartók, and Stravinsky. For a time I also became a pupil of Schönberg's pupil Erwin Stein, but I had scarcely any lessons with him: instead I helped him a little with his rehearsals for the Society's performances. In this way I got to know some of Schönberg's music intimately, especially the *Kammersymphonie* and *Pierrot Lunaire*. I also went to rehearsals of Webern, especially of his *Orchesterstücke*, and of Berg.

After about two years I found I had succeeded in getting to know something—about a kind of music which now I liked even less than I had to begin with. So I became, for about a year, a pupil in a very different school of music: the department of Church music in the Vienna *Konservatorium* ("Academy of Music"). I was admitted on the basis of a fugue I had written. It was at the end of this year that I came to the decision mentioned earlier: that I was not good enough to become a musician. But all this added to my love for "classical" music, and to my boundless admiration for the great composers of old.

The connection between music and my intellectual development in the narrow sense is that out of my interest in music there came at least three ideas which influenced me for life. One was closely connected with my ideas on dogmatic and critical thinking, and with the significance of dogmas and traditions. The second was a distinction between two kinds of musical composition, which I then felt to be immensely important, and for which I appropriated for my own use the terms "objective" and "subjective". The third was a realization of the intellectual poverty and destructive power of historicist ideas in music and in the arts in general. I shall now discuss these three ideas.[57]

12. Speculations about the Rise of Polyphonic Music: Psychology of Discovery or Logic of Discovery?

The speculations which I shall recount briefly here were closely related to my speculations, reported earlier, on dogmatic and critical thinking. I believe they were among my earliest attempts to apply those psychological ideas to another field; later they led me to an interpretation of the rise of Greek science. The ideas on Greek science I found to be historically fruitful; those on the rise of polyphony may well be historically mistaken. I later chose the history of music as a second subject for my Ph.D. examination, in the hope that this would give me an opportunity to investigate whether there was anything in them, but I did not get anywhere and my attention soon turned to other problems. In fact, I have now forgotten almost everything I ever knew in this field. Yet these ideas later greatly influenced my reinterpretation of Kant and my change of interest from the psychology of discovery to an objectivist epistemology—that is, to the logic of discovery.

My problem was this. Polyphony, like science, is peculiar to our Western civilization. (I am using the term "polyphony" to denote not only counterpoint but also Western harmony.) Unlike science it does not seem to be of Greek origin but to have arisen between the ninth and fifteenth centuries A.D. If so, it is possibly the most unprecedented, original, indeed miraculous achievement of our Western civilization, not excluding science.

The facts seem to be these. There was much melodic singing—dance-song, folk music, and above all Church music. The melodies—especially slow ones, as sung in Church—were, of course, sometimes sung in parallel octaves. There are reports that they were also sung in parallel fifths (which, taken with the octave, also make fourths, though not if reckoned from the bass). This way of singing ("*organum*") is reported from the tenth century, and probably existed earlier. Plainsong was also sung in parallel thirds, and/or in parallel sixths (both reckoned from the bass: "*fauxbourdon*", "*faburden*").[58] This it seems was felt to be a real innovation, like an accompaniment, or even an embellishment.

What might have been the next step (though its origins are said to go back even to the ninth century) seems to have been that, while the plainsong melody remained unaltered, the accompanying voices no longer proceeded only in parallel thirds and sixths. Antiparallel movement of note against note (*punctum contra punctum,* point counter point) was now also permitted, and could lead not only to thirds and sixths but to fifths, reckoned from the bass, and therefore to fourths between these and some of the other voices.

In my speculations I regarded this last step, the invention of counterpoint, as the decisive one. Although it does not seem to be quite certain that it was temporarily the last step, it was the one that led to polyphony.

The "*organum*" may not at the time have been felt to be an addition to the one-voice melody, except perhaps by those responsible for Church music. It is quite possible that it arose simply from the different voice levels of a congregation which was trying to sing the melody. Thus it may have been an unintended result of a religious practice, namely the intoning of responses by the congregation. Mistakes of this kind in the singing of congregations are bound to occur. It is well known, for example, that in the Anglican festal responses, with the *cantus firmus* in the tenor, congregations are liable to make the mistake of following (in octaves) the highest voice, the treble, instead of the tenor. At all events as long as the singing is in strict parallels there is no polyphony. There may be more than one voice but there is only one melody.

It is perfectly conceivable that the origin also of counterpoint singing lay in mistakes made by the congregation. For when singing in parallels would lead a voice to a note higher than it could sing it may have dropped down to the note sung by the next voice below, thus moving *contra punctum* rather than in parallel *cum puncto*. This may have happened in either *organum* or *fauxbourdon* singing. At any rate, it would explain the first basic rule of simple one-to-one note counterpoint: that the result of the countermovement must be only an octave or fifth or third or sixth (always reckoned from the bass). But though this may be the way the counterpoint *originated*, the *invention* of it must have been due to the musician who first realized that here was a possibility for a more or less independent second melody, to be sung together with the original or fundamental melody, the *cantus firmus*, without disturbing it or interfering with it any more than did *organum* or *fauxbourdon* singing. And this leads to the second basic rule of counterpoint: parallel octaves and fifths are to be avoided *because these would destroy the intended effect of an independent second melody*. Indeed they would lead to an unintended (though temporary) *organum* effect, and thus to the disappearance of the second melody as such, for the second voice would (as in *organum* singing) merely enforce the *cantus firmus*. Parallel thirds and sixths (as in *fauxbourdon*) are permitted steps provided they are preceded or followed fairly soon by a real countermovement (with respect to some of the parts).

Thus the basic idea is this. The fundamental or given melody, the *cantus firmus*, puts limitations on any second melody (or counterpoint), but in spite of these limitations the counterpoint should appear as if it were a freely invented independent melody—a melody melodious in itself and yet almost miraculously fitting the *cantus firmus* though, unlike both *organum* and *fauxbourdon,* in no way dependent on it. Once this basic idea is grasped, we are on the way to polyphony.

I will not enlarge on this. Instead I will explain the historical conjecture I made in this connection—a conjecture which, though it may in fact be false, was nevertheless of great significance for all my further ideas. It was this.

Given the heritage of the Greeks, and the development (and canonization) of the Church modes in the time of Ambrose and Gregory the Great, there would hardly have been any need for, or any incitement to, the invention of polyphony if Church musicians had had the same freedom as, let us say, the originators of folk song. My conjecture was that it was the canonization of Church melodies, the *dogmatic restrictions* on them, which produced the *cantus firmus* against which the counterpoint could develop. It was the established *cantus firmus* which provided the framework, the order, the regularity that made possible inventive freedom without chaos.

In some non-European music we find that *established* melodies give rise to *melodic* variations: this I regarded as a similar development. Yet the combination of a tradition of melodies sung in parallels with the security of a *cantus firmus* which remains undisturbed even by a countermovement opened to us, according to this conjecture, a whole new ordered world, a new cosmos.

Once the possibilities of this cosmos had been to some extent explored—by bold trials and by error elimination—the original authentic melodies, accepted by the Church, could be done without. New melodies could be invented to serve in place of the original *cantus firmus,* some to become traditional for a time, while others might be used in only one musical composition; for example as the subject of a fugue.

According to this perhaps untenable historical conjecture it was thus the canonization of the Gregorian melodies, a piece of dogmatism, that provided the necessary framework or rather the necessary scaffolding for us to build a new world. I also formulated it like this: the dogma provides us with the frame of coordinates needed for exploring the order of this new unknown and possibly in itself even somewhat chaotic world, and also for creating order where order is missing. Thus musical and scientific creation seem to have this much in common: the use of dogma, or myth, as a man-made path along which we move into the unknown, exploring the world, both creating regularities or rules and probing for existing regularities. And once we have found, or erected, some landmarks, we proceed by trying new ways of ordering the world, new coordinates, new modes of exploration and creation, new

ways of building a new world, undreamt of in antiquity unless
in the myth of the music of the spheres.

Indeed, a great work of music (like a great scientific theory)
is a cosmos imposed upon chaos—in its tensions and har-
monies inexhaustible even for its creator. This was described
with marvellous insight by Kepler in a passage devoted to the
music of the heavens: [59]

> Thus the heavenly motions are nothing but a kind of perennial
> concert, rational rather than audible or vocal. They move
> through the tension of dissonances which are like syncopations
> or suspensions with their resolutions (by which men imitate the
> corresponding dissonances of nature), reaching secure and pre-
> determined closures, each containing six terms like a chord con-
> sisting of six voices. And by these marks they distinguish and
> articulate the immensity of time. Thus there is no marvel
> greater or more sublime than the rules of singing in harmony
> together in several parts, unknown to the ancients but at last
> discovered by man, the ape of his Creator; so that, through the
> skilful symphony of many voices, he should actually conjure up
> in a short part of an hour the vision of the world's total per-
> petuity in time; and that, in the sweetest sense of bliss enjoyed
> through Music, the echo of God, he should almost reach the
> contentment which God the Maker has in His Own works.

Here were some more ideas which distracted me and which
interfered with my work on those writing desks during my
apprenticeship as a cabinetmaker.[60] It was during a time when
I was reading Kant's first *Critique* again and again. I soon decided that his central idea was that *scientific theories are man-
made, and that we try to impose them upon the world*: "Our
intellect does not derive its laws from nature, but imposes its
laws upon nature." Combining this with my own ideas, I
arrived at something like the following.

Our theories, beginning with primitive myths and evolving
into the theories of science, are indeed man-made, as Kant
said. We *do* try to impose them on the world, and we *can*
always stick to them dogmatically if we so wish, even if they
are false (as are not only most religious myths, it seems, but
also Newton's theory, which is the one Kant had in mind).[61]
But although at first we have to stick to our theories—*without
theories we cannot even begin*, for we have nothing else to go
by—we can, in the course of time, adopt a more critical attitude towards them. We can try to replace them by something

better if we have learned, with their help, where they let us
down. Thus there may arise a scientific or critical phase of
thinking, *which is necessarily preceded by an uncritical phase*.

Kant, I felt, had been right when he said that it was impossible that knowledge was, as it were, a copy or impression
of reality. He was right to believe that knowledge was *genetically or psychologically* a priori, but quite wrong to suppose
that any knowledge could be a priori *valid*.[62] Our theories are
our inventions; but they may be merely ill-reasoned guesses,
bold conjectures, *hypotheses*. Out of these we create a world:
not the real world, but our own nets in which we try to catch
the real world.

If this was so, then what I originally regarded as the psychology of discovery had a basis in logic: there was no other
way into the unknown, for logical reasons.

13. Two Kinds of Music

It was my interest in music that led me to what I then felt
was a minor intellectual discovery (in 1920, I should say, even
before the rise of my interest in the psychology of discovery
described in the preceding section and in section 10). This discovery later greatly influenced my ways of thinking in philosophy, and it ultimately led even to my distinction between
world 2 and world 3, which plays such a role in the philosophy
of my old age. At first it took the form of an interpretation of
the difference between Bach's and Beethoven's music, or their
ways of approaching music. I still think that there is something
in my idea, even though this particular interpretation, I later
thought, greatly exaggerated the difference between Bach and
Beethoven. Yet the origin of this intellectual discovery is for
me so closely connected with these two great composers that
I will relate it in the form in which it occurred to me at the
time. I do not wish to suggest, however, that my remarks do
justice to them or to other composers, or that they add something new to the many things, good and bad, which have been
written about music: my remarks are essentially autobiographical.

To me the discovery came as a great shock. I loved both
Bach and Beethoven—not only their music but also their
personalities, which, I felt, became visible through their music.

(It was not the same with Mozart: there is something un-fathomable behind his charm.) The shock came one day when it struck me that Bach's and Beethoven's relations to their own work were utterly different, and that although it was permissible to take Bach as one's model, it was quite impermissible to adopt this attitude towards Beethoven.

Beethoven, I felt, had made music an instrument of self-expression. For him in his despair this may have been the only way to go on living. (I believe that this is suggested in his *"Heiligenstädter Testament"* of October 6, 1802.) There is no more moving work than *Fidelio*; no more moving expression of a man's faith, and his hopes, and his secret dreams, and his heroic fight against despair. Yet his purity of heart, his dra-matic powers, his unique creative gifts allowed him to work in a way which, I felt, was not permissible for others. I felt that there could be no greater danger to music than an attempt to make Beethoven's ways an ideal, or a standard, or a model.

It was to distinguish the two distinct attitudes of Bach and of Beethoven towards their compositions that I introduced— only for myself—the terms "objective" and "subjective". These terms may not be well chosen (this does not matter much), and in a context such as this they may mean little to a philosopher; but I was glad to find, many years later, that Albert Schweitzer had used them in 1905, at the beginning of his great book on Bach.[63] For my own thinking the contrast between an objective and a subjective approach, or attitude, especially in relation to one's own work, became decisive. And it soon influenced my views on epistemology. (See, for example, the titles of some of my more recent papers, like "Epistemology Without a Know-ing Subject", or "On the Theory of the Objective Mind", or "Quantum Mechanics without 'The Observer' ".)[64]

I will now try to explain what I have had in mind when speaking (to this day only to myself, and perhaps a few friends) about "objective" and "subjective" music or art. In order to give a better explanation of some of my early ideas I shall sometimes use formulations which I should scarcely have been capable of at that time.

I should perhaps start with a criticism of a widely accepted theory of art: the theory that art is self-expression, or the ex-pression of the artist's personality, or perhaps the expression of his emotions. (Croce and Collingwood are two of the many proponents of this theory. My own anti-essentialist point of view implies that *what-is?* questions like "What is art?" are never genuine problems.)[65] My main criticism of this theory is simple: *the expressionist theory of art is empty.* For everything a man or an animal can do is (among other things) an expression of an internal state, of emotions, and of a personality. This is trivially true for all kinds of human and animal languages. It holds for the way a man or a lion walks, the way a man coughs or blows his nose, the way a man or a lion may look at you, or ignore you. It holds for the ways a bird builds its nest, a spider constructs its web, and a man builds his house. In other words it is not a characteristic of art. For the same reason expressionist or emotive theories of language are trivial, uninformative, and useless.[65a]

I do not of course propose to answer the *what-is?* question "What is art?", but I do suggest that what makes a work of art interesting or significant is something quite different from self-expression. Regarded from a psychological point of view there are certain abilities needed in the artist, which we may describe as creative imagination, perhaps playfulness, taste, and—of some significance—utter devotion to his work. The work must be everything to him, it must transcend his personality. But this is merely a psychological aspect of the matter, and for this very reason of minor importance. The important thing is the work of art. And here I wish to say some negative things first.

There can be great works of art without great originality. There can hardly be a great work of art which the artist *intended mainly* to be original or "different" (except perhaps in a playful way). The main aim of the true artist is the perfection of the work. Originality is a gift of the gods—like naivety, it cannot be had for the asking or gained by seeking. Trying seriously to be original or different, and also trying to express one's own personality, must interfere with what has been called the "integrity" of the work of art. In a great work of art the artist does not try to impose his little personal ambitions on the work but uses them to *serve* his work. In this way he may grow, as a person, through interaction with what he does. By a kind of feedback he may gain in craftsmanship and other powers that make an artist.[66]

What I have said may indicate what the difference was between Bach and Beethoven which so impressed me: Bach forgets himself in his work, he is a servant of his work. Of course, he cannot fail to impress his personality on it; this is unavoidable. But he is not, as Beethoven is, at times, conscious of expressing himself and even his moods. It was for this reason that I saw them as representing two opposite attitudes towards music.

Thus Bach said, when dictating instructions to his pupils concerning continuo playing: "It should make a euphonious harmony for the glory of God and the permitted delectation of the mind; and like all music its *finis* and final cause should never be anything else but the glory of God and the recreation of the mind. When this is not heeded, there really is no music, but a hellish howl and clatter."[67]

I suggest that Bach wished to exclude from the final cause of music the making of a noise for the greater glory of the musician.

In view of my quotation from Bach I should make it quite clear that the difference I have in mind is not one between religious and secular art. Beethoven's *Mass in D* shows this. It is inscribed "From the heart—may it again go to the heart" ("Vom Herzen—möge es wieder—zu Herzen gehen"). It should also be said that my emphasis upon this difference has nothing to do with a denial of the emotional content or the emotional impact of music. A dramatic oratorio such as Bach's *St Matthew Passion depicts* strong emotions and thus, by sympathy, arouses strong emotions—stronger perhaps even than Beethoven's *Mass in D*. There is no reason to doubt that the composer felt these emotions too; but, I suggest, he felt them because the music which he invented must have made its impact on him (otherwise he would, no doubt, have scrapped the piece as unsuccessful), and not because he was first in an emotional mood which he then expressed in his music.

The difference between Bach and Beethoven has its characteristic technical aspects. For example, the structural role of the dynamic element (forte *versus* piano) is different. There are, of course, dynamic elements in Bach. In the concertos there are the changes from tutti to solo. There is the shout "*Barrabam!*" in the *St Matthew Passion*. Bach is often highly dramatic. Yet although dynamic surprises and contrasts occur, they are rarely important determinants of the structure of the composition. As a rule, fairly long periods occur without major dynamic contrasts. Something similar may be said of Mozart. But it cannot be said of, say, Beethoven's *Appassion-*

ata, where dynamic contrasts are nearly as important as harmonic ones.

Schopenhauer says that, in a Beethoven symphony, "all human emotions and passions speak: joy and grief, love and hate, fear and hope, . . . in countless delicate shades";[68] and he stated the theory of emotional expression and resonance in the form: "The way in which all music touches our hearts . . . is due to the fact that it reflects every impulse of our inmost essence." One might say that Schopenhauer's theory of music, and of art in general, escapes subjectivism (if at all) only because according to him "our inmost essence"—our will—is also objective, since it is the essence of the objective world.

But to return to objective music. Without asking a *what-is?* question, let us look at Bach's *Inventions,* and his own somewhat longish title page, in which he makes it clear that he has written for people wanting to play the piano. They will, he assures them, learn "how to play with two and three parts clearly . . . and in a melodious way";[69] and they will be stimulated to be inventive, and so "incidentally get a first taste of composition". Here music is to be learned from examples. The musician is to grow up in Bach's workshop, as it were. He learns a discipline, but he is also encouraged to use his own musical ideas and he is shown how they can be worked out clearly and skilfully. His ideas may develop, no doubt. Through work the musician may, like a scientist, learn by trial and error. And with the growth of his work his musical judgement and taste may also grow—and perhaps even his creative imagination. But this growth will depend on effort, industry, dedication to his work; on sensitivity to the work of others, and on self-criticism. There will be a constant give-and-take between the artist and his work rather than a one-sided "give"— a mere expression of his personality in his work.

From what I have said it should be clear that I am far from suggesting that great music, and great art in general, may not have a deep emotional impact. And least of all do I suggest that a musician may not be deeply moved by what he is writing or playing. Yet to admit the emotional impact of music is not, of course, to accept musical expressionism, which is *a theory about music* (and a theory which has led to certain musical practices). It is, I think, a mistaken theory of the relation between human emotions on the one side and music— and art in general—on the other.

The relation between music and the human emotions can be viewed in a number of very different ways. One of the earliest and most seminal theories is the theory of divine inspiration which manifests itself in the divine madness or divine frenzy of the poet or musician: the artist is possessed by a spirit, though by a benign spirit rather than an evil one. A classical formulation of this view can be found in Plato's *Ion*.[70] The views which Plato formulates there are many-sided and incorporate several distinct theories. Indeed, Plato's treatment may be used as the basis for a systematic survey:

(1) What the poet or musician composes is not his own work but rather a message or dispensation from the gods, especially the Muses. The poet or musician is only an instrument through which the Muses speak; he is merely the mouthpiece of a god and "to prove this, the god sang on purpose the finest of songs through the meanest of poets".[71]

(2) The artist (whether creative or performing) who is possessed by a divine spirit gets frantic, that is, emotionally overexcited; and his state communicates itself to his audience by a process of sympathetic resonance. (Plato compares it with magnetism.)

(3) When the poet or the performer composes or recites he is deeply moved, and indeed possessed (not only by the god but also) by the message; for example, by the scenes he describes. And the work, rather than merely his emotional state, induces similar emotions in his audience.

(4) We have to distinguish between a mere craft or skill or "art" acquired by training or study, and divine inspiration; the latter alone makes the poet or musician.

It should be noted that in developing these views Plato is far from serious: he speaks with his tongue in his cheek. One little joke, especially, is significant and quite amusing. To Socrates' remark that the rhapsode, when possessed by the god, is obviously quite deranged (for example, when he is shaking with fear even though he is in no danger) and that he induces the same nonsensical emotions in his audience, the rhapsode Ion replies: "Exactly: when I watch them from my platform I see how they cry, and how they look at me with awestruck eyes . . . . And I am obliged to watch them very closely indeed; for if they cry I shall laugh because of the money I take, and if they laugh I shall cry because of the money I lose."[72] Clearly Plato wants us to understand that if the rhapsode is possessed by these mundane and far from "deranged" anxieties while watching his listeners in order to regulate his behaviour by their response, then he cannot be serious when he suggests (as Ion does at that very place) that his great effect on them depends entirely on his sincerity—that is, on his being completely and genuinely possessed by the god and out of his mind. (Plato's joke here is a typical self-referring joke—an almost paradoxical self-reference.)[73] In fact, Plato hints strongly[74] that any knowledge or skill (say, of keeping his audience spellbound) would be dishonest trickery and deception, since it would necessarily interfere with the divine message. And he suggests that the rhapsode (or the poet or the musician) is at least sometimes a skilful deceiver, rather than genuinely inspired by the gods.

I will now make use of my list (1) to (4) of Plato's theories in order to derive a modern theory of art as expression. My main contention is that if we take the theory of inspiration and frenzy, *but discard its divine source,* we arrive immediately at the modern theory that art is self-expression, or more precisely, self-inspiration and the expression and communication of emotion. In other words the modern theory is a kind of theology without God—with the hidden nature or essence of the artist taking the place of the gods: the artist inspires himself.

Clearly, this subjectivist theory must discard, or at least play down, point (3): the view that the artist and his audience are emotionally moved *by the work of art.* Yet to me (3) seems to be precisely the theory that gives a correct account of the relationship between art and the emotions. It is an objectivist theory which holds that poetry or music may describe or depict or dramatize scenes which have emotional significance, and that they may even describe or depict emotions as such. (Note that it is not implied by this theory that this is the only way in which art can be significant.)

This objectivist theory of the relationship between art and the emotions may be discerned in the passage from Kepler quoted in the preceding section.

It played an important part in the rise of the opera and the oratorio. It was certainly acceptable to Bach and Mozart. It is, incidentally, perfectly compatible with Plato's theory, expounded for example in the *Republic* and also in the *Laws,* that music has the power to arouse emotions, and to soothe them (like a lullaby), and even to form a man's character: some kinds of music may make him brave, others turn him into a coward; a theory which exaggerates the power of music, to say the least.[75]

According to my objectivist theory (which does not deny self-expression but stresses its utter triviality) the really interesting function of the composer's emotions is not that they are to be expressed, but that they may be used to test the success or the fittingness or the impact of the (objective) work: the composer may use himself as a kind of test body, and he may modify and rewrite his composition (as Beethoven often did) when he is dissatisfied by his own reaction to it; or he may even discard it altogether. (Whether or not the composition is primarily emotional, he will in this way make use of his own reactions—his own "good taste": it is another application of the method of trial and error.)

It should be noted that Plato's theory (4), in its nontheological form, is hardly compatible with an objectivist theory which sees the sincerity of the work less in the genuineness of the artist's inspiration than in the result of the artist's self-criticism. Yet an expressionist view such as Plato's theory (4), Ernst Gombrich informs me, became part of the classical tradition of rhetoric and poetic theory. It even went so far as to suggest that successful description or depiction of emotions depended on the depth of the emotions of which the artist was capable.[76] And it may well have been this dubious last view, the secularized form of Plato's (4) which regards anything that is not pure self-expression as "playing false"[77] or "insincere", that led to the modern expressionist theory of music and art.[78]

To sum up; (1), (2), and (4), without the gods, may be regarded as a formulation of the subjectivist or expressionist theory of art and of its relation to the emotions, and (3) as a partial formulation of an objectivist theory of this relation. According to this objectivist theory it is the work which is mainly responsible for the emotions of the musician rather than the other way round.

To turn now to the objectivist view of music, it is clear that (3) cannot suffice for this, since it is merely concerned with the relation of music to the emotions, which are not the only or even the main thing that makes art significant. The musician *may* make it his problem to depict emotions and to move us to sympathy, as in the *St Matthew Passion*; but there are many other problems he tries to solve. (This is obvious in such an art as architecture, where there are always practical and technical problems to be solved.) In writing a fugue the composer's problem is to find an interesting subject and a contrasting counterpoint, and then to exploit this material as well as he can. What leads him may be a trained sense of general fittingness or "balance". The result may still be moving; but our appreciation may be based on the sense of fittingness—of a cosmos emerging from near chaos—rather than on any depicted emotion. The same may be said of some of Bach's *Inventions,* whose problem was to give the student a first taste of composition, of musical problem solving. Similarly, the task of writing a minuet or a trio poses a definite *problem* for the musician; and the problem may be made more specific by the demand that it should fit into a certain half-completed suite. To see the musician as struggling to solve musical problems is of course very different from seeing him engaged in expressing his emotions (which, trivially, nobody can avoid doing).

I have tried to give a reasonably clear idea of the difference between these two theories of music, objectivist and subjectivist, and to relate them to the two kinds of music—Bach's and Beethoven's—which seemed to me so different at the time, though I loved them both.

The distinction between an objective and a subjective view of one's work became most important for me; and it has, I may say, coloured my views of the world and of life, ever since I was about 17 or 18.

14. *Progressivism in Art, Especially in Music*

I certainly was not quite just when I thought that Beethoven was responsible for the rise of expressionism in music. No doubt he was influenced by the romantic movement, but we can see from his notebooks that he was far removed from merely expressing his feelings or his whims. He often worked very hard through version after version of an idea, trying to clarify and to simplify it, as a comparison of the *Choral Fantasy* with the notebooks for his Ninth Symphony will show. And yet, the indirect influence of his tempestuous personality, and the attempts to emulate him led, I believe, to a decline in

music. It still seems to me that this decline was brought about
largely by expressionist theories of music. But I would not
now contend that there are not other equally pernicious creeds,
and among them some anti-expressionist creeds, which have
led to all kinds of formalistic experiments, from serialism to
musique concrète. All these movements, however, and especially the "anti-" movements, largely result from that brand of
"historicism" which I will discuss in this section, and especially
from the historicist attitude towards "progress".

Of course, there can be something like progress in art, in
the sense that certain new possibilities may be discovered, and
also new problems.[79] In music such inventions as counterpoint
revealed almost an infinity of new possibilities and problems.
There is also purely technological progress (for example in
certain instruments). But although this may open new possibilities, it is not of fundamental significance. (Changes in the
"medium" may remove more problems than they create.)
There could conceivably be progress even in the sense that
musical knowledge grows—that is, a composer's mastery of
the discoveries of all his great predecessors; but I do not think
that anything like this has been achieved by any musician.
(Einstein may not have been a greater physicist than Newton,
but he mastered Newtonian technique completely; no similar
relation seems ever to have existed in the field of music.) Even
Mozart, who may have come closest to it, did not attain it
and Schubert did not come close to it. There is also always the
danger that newly realized possibilities may kill old ones:
dynamic effects, dissonance, or even modulation may, if used
too freely, dull our sensitivity to the less obvious effects of
counterpoint or, say, to an allusion to the old modes.

The loss of possibilities which may be the result of any
innovation is an interesting problem. Thus counterpoint
threatened the loss of monodic and especially of rhythmic
effects, and contrapuntal music was criticized for this reason,
as well as for its complexity. There is no doubt that this criticism had some wholesome effects, and that some of the great
masters of counterpoint, Bach included, took the greatest interest in the intricacies and contrasts resulting from combining
recitatives, arias, and other monodic alternatives with contrapuntal writing. Many recent composers have been less imaginative. (Schönberg realized that, in a context of dissonances,
consonances have to be carefully prepared, introduced, and

perhaps even resolved. But this meant that their old function was lost.)

It was Wagner[80] who introduced into music an idea of progress which (in 1935 or thereabouts) I called "historicist", and who thereby, I still believe, became the main villain of the piece. He also sponsored the uncritical and almost hysterical idea of the unappreciated genius: the genius who not only expresses the spirit of his time but who actually is "ahead of his time"; a leader who is normally misunderstood by all his contemporaries except a few "advanced" connoisseurs.

My thesis is that the doctrine of art as self-expression is merely trivial, muddleheaded and empty—though not necessarily vicious, unless taken seriously, when it may easily lead to self-centred attitudes and megalomania. But the doctrine that the genius must be in advance of his time is almost wholly false and vicious, and opens up the universe of art to evaluations which have nothing to do with the values of art.

Intellectually, both theories are on such a low level that it is astonishing that they were ever taken seriously. The first can be dismissed as trivial and muddled on purely intellectual grounds, without even looking more closely at art itself. The second—the theory that art is the expression of the genius in advance of his time—can be refuted by countless examples of geniuses genuinely appreciated by many patrons of the arts of their own time. Most of the great painters of the Renaissance were highly appreciated. So were many great musicians. Bach was appreciated by King Frederick of Prussia—besides, he obviously was not ahead of his time (as was, perhaps, Telemann): his son Carl Philipp Emanuel thought him *passé* and spoke of him habitually as "The Old Fusspot" (*"der alte Zopf"*). Mozart, though he died in poverty, was appreciated throughout Europe. An exception is perhaps Schubert, appreciated only by a comparatively small circle of friends in Vienna; but even he was getting more widely known at the time of his premature death. The story that Beethoven was not appreciated by his contemporaries is a myth. Yet let me say here again (see the text between notes 47 and 48 in section 10 above) that I think that success in life is largely a matter of luck. It has little correlation with merit, and in all fields of life there have always been many people of great merit who did not succeed. Thus it is only to be expected that this happened also in the sciences and in the arts.

The theory that art advances with the great artists in the van is not just a myth; it has led to the formation of cliques and pressure groups which, with their propaganda machines, almost resemble a political party or a church faction.

Admittedly there were cliques before Wagner. But there was nothing quite like the Wagnerians (unless later the Freudians): a pressure group, a party, a church with rituals. But I shall say no more about this, since Nietzsche has said it all much better.[81]

I saw some of these things at close quarters in Schönberg's Society for Private Performances. Schönberg started as a Wagnerian, as did so many of his contemporaries. After a time his problem and that of many members of his circle became, as one of them said in a lecture, "How can we supersede Wagner?" or even "How can we supersede the remnants of Wagner in ourselves?". Still later it became: "How can we remain ahead of everybody else, and even constantly supersede ourselves?". Yet I feel that the will to be ahead of one's time has nothing to do with service to music, and nothing to do with genuine dedication to one's own work.

Anton von Webern was an exception to this. He was a dedicated musician and a simple, lovable man. But he had been brought up in the philosophical doctrine of self-expression, and he never doubted its truth. He once told me how he wrote his *Orchesterstücke*: he just listened to sounds that came to him, and he wrote them down; and when no more sounds came, he stopped. This, he said, was the explanation of the extreme brevity of his pieces. Nobody could doubt the purity of his heart. But there was not much music to be found in his modest compositions.

There may be something in the ambition to write a great work; and such an ambition may indeed be instrumental in creating a great work, though many great works have been produced without any ambition other than to do one's work well. But the ambition to write a work which is ahead of its time and which will preferably not be understood too soon —which will shock as many people as possible—has nothing to do with art, even though many art critics have fostered this attitude and popularized it.

Fashions, I suppose, are as unavoidable in art as in many other fields. But it should be obvious that those rare artists who were not only masters of their art but blessed with the gift of originality were seldom anxious to follow a fashion, and never tried to be leaders of fashion. Neither Johann Sebastian Bach nor Mozart nor Schubert created a new fashion or "style" in music. Yet one who did was Carl Philipp Emanuel Bach, a well-trained musician of talent and charm—and less originality of invention than the great masters. This holds for all fashions, including that of primitivism—though primitivism may be partly motivated by a preference for simplicity; and one of Schopenhauer's wisest remarks (though not perhaps his most original one) was: "In all art . . . simplicity is essential . . . ; at least it is always dangerous to neglect it."[82] I think what he meant was the striving for the kind of simplicity which we find especially in the subjects of the great composers. As we may see from the *Seraglio,* for example, the final result may be complex; but Mozart could still proudly reply to the Emperor Joseph that there was not one note too many in it.

But although fashions may be unavoidable, and although new styles may emerge, we ought to despise attempts to be fashionable. It should be obvious that "modernism"—the wish to be new or different at any price, to be ahead of one's time, to produce *"The Work of Art of the Future"* (the title of an essay by Wagner)—has nothing to do with the things an artist should value and should try to create.

Historicism in art is just a mistake. Yet one finds it everywhere. Even in philosophy one hears of a new style of philosophizing, or of a "Philosophy in a New Key"—as if it were the key that mattered rather than the tune played, and as if it mattered whether the key was old or new.

Of course I do not blame an artist or a musician for trying to say something new. What I really blame many of the "modern" musicians for is their failure to love great music—the great masters and their miraculous works, the greatest perhaps that man has produced.

15. Last Years at the University

In 1925, while I was working with neglected children, the City of Vienna founded a new institute of education, called the Pedagogic Institute. The Institute was to be linked, somewhat loosely, with the University. It was to be autonomous, but its students were to take courses at the University in addition to the courses at the Institute. Some of the University courses (such as psychology) were made compulsory by the Institute, others were left to the choice of the students. The purpose of the new Institute was to further and support the reform, then in progress, of the primary and secondary schools in Vienna, and some social workers were admitted as students; I was among them. So also were some lifelong friends of mine—Fritz Kolb, who after the Second World War served as Austrian Ambassador in Pakistan, and Robert Lammer, with both of whom I enjoyed many fascinating discussions.

This meant that after a short period as social workers we had to give up our work (without unemployment relief, or income of any kind—except, in my case, the occasional coaching of American students). But we were enthusiastic for school reform, and enthusiastic for studying—even though our experience with neglected children made some of us sceptical of the educational theories we had to swallow in huge doses. These were imported mainly from America (John Dewey) and from Germany (Georg Kerschensteiner).

From a personal and intellectual point of view the years at the Institute were most significant for me because I met my wife there. She was one of my fellow students, and was to become one of the severest judges of my work. Her part in it ever since has been at least as strenuous as my own. Indeed, without her much of it would never have been done at all.

My years in the Pedagogic Institute were years of studying, of reading and of writing—but not of publishing. They were my first years of (quite unofficial) academic teaching. Throughout these years I gave seminars for a group of fellow students. Although I did not realize it then, they were good seminars. Some of them were most informal, and took place while hiking, or skiing, or spending the day on a river island in the Danube. From my teachers at the Institute I learned very little, but I learned much from Karl Bühler, Professor of Psychology at the University. (Though students of the Pedagogic Institute went to his lectures, he did not teach at the Pedagogic Institute, or hold a position there.)

In addition to the seminars I gave classes, also quite unofficially, to prepare my fellow students for some of the countless examinations we had to sit, among which were psychology examinations set by Bühler. He told me afterwards (in the first private conversation I ever had with a university

teacher) that this had been the best-prepared batch of students
he had ever examined. Bühler had only recently been called to
Vienna to teach psychology, and at that time was best known
for his book on *The Mental Development of the Child*.[83] He
had also been one of the first *Gestalt* psychologists. Most important for my future development was his theory of the three
levels or functions of language (already referred to in note 78):
the expressive function (*Kundgabefunktion*), the signal or release function (*Auslösefunktion*), and, on a higher level, the
descriptive function (*Darstellungsfunktion*). He explained that
the two lower functions were common to human and animal
languages and were always present, while the third function
was characteristic of human language alone and sometimes (as
in exclamations) absent even from that.

This theory became important to me for many reasons. It
confirmed my view of the emptiness of the theory that art is
self-expression. It led me later to the conclusion that the theory
that art was "communication" (that is, release)[84] was equally
empty, since these two functions were trivially present in all
languages, even in animal languages. It led me to a strengthen-
ing of my "objectivist" approach. And it led me—a few years
later—to add to Bühler's three functions what I called the
argumentative function.[85] The argumentative function of language became particularly important for me because I regarded
it as the basis of all critical thought.

I was in my second year at the Pedagogic Institute when I
met Professor Heinrich Gomperz, to whom Karl Polanyi had
given me an introduction. Heinrich Gomperz was the son of
Theodor Gomperz (author of *Greek Thinkers*, and a friend
and translator of John Stuart Mill). Like his father, he was an
excellent Greek scholar, and also greatly interested in epistemology. He was only the second professional philosopher I had
met, and the first university teacher of philosophy. Previously
I had met Julius Kraft (of Hanover, a distant relation of mine,
and a pupil of Leonard Nelson),[86] who later became a teacher
of philosophy and sociology at Frankfurt; my friendship with
him lasted until his death in 1960.[87]

Julius Kraft, like Leonard Nelson, was a non-Marxist
socialist, and about half our discussions, often lasting into the
small hours of the morning, were centred on my criticism of
Marx. The other half were about the theory of knowledge:
mainly Kant's so-called "transcendental deduction" (which I

regarded as question-begging), his solution of the antinomies, and Nelson's "Impossibility of the Theory of Knowledge".[88] Over these we fought a hard battle, which went on from 1926 to 1956, and we did not reach anything approaching agreement until a few years before his untimely death in 1960. On Marxism we reached agreement fairly soon.

Heinrich Gomperz was always patient with me. He had the reputation of being scathing and ironical, but I never saw anything of it. He could be most witty, though, when telling stories about some of his famous colleagues, such as Brentano and Mach. He invited me from time to time to his house, and let me talk. Usually I gave him portions of manuscript to read, but he made few comments. He was never critical of what I had to say, but he very often drew my attention to related views, and to books and articles bearing on my own topic. He never indicated that he found what I said important until I gave him, some years later, the manuscript of my first book (still unpublished—see section 16 below). He then (in December, 1932) wrote me a highly appreciative letter, the first I had ever received about something I had written.

I read all his writings, which were outstanding for their historical approach: he could follow a historical problem through all its vicissitudes from Heraclitus to Husserl, and (in conversations anyway) to Otto Weininger, whom he had known personally, and regarded as almost a genius. We did not agree on psychoanalysis. At this time he believed in it, and he even wrote for *Imago*.

The problems I discussed with Gomperz belonged to the psychology of knowledge or of discovery; it was during this period that I was exchanging them for problems of the logic of discovery. I was reacting more and more strongly against any "psychologistic" approach, including the psychologism of Gomperz.

Gomperz himself had criticized psychologism—only to fall back into it.[89] It was mainly in discussions with him that I began to stress my realism, my conviction that there is a real world, and that the problem of knowledge is the problem of how to discover this world. I became convinced that, if we want to argue about it, we cannot start from our sense experiences (or even our feelings, as his theory demanded) without falling into the traps of psychologism, idealism, positivism, phenomenalism, even solipsism—all views which I refused to take seriously. My sense of social responsibility told me that taking such problems seriously was a kind of treason of the intellectuals—and a misuse of the time we ought to be spending on real problems.

Since I had access to the psychological laboratory I conducted a few experiments, which soon convinced me that sense data, "simple" ideas or impressions, and other such things, did not exist: they were fictitious—inventions based on mistaken attempts to transfer atomism (or Aristotelian logic—see below) from physics to psychology. The proponents of *Gestalt* psychology held similarly critical views; but I felt that their views were insufficiently radical. I found that my views were similar to those of Oswald Külpe and his school (the *Würzburger Schule*), especially Bühler[90] and Otto Selz.[91] They had found that we do not think in images but in terms of problems and their tentative solutions. Finding that some of my results had been anticipated, especially by Otto Selz, was, I suspect, one of the minor motives of my move away from psychology.

Abandoning the psychology of discovery and of thinking, to which I had devoted years, was a lengthy process which culminated in the following insight. I found that association psychology—the psychology of Locke, Berkeley, and Hume—was merely a translation of Aristotelian subject-predicate logic into psychological terms.

Aristotelian logic deals with statements like "Men are mortal". Here are two "terms" and a "copula" which couples or associates them. Translate this into psychological terms, and you will say that thinking consists in having the "ideas" of man and of mortality "associated". One has only to read Locke with this in mind to see how it happened: his main assumptions are the validity of Aristotelian logic, and that it describes our subjective, psychological thought processes. But subject-predicate logic is a very primitive thing. (It may be regarded as an interpretation of a small fragment of Boolean algebra, untidily mixed up with a small fragment of naive set theory.) It is incredible that anybody should still mistake it for empirical psychology.

A further step showed me that the mechanism of translating a dubious logical doctrine into one of an allegedly empirical psychology was still at work, and had its dangers, even for such an outstanding thinker as Bühler.

For in Külpe's *Logic*,[92] which Bühler accepted and greatly admired, arguments were regarded as complex judgements (which is a mistake from the point of view of modern logic).[93] In consequence there could be no real distinction between judging and arguing. As a further consequence the descriptive function of language (which corresponds to "judgements") and the argumentative function amounted to the same thing; thus Bühler failed to see that they could be as clearly separated as the three functions of language which he had already distinguished.

Bühler's expressive function could be separated from his communicative function (or signal function, or release function) because an animal or a man could express himself even if there were no "receiver" to be stimulated. The expressive and communicative functions together could be distinguished from Bühler's descriptive function because an animal or a man could communicate fear (for example) without describing the object feared. The descriptive function (a higher function, according to Bühler, and exclusive to man) was, I then found, clearly distinguishable from the argumentative function, since there exist languages, such as maps, which are descriptive but not argumentative.[94] (This, incidentally, makes the familiar analogy between maps and scientific theories a particularly unfortunate one. Theories are essentially argumentative systems of statements: their main point is that they explain deductively. Maps are non-argumentative. Of course every theory is also descriptive, like a map—just as it is, like all descriptive language, communicative, since it may make people act; and also expressive, since it is a symptom of the "state" of the communicator—which may happen to be a computer.) Thus there was a second case where a mistake in logic led to a mistake in psychology; in this particular case the psychology of linguistic dispositions and of the innate biological needs that underlie the uses and achievements of human language.

All this showed me *the priority of the study of logic over the study of subjective thought processes*. And it made me highly suspicious of many of the psychological theories accepted at the time. For example, I came to realize that *the theory of conditioned reflex was mistaken. There is no such thing as a conditioned reflex.* Pavlov's dogs have to be interpreted as searching for invariants in the field of food acquisition (a field that is essentially "plastic", or in other words open to exploration by trial and error) and as fabricating expectations, or anticipations, of impending events. One might call this "conditioning"; but it is not a reflex formed as a result of the learning process, it is a discovery (perhaps a mistaken one) of what to anticipate.[95] Thus even the apparently empirical results of Pavlov, and the Reflexology of Bechterev,[96] and most of the results of modern learning theory, turned out, in this light, to misinterpret their findings under the influence of Aristotle's logic; for reflexology and the theory of conditioning were merely association psychology translated into neurological terms.

In 1928 I submitted a Ph.D. thesis in which, though indirectly it was the result of years of work on the psychology of thought and discovery, I finally turned away from psychology. I had left the psychological work unfinished; I had not even a fair copy of most of what I had written; and the thesis, "On the Problem of Method in the Psychology of Thinking",[97] was a kind of hasty last minute affair originally intended only as a methodological introduction to my psychological work, though now indicative of my changeover to methodology.

I felt badly about my thesis, and I have never again even glanced at it. I also felt badly about my two "rigorous" examinations (*"Rigorosum"* was the name of the public oral examinations for Ph.D.), one in the history of music, the other in philosophy and psychology. Bühler, who had previously examined me in psychology, did not ask me any questions in this field, but encouraged me to talk about my ideas on logic and the logic of science. Schlick examined me mainly on the history of philosophy, and I did so badly on Leibniz that I thought I had failed. I could hardly believe my ears when I was told that I had passed in both examinations with the highest grade, *"einstimmig mit Auszeichnung"*. I was relieved and happy, of course, but it took quite a time before I could get over the feeling that I had deserved to fail.

16. *Theory of Knowledge:* Logik der Forschung

I got my Ph.D. in 1928, and in 1929 I qualified as a teacher of mathematics and physical science in (lower) secondary schools. For this qualifying examination I wrote a thesis on problems of axiomatics in geometry, which also contained a chapter on non-Euclidean geometry.

It was only after my Ph.D. examination that I put two and two together, and my earlier ideas fell into place. I understood why the mistaken theory of science which had ruled since Bacon—that the natural sciences were the *inductive* sciences, and that induction was a process of establishing or justifying theories by *repeated* observations or experiments—was so deeply entrenched. The reason was that scientists had to *demarcate* their activities from pseudoscience as well as from theology and metaphysics, and they had taken over from Bacon the inductive method as their criterion of demarcation. (On the other hand, they were anxious to justify their theories by an appeal to sources of knowledge comparable in reliability to the sources of religion.) But I had held in my hands for many years a better criterion of demarcation: testability or falsifiability.

Thus I could discard induction without getting into trouble over demarcation. And I could apply my results concerning the method of trial and error in such a way as to replace the whole inductive methodology by a deductive one. The falsification or refutation of theories through the falsification or refutation of their deductive consequences was, clearly, a deductive inference (*modus tollens*). This view implied that *scientific theories, if they are not falsified, for ever remain hypotheses or conjectures.*

Thus the whole problem of scientific method cleared itself up, and with it the problem of scientific progress. Progress consisted in moving towards theories which tell us more and more—theories of ever greater content. But the more a theory says the more it excludes or forbids, and the greater are the opportunities for falsifying it. So a theory with greater content is one which can be more severely tested. This consideration led to a theory in which scientific progress turned out not to consist in the accumulation of observations but in the overthrow of less good theories and their replacement by better ones, in particular by theories of greater content. Thus there was competition between theories—a kind of Darwinian struggle for survival.

Of course theories which we claim to be no more than conjectures or hypotheses need no justification (and least of all a justification by a nonexistent "method of induction", of which nobody has ever given a sensible description). We can, however, sometimes give reasons for preferring one of the

competing conjectures to the others, in the light of their critical discussion.[98]

All this was straightforward and, if I may say so, highly
coherent. But it was very different from what the Machian
positivists and the Wittgensteinians of the Vienna Circle were
saying. I had heard about the Circle in 1926 or 1927, first from
a newspaper article by Otto Neurath and then in a talk he
gave to a social democratic youth group. (This was the only
party meeting I ever attended; I did so because I had known
Neurath a little since 1919 or 1920.) I had read the programmatic literature of the Circle, and of the *Verein* Ernst Mach;
in particular a pamphlet by my teacher, the mathematician
Hans Hahn. In addition I had read Wittgenstein's *Tractatus*,
some years before writing my Ph.D. thesis, and Carnap's
books as they were published.

It was clear to me that all these people were looking for a
criterion of demarcation not so much between science and
pseudoscience as between science and metaphysics. And it was
also clear to me that my old criterion of demarcation was
better than theirs. For, first of all, they were trying to find a
criterion which made metaphysics meaningless nonsense, sheer
gibberish, and any such criterion was bound to lead to trouble,
since metaphysical ideas are often the forerunners of scientific
ones. Secondly, demarcation by meaningfulness versus mean-
inglessness merely shifted the problem. As the Circle recognized, it created the need for another criterion, one to distinguish between meaning and lack of meaning. For this, they
had adopted verifiability, which was taken as being the same
as provability by observation statements. But this was only
another way of stating the time-honoured criterion of the in-
ductivists; there was no real difference between the ideas of
induction and of verification. Yet according to my theory,
science was not inductive; induction was a myth which had
been exploded by Hume. (A further and less interesting point,
later acknowledged by Ayer, was the sheer absurdity of the
use of verifiability as a meaning criterion: how could one
ever say that a theory was gibberish because it could not be
verified? Was it not necessary to *understand* a theory in order
to judge whether or not it could be verified? And could an
understandable theory be sheer gibberish?) All this made me
feel that, to every one of their main problems, I had better
answers—more coherent answers—than they had.

Perhaps the main point was that they were positivists, and therefore epistemological idealists in the Berkeley-Mach tradition. Of course they did not admit that they were idealists. They described themselves as "neutral monists". But in my opinion this was merely another name for idealism—and in Carnap's books[99] idealism (or, as he called it, methodological solipsism) was pretty openly accepted as a kind of working hypothesis.

I wrote (without publishing) a great amount on these issues, working through Carnap's and Wittgenstein's books in considerable detail. From the point of view I had reached this turned out to be fairly straightforward. I knew only one man to whom I could explain these ideas, and that was Heinrich Gomperz. In connection with one of my main points—that scientific theories always remain hypotheses or conjectures—he referred me to Alexis Meinong, *On Assumptions (Über Annahmen*, 1902), which I found not only to be psychologistic but also to assume implicitly—as did Husserl in his *Logical Investigations (Logische Untersuchungen*, 1900, 1901)—that scientific theories are true. For years I found that people had great difficulty in admitting that theories are, logically considered, the same as hypotheses. The prevailing view was that hypotheses are as yet unproved theories, and that theories are proved, or established, hypotheses. And even those who admitted the hypothetical character of all theories still believed that they needed some justification; that, if they could not be shown to be true, their truth had to be highly probable.

The decisive point in all this, the hypothetical character of all scientific theories, was to my mind a fairly commonplace consequence of the Einsteinian revolution, which had shown that not even the most successfully tested theory, such as Newton's, should be regarded as more than a hypothesis, an approximation to the truth.

In connection with my espousal of deductivism—the view that theories are hypothetico-deductive systems, and that the method of science is not inductive—Gomperz referred me to Professor Victor Kraft, a member of the Vienna Circle and author of a book on *The Basic Forms of Scientific Method*.[100] This book was a most valuable description of a number of the methods actually used in science, and it showed that at least some of these methods are not inductive but deductive—*hypothetico-deductive*. Gomperz gave me an introduction to

Victor Kraft (no relation to Julius Kraft) and I met him several times in the *Volksgarten*, a park near the University. Victor Kraft was the first member of the Vienna Circle I met (unless I include Zilsel, who, according to Feigl[101] was not a member). He was ready to pay serious attention to my criticisms of the Circle—more so than most of the members I met later. But I remember how shocked he was when I predicted that the philosophy of the Circle would develop into a new form of scholasticism and verbalism. This prediction has, I think, come true. I am alluding to the programmatic view that the task of philosophy is "the explication of concepts".

In 1929 or 1930 (in the latter year I was, at last, appointed to a teaching position in a secondary school) I met another member of the Vienna Circle, Herbert Feigl.[102] The meeting, arranged by my uncle Walter Schiff, Professor of Statistics and Economics at the University of Vienna, who knew of my philosophical interests, became decisive for my whole life. I had found some encouragement before in the interest shown by Julius Kraft, Gomperz, and Victor Kraft. But although they knew that I had written many (unpublished) papers,[103] none of them had encouraged me to publish my ideas. Gomperz had indeed impressed upon me the fact that publishing *any* philosophical ideas was hopelessly difficult. (Times have changed.) This was supported by the fact that Victor Kraft's great book on the methods of science had been published only with the support of a special fund.

But Herbert Feigl, during our nightlong session, told me not only that he found my ideas important, almost revolutionary, but also that I should publish them in book form.[104]

It had never occurred to me to write a book. I had developed my ideas out of sheer interest in the problems, and then written some of them down for myself because I found that this was not only conducive to clarity but necessary for self-criticism. At that time I looked upon myself as an unorthodox Kantian, and as a realist.[105] I conceded to idealism that our theories are actively produced by our minds rather than impressed upon us by reality, and that they transcend our "experience"; yet I stressed that a falsification may be a head-on clash with reality. I also interpreted Kant's doctrine of the impossibility of knowing things in themselves as corresponding to the for ever hypothetical character of our theories. I also regarded myself as a Kantian in ethics. And I used to think in those days that my criticism of the Vienna Circle was simply the result of having read Kant, and of having understood some of his main points.

I think that without encouragement from Herbert Feigl it is unlikely that I should ever have written a book. Writing a book did not fit my way of life nor my attitude towards myself. I just did not have the confidence that what interested me was of sufficient interest to others. Moreover, nobody encouraged me after Feigl left for America. Gomperz, to whom I told the story of my exciting meeting with Feigl, definitely discouraged me, and so did my father, who was afraid that it all would end in my becoming a journalist. My wife opposed the idea because she wanted me to use any spare time to go skiing and mountain climbing with her—the things we both enjoyed most. But once I started on the book she taught herself to type, and she has typed many times everything I have written since. (I have always been unable to get anywhere when typing—I am in the habit of making far too many corrections.)

The book I wrote was devoted to two problems—the problems of induction and of demarcation—and their interrelation. So I called it *The Two Fundamental Problems of the Theory of Knowledge* (*Die beiden Grundprobleme der Erkenntnistheorie*), an allusion to a title of Schopenhauer's (*Die beiden Grundprobleme der Ethik*).

As soon as I had a number of chapters typed I tried them out on my friend and onetime colleague at the Pedagogic Institute, Robert Lammer. He was the most conscientious and critical reader I have ever come across: he challenged every point which he did not find crystal clear, every gap in the argument, every loose end I had left. I had written my first draft pretty quickly, but thanks to what I learned from Lammer's insistent criticism I never again wrote anything quickly. I also learned never to defend anything I had written against the accusation that it is not clear enough. If a conscientious reader finds a passage unclear, it has to be rewritten. So I acquired the habit of writing and rewriting, again and again, clarifying and simplifying all the time. I think I owe this habit almost entirely to Robert Lammer. I write, as it were, with somebody constantly looking over my shoulder and constantly pointing out to me passages which are not clear. I know of course very well that one can never anticipate all possible misunderstandings; but I think one can avoid some misunderstandings, assuming readers who want to understand.

Through Lammer I had earlier met Franz Urbach, an experimental physicist working at the University of Vienna's Institute for Radium Research. We had many common interests (music among them), and he gave me much encouragement. He also introduced me to Fritz Waismann, who had been the first to formulate the famous criterion of meaning with which the Vienna Circle was identified for so many years —the verifiability criterion of meaning. Waismann was very interested in my criticism. I believe it was through his initiative that I received my first invitation to read some papers criticizing the views of the Circle in some of the "epicyclic" groups which formed its halo, so to speak.

The Circle itself was, so I understood, Schlick's private seminar, meeting on Thursday evenings. Members were simply those whom Schlick invited to join. I was never invited, and I never fished for an invitation.[106] But there were other groups, meeting in Victor Kraft's or Edgar Zilsel's apartments, and in other places; and there was also Karl Menger's famous *"mathematisches Colloquium"*. Several of these groups, of whose existence I had not even heard, invited me to present my criticisms of the central doctrines of the Vienna Circle. It was in Edgar Zilsel's apartment, in a crowded room, that I read my first paper. I still remember the stage fright.

In some of those early talks I also discussed problems connected with the theory of probability. Of all existing interpretations I found the so-called "frequency interpretation" the most convincing, and Richard von Mises's form of it the one which seemed most satisfactory. But there were still a number of difficult problems left open, especially if one looked at it from the point of view that *statements about probability are hypotheses*. The central question then was: *are they testable?* I tried to discuss this and some subsidiary questions, and I have worked on various improvements of my treatment of them ever since.[107] (Some are still unpublished.)

Several members of the Circle, some of whom had been at these meetings, invited me to discuss these points with them personally. Among them were Hans Hahn, who had so impressed me through his lectures, and Philipp Frank and Richard von Mises (on their frequent visits to Vienna). Hans Thirring, the theoretical physicist, invited me to address his seminar; and Karl Menger invited me to become a member of his colloquium. It was Karl Menger (whom I had asked for advice on the point) who suggested to me that I should try to apply his theory of dimension to the comparison of degrees of testability.

Very early in 1932 I completed what I then regarded as the first volume of *The Two Fundamental Problems of the Theory of Knowledge*. It was conceived, from the beginning, largely as a critical discussion and as a correction of the doctrines of the Vienna Circle; long sections were also devoted to criticisms of Kant and of Fries. The book, which is still unpublished, was read first by Feigl and then by Carnap, Schlick, Frank, Hahn, Neurath, and other members of the Circle; and also by Gomperz.

Schlick and Frank accepted the book in 1933 for publication in the series *Schriften zur wissenschaftlichen Weltauffassung* of which they were the editors. (This was a series of books most of which were written by members of the Vienna Circle.) But the publishers, Springer, insisted that it must be radically shortened. By the time the book was accepted I had written most of the second volume. This meant that little more than an outline of my work could be given within the number of pages the publishers were prepared to publish. With the agreement of Schlick and Frank I put forward a new manuscript which consisted of extracts from both volumes. But even this was returned by the publishers as too long. They were insisting on a maximum of fifteen sheets (two hundred and forty pages). The final extract—which was ultimately published as *Logik der Forschung*—was made by my uncle, Walter Schiff, who ruthlessly cut about half the text.[108] I do not think that, after having tried so hard to be clear and explicit, I could have done this myself.

I can hardly give here an outline of that outline which became my first published book. But there are one or two points I will mention. The book was meant to provide a theory of knowledge and, at the same time, to be a treatise on method—the method of science. The combination was possible because I looked on human knowledge as consisting of our theories, our hypotheses, our conjectures; as the *product* of our intellectual activities. There is of course another way of looking at "knowledge": we can regard "knowledge" as a subjective "state of mind", as a subjective state of an organism. But I chose to treat it as a system of statements—theories submitted to discussion. "Knowledge" in this sense is *objective*; and it is hypothetical or conjectural.

This way of looking at knowledge made it possible for me to reformulate Hume's *problem of induction*. In this objective reformulation the problem of induction is no longer a problem of our beliefs—or of the rationality of our beliefs—but a problem of the logical relationship between singular statements (descriptions of "observable" singular facts) and universal theories.

In this form, the problem of induction becomes soluble: [109] there is no induction, because universal theories are not deducible from singular statements. But they may be refuted by singular statements, since they may clash with descriptions of observable facts.

Moreover, we may speak of "better" and of "worse" theories in an objective sense even before our theories are put to the test: the better theories are those with the greater content and the greater explanatory power (both relative to the problems we are trying to solve). And these, I showed, are also the better testable theories; and—if they stand up to tests—the better tested theories.

This solution of the problem of induction gives rise to a new theory of the method of science, to an analysis of the *critical method*, the method of trial and error: the method of proposing bold hypotheses, and exposing them to the severest criticism, in order to detect where we have erred.

From the point of view of this methodology, we start our investigation with *problems*. We always find ourselves in a certain problem situation; and we choose a problem which we hope we may be able to solve. The solution, always tentative, consists in a theory, a hypothesis, a conjecture. The various competing theories are compared and critically discussed, in order to detect their shortcomings; and the always changing, always inconclusive results of the critical discussion constitute what may be called "the science of the day".

Thus *there is no induction*: we never argue from facts to theories, unless by way of refutation or "falsification". This view of science may be described as selective, as Darwinian. By contrast, theories of method which assert that we proceed by induction or which stress *verification* (rather than *falsification*) are typically Lamarckian: they stress *instruction* by the environment rather than *selection* by the environment.

It may be mentioned (although this was not a thesis of *Logik der Forschung*) that the proposed solution of the problem of induction also shows the way to a solution of the older problem—the problem of the rationality of our beliefs. For we may first replace the idea of belief by that of action; and we may say that actions (or inactions) are "rational" if they are carried out in accordance with the state, prevailing at the time, of the critical scientific discussion. There is no better synonym for "rational" than "critical". (Belief, of course, is never rational: it is rational to *suspend* belief; cp. note 226 below.)

My solution of the problem of induction has been widely misunderstood. I intend to say more about it in my *Replies to my Critics*.[109a]

17. Who Killed Logical Positivism?

> Logical positivism, then, is dead, or as dead as a philosophical movement ever becomes.
>
> JOHN PASSMORE[110]

Owing to the manner in which it originated, my book *Logik der Forschung*, published late in 1934, was cast partly in the form of a criticism of positivism. So were its unpublished predecessor of 1932 and my brief letter to the Editors of *Erkenntnis* in 1933.[111] Since at this time my position was being widely discussed by leading members of the Circle and, moreover, since the book was published in a mainly positivistic series edited by Frank and Schlick, this aspect of *Logik der Forschung* had some curious consequences. One was that until its English publication in 1959 as *The Logic of Scientific Discovery* philosophers in England and America (with only a few exceptions, such as J. R. Weinberg)[112] seem to have taken me for a logical positivist—or at best for a dissenting logical positivist who replaced verifiability by falsifiability.[113] Even some logical positivists themselves, remembering that the book had come out in this series, preferred to see in me an ally rather than a critic.[113a] They thought they could ward off my criticism with a few concessions—preferably mutual ones—and some verbal stratagems.[114] (For example, they persuaded themselves that I would agree to substitute falsifiability for verifiability as a criterion of *meaningfulness*.) And because I did not press my attack home (fighting logical positivism being by no means a major interest of mine) the logical positivists did not feel that logical positivism was seriously challenged. Before, and even after, the Second World War books and papers went on appearing which continued this method of concessions and small adjustments. But by then logical positivism had really been dead some years.

Everybody knows nowadays that logical positivism is dead. But nobody seems to suspect that there may be a question to be asked here—the question "Who is responsible?" or, rather, the question "Who has done it?". (Passmore's excellent historical article [cited in note 110] does not raise this question.) I fear that I must admit responsibility. Yet I did not do it on purpose: my sole intention was to point out what seemed to me a number of fundamental mistakes. Passmore correctly ascribes the dissolution of logical positivism to insuperable internal difficulties. Most of these difficulties had been pointed out in my lectures and discussions, and especially in my *Logik der Forschung*.[114a] Some members of the Circle were impressed by the need to make changes. Thus the seeds were sown. They led, in the course of many years, to the disintegration of the Circle's tenets.

Yet the disintegration of the Circle preceded that of its tenets. The Vienna Circle was an admirable institution. Indeed, it was a unique seminar of philosophers working in close cooperation with first-rate mathematicians and scientists, keenly interested in problems of logic and the foundations of mathematics, and attracting two of the greatest innovators in the field, Kurt Gödel and Alfred Tarski. Its dissolution was a most serious loss. Personally I owe a debt of gratitude to some of its members, especially to Herbert Feigl, Victor Kraft, and Karl Menger—not to mention Philipp Frank and Moritz Schlick, who had accepted my book in spite of its severe criticism of their views. Again, it was indirectly through the Circle that I met Tarski, first at the Prague conference in August, 1934, when I had with me the page proofs of *Logik der Forschung*; in Vienna in 1934-35; and again at the Congress in Paris in September, 1935. And from Tarski I learned more, I think, than from anybody else.

But what attracted me perhaps most to the Vienna Circle was the "scientific attitude" or, as I now prefer to call it, the rational attitude. This was beautifully stated by Carnap in the last three paragraphs of the Preface to the first edition of his first major book, *Der logische Aufbau der Welt*. There is much in Carnap with which I disagree; and even in these three paragraphs there are things which I regard as mistaken: for although I agree that there is something "depressing" (*"nieder-drückend"*) about most philosophical systems, I do not think that it is their "plurality" which is to be blamed; and I feel that it is a mistake to demand the elimination of metaphysics, and another to give as a reason that "its theses cannot be rationally justified". But although especially Carnap's repeated demand for "justification" was (and still is) to my mind a serious mistake, such a matter is almost insignificant in this context. For Carnap pleads here for rationality, for greater intellectual responsibility; he asks us to learn from the way in which mathematicians and scientists proceed, and he contrasts with this the depressing ways of the philosophers: their pretentious wisdom, and their arrogation of knowledge which they present to us with a minimum of rational, or critical, argument.

It is in this general attitude, the attitude of the enlightenment, and in this critical view of philosophy—of what philosophy unfortunately is, and of what it ought to be—that I still feel very much at one with the Vienna Circle and with its spiritual father, Bertrand Russell. This explains perhaps why I was sometimes thought by members of the Circle, such as Carnap, to be one of them, and to overstress my differences with them.

Of course I never intended to overstress these differences. When writing my *Logik der Forschung* I hoped only to challenge my positivist friends and opponents. I was not altogether unsuccessful. When Carnap, Feigl, and I met in the Tyrol[115] in the summer of 1932, Carnap read the unpublished first volume of my *Grundprobleme* and, to my surprise, published shortly afterwards an article in *Erkenntnis*, "Über Protokoll-sätze",[116] in which he gave a detailed account, with ample acknowledgements, of some of my views. He summed up the situation by explaining that—and why—he now regarded what he called my "procedure" (*"Verfahren B"*) as the best so far available in the theory of knowledge. This procedure was *the deductive procedure of testing statements in physics*, a procedure that looks on *all statements, even the test statements themselves, as hypothetical or conjectural,* as being soaked in theory. Carnap adhered to this view for a considerable time,[117] and so did Hempel.[118] Carnap's and Hempel's highly favourable reviews of *Logik der Forschung*[119] were promising signs, and so, in another way, were attacks by Reichenbach and Neurath.[120]

Since I mentioned Passmore's article at the beginning of this section, I may perhaps say here that what I regard as the ultimate cause of the dissolution of the Vienna Circle and of Logical Positivism is not its various grave mistakes of doctrine (many of which I had pointed out) but a decline of interest in the great problems: the concentration upon *minutiae* (upon "puzzles") and especially upon the meanings of words; in brief, its scholasticism. This was inherited by its successors, in England and in the United States.

18. Realism and Quantum Theory

Although my *Logik der Forschung* may have looked to some like a criticism of the Vienna Circle, its main aims were positive. I tried to propound a theory of human knowledge. But I looked upon human knowledge in a way quite different from the way of the classical philosophers. Down to Hume and Mill and Mach, most philosophers took human knowledge as something settled. Even Hume, who thought of himself as a sceptic, and who wrote the *Treatise* in the hope of revolutionizing the social sciences, almost identified human knowledge with human habits. Human knowledge was what almost everybody knew: that the cat was on the mat; that Julius Caesar had been assassinated; that grass was green. All this seemed to me incredibly uninteresting. What was interesting was problematic knowledge, growth of knowledge—*discovery*.

If we are to look upon the theory of knowledge as a theory of discovery, then it will be best to look at *scientific* discovery. A theory of the growth of knowledge should have something to say especially about the growth of physics, and about the clash of opinions in physics.

At the time (1930) when, encouraged by Herbert Feigl, I began writing my book, modern physics was in turmoil. Quantum mechanics had been created by Werner Heisenberg in 1925;[121] but it was several years before outsiders—including professional physicists—realized that a major breakthrough

had been achieved. And from the very beginning there was
dissension and confusion. The two greatest physicists, Einstein
and Bohr, perhaps the two greatest thinkers of the twentieth
century, disagreed with one another. And their disagreement
was as complete at the time of Einstein's death in 1955 as it
had been at the Solvay meeting in 1927. There is a widely
accepted myth that Bohr won a victory in his debate with
Einstein;[122] and the majority of creative physicists supported
Bohr and subscribed to this myth. But two of the greatest
physicists, de Broglie and Schrödinger, were far from happy
with Bohr's views (later called "the Copenhagen interpretation
of quantum mechanics") and proceeded on independent lines.
And after the Second World War, there were several important
dissenters from the Copenhagen School, in particular Bohm,
Bunge, Landé, Margenau, and Vigier.

The opponents of the Copenhagen interpretation are still in
a small minority, and they may well remain so. They do not
agree among themselves. But quite a lot of disagreement is also
discernible within the Copenhagen orthodoxy. The members
of this orthodoxy do not seem to notice these disagreements
or at any rate to worry about them, just as they do not seem
to notice the difficulties inherent in their views. But both are
very noticeable to outsiders.

These all too superficial remarks will perhaps explain why
I felt at a loss when I first tried to get to grips with quantum
mechanics, then often called "the new quantum theory". I was
working on my own, from books and from articles; the only
physicist with whom I sometimes talked about my difficulties
was my friend Franz Urbach. I tried to *understand* the theory,
and he had doubts whether it was understandable—at least by
ordinary mortals.

I began to see light when I realized the significance of
Born's statistical interpretation of the theory. At first I had not
liked Born's interpretation: Schrödinger's original interpretation appealed to me, aesthetically, and as *an explanation of
matter*; but once I had accepted the fact that it was not tenable,
and that Born's interpretation was highly successful, I stuck to
the latter, and was thus puzzled to know how one could uphold
Heisenberg's interpretation of his indeterminacy formulae if
Born's interpretation was accepted. It seemed obvious that if
quantum mechanics was to be interpreted statistically, then so
must be Heisenberg's formulae: they had to be interpreted as

scatter relations, that is, as stating the lower bounds of the statistical scatter, or the upper bounds of the homogeneity, of any sequence of quantum-mechanical experiments. This view has now been widely accepted.[123] (I should make clear, however, that originally I did not always clearly distinguish between the scatter of the results of a set of experiments and the scatter of a set of particles in one experiment; although I had found in "formally singular" probability statements the means for solving this problem, it was only completely cleared up with the help of the idea of propensities.)[124]

A second problem of quantum mechanics was the famous problem of the "reduction of the wave packet". Few perhaps will agree that this problem was solved in 1934 in my *Logik der Forschung*; yet some very competent physicists have accepted the correctness of this solution. The proposed solution consists in pointing out that the probabilities occurring in quantum mechanics were *relative probabilities* (or conditional probabilities).[125]

The second problem is connected with what was perhaps the central point of my considerations—a conjecture, which grew into a conviction, that the *problems of the interpretation of quantum mechanics can all be traced to problems of the interpretation of the calculus of probability.*

A third problem solved was the distinction between a preparation of a state and a measurement. Although my discussion of this was quite correct and, I think, very important, I made a serious mistake over a certain thought experiment (in section 77 of *Logik der Forschung*). I took this mistake very much to heart; I did not know at that time that even Einstein had made some similar mistakes, and I thought that my blunder proved my incompetence. It was in Copenhagen in 1936, after the Copenhagen "Congress for Scientific Philosophy", that I heard of Einstein's mistakes. On the initiative of Victor Weisskopf, the theoretical physicist, I had been invited by Niels Bohr to stay a few days for discussion at his Institute. I had previously defended my thought experiment against von Weizsäcker and Heisenberg, whose arguments did not quite convince me, and against Einstein, whose arguments did convince me. I had also discussed the matter with Thirring and (in Oxford) with Schrödinger, who told me that he was deeply unhappy about quantum mechanics and thought that nobody really understood it. Thus I was in a defeatist mood when Bohr told me of his discussions with Einstein—the same discussions he described later in Schilpp's *Einstein* volume.[126] It did not occur to me to derive comfort from the fact that, according to Bohr, Einstein had been as mistaken as I; I felt defeated, and I was unable to resist the tremendous impact of Bohr's personality. (In those days Bohr was irresistible anyway.) I more or less caved in, though I still defended my explanation of the "reduction of the wave packet". Weisskopf seemed willing to accept it, but Bohr was much too eager to expound his theory of complementarity to take any notice of my feeble efforts to sell my explanation, and I did not press the point, content to learn rather than to teach. I left with an overwhelming impression of Bohr's kindness, brilliance, and enthusiasm; I also felt little doubt that he was right and I wrong. Yet I could not persuade myself that I understood Bohr's "complementarity", and I began to doubt whether anybody else understood it, though clearly some were persuaded that they did. This doubt was shared by Einstein, as he later told me, and also by Schrödinger.

This set me thinking about "understanding". Bohr, in a way, was asserting that quantum mechanics was not understandable; that only classical physics was understandable and that we had to resign ourselves to the fact that quantum mechanics could be only partially understood, and then only through the medium of classical physics. Part of this understanding was achieved through the classical "particle picture", part through the classical "wave picture"; these two pictures were incompatible, and they were what Bohr called "*complementary*". There was no hope for a fuller or more direct understanding of the theory; and what was required was a "*renunciation*" of any attempt to reach a fuller understanding.

I suspected that Bohr's theory was based on a very narrow view of what *understanding* could achieve. Bohr, it appeared, thought of understanding in terms of pictures and models—in terms of a kind of visualization. This was too narrow, I felt; and in time I developed an entirely different view. According to this view what matters is the understanding not of pictures but of the logical force of a theory: its explanatory power, its relation to the relevant problems and to other theories. I developed this view over many years in lectures, first I think in Alpbach (1948) and in Princeton (1950), in Cambridge in a lecture on quantum mechanics (1953 or 1954), in Minneapolis (1962), and later again in Princeton (1963), and other places (London too, of course). It will be found, though only sketchily, in some of my later papers.[127]

Concerning quantum physics I remained for years greatly discouraged. I could not get over my mistaken thought experiment, and although it is, I think, quite right to grieve over any of one's mistakes, I think now that I attributed too much weight to it. Only after some discussions, in 1948 or 1949, with Arthur March, a quantum physicist whose book on the foundations of quantum mechanics[128] I had quoted in my *Logik der Forschung*, did I return to the problem with something like renewed courage.

I went again into the old arguments, and I arrived at the following:[129]

(A) The problem of determinism and indeterminism.
(1) There is no such thing as a specifically quantum-mechanical argument against determinism. Of course, quantum mechanics is a statistical theory and not a prima facie deterministic one, but this does not mean that it is incompatible with a prima facie deterministic theory. (More especially, von Neumann's famous proof of this alleged incompatibility— of the nonexistence of so-called "hidden variables"—is invalid, as was shown by David Bohm and more recently, by more direct means, by John S. Bell.)[130] The position at which I had arrived in 1934 was that nothing in quantum mechanics justifies the thesis that determinism is refuted because of its incompatibility with quantum mechanics. Since then I have changed my mind on this issue more than once.

A model showing that the existence of a prima facie deterministic theory was indeed formally compatible with the results of quantum mechanics was given by David Bohm in 1951. (The basic ideas underlying this proof had been anticipated by de Broglie.)

(2) There is, on the other hand, no valid reason whatever for the assertion that determinism has a basis in physical science; in fact there are strong reasons against it, as pointed out by C. S. Peirce,[131] Franz Exner, Schrödinger,[132] and von Neumann:[133] all these drew attention to the fact that the deterministic character of Newtonian mechanics was compatible with indeterminism.[134] Moreover, while it is possible to explain the existence of prima facie deterministic theories as macro-theories on the basis of indeterministic and probabilistic micro-

theories, the opposite is not possible: *nontrivial probabilistic conclusions can only be derived (and thus explained) with the help of probabilistic premises.*[135] (In this connection some very interesting arguments of Landé's should be consulted.)[136]

     (B) Probability.

In quantum mechanics we need an interpretation of the probability calculus which

     (1) is physical and objective (or "realistic");

     (2) yields probability hypotheses which can be statistically tested.

Moreover,

     (3) these hypotheses are applicable to single cases; and

     (4) they are relative to the experimental setup.

In *Logik der Forschung* I developed a "formalistic" interpretation of the probability calculus which satisfied all these demands. I have since improved upon this, replacing it by the "propensity interpretation".[137]

     (C) Quantum Theory.

     (1) Realism. Although I had no objections of principle to "wavicles" (wave-*cum*-particles) or similar nonclassical entities, I did not see (and I still do not see) any reason to deviate from the classical, naive, and realistic view that electrons and so on are just particles; that is to say, *that they are localized, and possess momentum.* (Of course, further developments of the theory *may* show that those who do not agree with this view are right.)[138]

     (2) Heisenberg's so-called "indeterminacy principle" is a misinterpretation of certain formulae, which assert *statistical scatter.*

     (3) The Heisenberg formulae *do not refer to measurements*; which implies that the whole of the current "quantum theory of measurement" is packed with misinterpretations. Measurements which according to the usual interpretation of the Heisenberg formulae are "forbidden" are according to my results not only allowed, but actually required for *testing* these very formulae.[139] However, the scatter relations refer to the *preparation of the states* of quantum mechanical systems. In preparing a state we always introduce a (conjugate) scatter.[139a]

     (4) What is indeed peculiar to quantum theory is the (phase-dependent) *interference of probabilities.* It is conceivable that we may have to accept this as something ultimate. However, this does not seem to be the case: while still oppos-

ing Compton's crucial tests of Einstein's photon theory Duane produced, in 1923, long before wave mechanics, a new quantum rule,[140] which may be regarded as the analogue with respect to momentum of Planck's rule with respect to energy. Duane's rule for the quantization of momentum can be applied not only to photons but (as stressed by Landé)[141] to particles, and it then gives a rational (though only qualitative) explanation of particle interference. Landé has further argued that quantitative interference rules of wave mechanics can be derived from simple additional assumptions.

(5) Thus a host of philosophical spectres can now be exorcized, and all those many staggering philosophical assertions about the intrusion of the subject or the mind into the world of the atom can now be dismissed. This intrusion can be largely explained as due to the traditional subjectivist misinterpretation of the probability calculus.[142]

19. Objectivity and Physics

In the preceding section I stressed some aspects of *Logik der Forschung* and of later work that emerged from it, which had little or nothing to do with my criticism of positivism. However, the criticism of positivism did play a subsidiary role even in my views on quantum theory. I think I was immunized against Heisenberg's early positivism by my rejection of Einstein's positivism.

As I mentioned before (section 8, text between notes 31 and 32), I was introduced to Einstein's theories of relativity by Max Elstein. He neither stressed nor criticized the observational point of view, but helped me to understand the problem of the special theory (I am afraid in the usual unhistorical manner, as a problem posed by the experiment of Michelson and Morley), and he discussed with me Minkowski's form of the solution. It may have been this initiation that prevented me from ever taking the operationalist approach to simultaneity seriously: one can read Einstein's paper[143] of 1905 as a realist, without paying any attention to "the observer"; or alternatively, one can read it as a positivist or operationalist, always attending to the observer and his doings.

It is an interesting fact that Einstein himself was for years a dogmatic positivist and operationalist. He later rejected this interpretation: he told me in 1950 that he regretted no mistake he ever made as much as this mistake. The mistake assumed a really serious form in his popular book *Relativity: The Special and the General Theory*.[144] There he says, on page 22 (pages 14 f. in the German original): "I would ask the reader not to proceed farther until he is fully convinced on this point." The point is, briefly, that "simultaneity" must be *defined*—and defined in an *operational* way—since otherwise "I allow myself to be deceived . . . when I imagine that I am able to attach a meaning to the statement of simultaneity". Or in other words, a term has to be operationally defined or else it is *meaningless*.[144a] (Here in a nutshell is the positivism later developed by the Vienna Circle under the influence of Wittgenstein's *Tractatus*, and in a very dogmatic form.)

But the situation in Einstein's theory is, simply, that for any inertial system (or "the stationary system")[145] events are simultaneous or not, just as they are in Newton's theory; and the following transitivity law (*Tr*) holds:

(*Tr*) In any inertial system, if the event *a* is simultaneous with *b*, and *b* with the event *c*, then *a* is simultaneous with *c*.

But (*Tr*) *does not hold in general for any three distant events unless the system in which a and b are simultaneous is the same as the system in which b and c are simultaneous:* it does not hold for distant events some of which occur in different systems, that is, in systems which are in relative motion. This is a consequence of the principle of the invariance of the velocity of light with respect to any two (inertial) systems in relative motion, that is, the principle that allows us to deduce the Lorentz transformations. There is no *need* even to mention simultaneity, except in order to warn the unwary that the Lorentz transformations are incompatible with an application of (*Tr*) to events that occur in different (inertial) systems.[146]

It will be seen that there is no occasion here to introduce operationalism and even less to insist on it. Moreover, since Einstein was in 1905—at least when he wrote his paper on relativity—unaware of the Michelson experiment, he had only scanty evidence at his disposal for the invariance of the velocity of light.

But many excellent physicists were greatly impressed by Einstein's operationalism, which they regarded (as did Einstein himself for a long time) as an integral part of relativity. And so it happened that operationalism became the inspiration of Heisenberg's paper of 1925, and of his widely accepted suggestion that the concept of the track of an electron, or of its classical position-*cum*-momentum, was *meaningless*.

Here, for me, was an occasion to test my realist epistemology, by applying it to a critique of Heisenberg's subjectivist interpretation of the quantum-mechanical formalism. About Bohr I said little in *Logik der Forschung* because he was less explicit than Heisenberg, and because I was reluctant to saddle Bohr with views which he might not hold. Anyway, it had been Heisenberg who had founded the new quantum mechanics on an operationalist programme, and whose success had converted the majority of theoretical physicists to positivism and to operationalism.

20. Truth; Probability; Corroboration

By the time *Logik der Forschung* was published I felt that there were three problems which I had to take further: truth, probability, and the comparison of theories with respect to their content and to their corroboration.

Although the notion of falsity—that is, of untruth—and thus, by implication, the notion of truth—played a big role in *Logik der Forschung*, I had used it quite naively, and had discussed it only in section 84, entitled "Remarks Concerning the Use of the Concepts 'True' and 'Corroborated' " (*Bemerkungen über den Gebrauch der Begriffe "wahr" und "bewährt"*). At the time I did not know Tarski's work, or the distinction between two kinds of metalinguistic theories (one called by Carnap "Syntax", and the other by Tarski "Semantics", later very clearly distinguished and discussed by Marja Kokoszyńska);[147] yet so far as the relation between truth and corroboration was concerned, my views[148] became more or less standard in the Circle—that is, among those of its members[149] who, like Carnap, accepted Tarski's theory of truth.

When in 1935 Tarski explained to me (in the *Volksgarten* in Vienna) the idea of his definition of the concept of truth, I realized how important it was, and that he had finally rehabilitated the much maligned correspondence theory of truth which, I suggest, is and always has been the commonsense idea of truth.

My later thoughts on this were largely an attempt to make

clear to myself what Tarski had done. It was not really that he had *defined* truth. To be sure, he had done so for a very simple formalized language, and he had sketched methods of defining it for a class of other formalized languages. Yet he had also made clear that there were other essentially equivalent ways of introducing truth: not by definition, but axiomatically; so the question of whether truth should be introduced axiomatically or by definition could not be fundamental. Moreover, all these precise methods were confined to formalized languages, and could not, as Tarski had shown, be applied to ordinary language (with its "universalistic" character). Nevertheless it was clear that we could learn from Tarski's analysis how to use, with a little care, the notion of truth in ordinary discourse, and to use it, moreover, in its ordinary sense—as correspondence to the facts. I decided in the end that what Tarski had done was to show that once we had understood the distinction between an object language and a (semantic) meta-language—a language in which we can speak about statements and about facts—there was no great difficulty left in *understanding* how a statement could correspond to a fact. (See section 32 below.)

Probability created problems for me, as well as much exciting and enjoyable work. The fundamental problem tackled in *Logik der Forschung* was the *testability of probability statements in physics.* I regarded this problem as offering an important challenge to my general epistemology, and I solved it with the help of an idea which was an integral part of this epistemology and not, I think, an *ad hoc* assumption. It was the idea that no test of any theoretical statement is final or conclusive, and that the empirical, or the critical, attitude involves the adherence to some "methodological rules" which tell us not to evade criticism but to accept refutations (though not too easily). These rules are essentially somewhat flexible. As a consequence the acceptance of a refutation is nearly as risky as the tentative adoption of a hypothesis: it is the acceptance of a conjecture.

A second problem was that of *the variety of possible interpretations of probability statements,* and this problem was closely related to two others which played a major role in my book (but which were utterly different in character). One was the problem of the interpretation of quantum mechanics—amounting, in my opinion, to the problem of the status of probability statements in physics; the other was the problem of the content of theories.

Yet in order to be able to attack the problem of the interpretation of probability statements in its most general form it was necessary to develop an *axiom system for the calculus of probability*. This was also necessary for another purpose— for establishing my thesis, proposed in *Logik der Forschung*, that *corroboration was not a probability in the sense of the probability calculus*; that is, that certain intuitive aspects of corroboration made it impossible to identify it with probability in the sense of the probability calculus.[149a] (See also the text between notes 155 and 159 below.)

In *Logik der Forschung* I had pointed out that there were *many possible interpretations* of the idea of probability, and I had insisted that in the physical sciences only a frequency theory like that proposed by Richard von Mises was acceptable. (I later modified this view by introducing the propensity interpretation, and I think that von Mises would have agreed with the modification; for propensity statements are still tested by frequencies.) But I had one major technical objection, quite apart from several minor ones, to all the known frequency theories operating with infinite sequences. It was this.

Take *any finite sequence* of 0's and 1's (or only of 0's or only of 1's), however long; and let its length be n, which may be thousands of millions. Continue from the $n + 1$st term with an *infinite random sequence* (a "collective"). Then for the combined sequence, only the properties of some *endpiece* (from some $m \geq n + 1$ on) are significant, for a sequence satisfies the demands of von Mises if, and only if, any endpiece of it satisfies them. But this means that any *empirical* sequence is simply irrelevant for judging any infinite sequence of which it is the initial segment.

I had the opportunity to discuss this problem (together with many others) with von Mises, with Helly, and with Hans Hahn. They agreed, of course; but von Mises did not worry much about it. His view (which is well known) was that a sequence which satisfied his demands—a "collective" as he called it— was an *ideal* mathematical concept like a sphere. Any empirical "sphere" could be only a rough approximation.

I was willing to accept the relation between an ideal mathematical sphere and an empirical sphere as a kind of model for that between a mathematical random sequence (a "collective")

and an infinite empirical sequence. But I stressed that there was
no satisfactory sense in which a *finite* sequence could be said
to be a rough approximation to a collective in von Mises's
sense. I therefore set out to construct something ideal but less
abstract: *an ideal infinite random sequence which had the
property of randomness from the very start*, so that every
finite initial segment of length *n* was as ideally random as
possible.

I had outlined the construction of such a sequence in *Logik
der Forschung*,[150] but I did not then fully realize that this construction actually solved (a) the problem of an *ideal infinite*
sequence capable of being compared with a *finite empirical*
sequence; (b) that of constructing a mathematical sequence
which could be used in place of von Mises's (nonconstructive)
definition of randomness; and (c) that of making superfluous
von Mises's postulate of the existence of a limit, since this
could now be proved. Or in other words, I did not realize at
the time that my construction superseded several of the
solutions proposed in *Logik der Forschung*.

My idealized random sequences were not "collectives" in
von Mises's sense: although they passed all statistical tests of
randomness, they were definite mathematical constructions:
their continuation could be mathematically predicted by anybody who knew the method of construction. But von Mises
had demanded that a "collective" should be unpredictable (the
"principle of the excluded gambling system"). This sweeping
demand had the unfortunate consequence that no example of
a collective could be constructed, so that a constructive proof
of the consistency of the demand was impossible. The only
way to get over this difficulty was, of course, to relax the demand. Thus arose an interesting problem: what was the minimum relaxation which would allow a proof of consistency (or
existence)?

This was interesting, but it was not my problem. My central
problem was the construction of *finite* randomlike sequences
of arbitrary length, and thus expandable into infinite ideal
random sequences.

Early in 1935 I lectured on this in one of the epicycles of
the Vienna Circle, and afterwards I was invited by Karl Menger to give a lecture to his famous "*mathematisches Colloquium*". I found a very select gathering of about thirty people,
among them Kurt Gödel, Alfred Tarski, and Abraham Wald;

and, according to Menger, I became the unwitting instrument for arousing Wald's interest in the field of probability and statistics, in which he became so famous. Menger describes the incident in his obituary of Wald as follows: [151]

> At that time there occurred a second event which proved to be of crucial importance in Wald's further life and work. The Viennese philosopher Karl Popper : . . tried to make precise the idea of a random sequence, and thus to remedy the obvious shortcomings of von Mises' definition of collectives. After I had heard (in Schlick's Philosophical Circle) a semitechnical exposition of Popper's ideas, I asked him to present the important subject in all details to the Mathematical Colloquium. Wald became greatly interested and the result was his masterly paper on the self-consistency of the notion of collectives : . : He based his existence proof for collectives on a twofold relativisation of that notion.

Menger proceeds to characterize his description of Wald's definition of a collective, and concludes: [152]

> Although Wald's relativisation restricts the original unlimited (but unworkable) idea of collectives, it is much weaker than the irregularity requirements of Copeland, Popper, and Reichenbach. In fact, it embraces these requirements as special cases.

This is very true, and I was most impressed by Wald's brilliant solution of the problem of a minimum relaxation of von Mises's demands. [153] But, as I had opportunity to point out to Wald, it did not solve my problem: a "Wald-collective" with equal probabilities for 0 and 1 could still *begin* with a block of thousands of millions of 0's, since randomness was only a matter of how it behaved in the limit. Admittedly, Wald's work provided a general method for dividing the class of all infinite sequences into collectives and noncollectives, whilst mine merely allowed the construction of *some* random sequences of any desired length—of some very special models, as it were. However, *any given finite sequence,* of any length, could always be so continued as to become either a collective or a noncollective in Wald's sense. (The same held for the sequences of Copeland, Reichenbach, Church, and others. [154])

I have felt for a long time that my solution of my problem, though it seems philosophically quite satisfactory, could be made mathematically more interesting by being generalized, and that Wald's method could be used for this purpose. I discussed the matter with Wald, with whom I became friendly, in the hope that he himself would do it. But these were difficult times: neither of us managed to return to the problem before we both emigrated, to different parts of the world.

There is another problem, closely connected with probability: that of (a measure of) the *content* of a statement or a theory. I had shown, in *Logik der Forschung*, that the probability of a statement is inversely related to its content, and that it could therefore be used to construct a measure of the content. (Such a measure of the content would be at best comparative, unless the statement was one about some game of chance, or perhaps about some statistics.)

This suggested that among the interpretations of the probability calculus at least two are of major importance: (1) an interpretation which allows us to speak of the *probability of (singular) events,* such as a toss of a penny or the arrival of an electron on a screen; and (2) the *probability of statements or propositions,* especially of conjectures (of varying degrees of universality).[155] This second interpretation is needed by those who maintain that degree of corroboration can be measured by a probability; and also by those, like myself, who wish to deny it.

As for my *degree of corroboration,* the idea was to sum up, in a short formula, a *report* of the manner in which a theory has passed—or not passed—its tests, including an evaluation of the severity of the tests: only tests undertaken in a *critical* spirit—attempted refutations—should count. By passing such tests, a theory may "prove its mettle"—its "fitness to survive".[156] Of course, it can only prove its "fitness" to survive those tests which it *did* survive; just as in the case of an organism, "fitness", unfortunately, only means actual survival, and past performance in no way ensures future success.

I regarded (and I still regard) the degree of corroboration of a theory merely as a critical report on the quality of past performance: *it could not be used to predict future performance.* (The *theory,* of course, may help us to predict *future events.*) Thus it had a time index: one could only speak of the degree of corroboration of a theory *at a certain stage of its critical discussion.* In some cases it provided a very good guide if one wished to assess *the relative merits of two or more competing theories in the light of past discussions.* When faced with the *need to act,* on one theory or another, the rational choice was to act on that theory—if there was one—

which so far had stood up to criticism better than its competitors had: there is no better idea of rationality than that of a readiness to accept criticism; that is, criticism which discusses the merits of competing theories from the point of view of the regulative idea of truth. Accordingly, the degree of corroboration of a theory is a rational guide to practice. Although we cannot justify a theory—that is, justify our belief in its truth—we can sometimes justify our *preference* for one theory over another; for example if its degree of corroboration is greater.[157]

I have been able to show, very simply, that Einstein's theory is (at least at the moment of writing) preferable to Newton's, by showing that its degree of corroboration is greater.[158]

A decisive point about degree of corroboration was that, because it increased with the severity of tests, it could be high only for *theories with a high degree of testability or content*. But this meant that degree of corroboration was linked to *improbability* rather than to *probability*: it was thus impossible to identify it with probability (although it could be defined in terms of probability—as can improbability).

All these problems were opened, or dealt with, in *Logik der Forschung*; but I felt that there was more to be done about them, and that an axiomatization of the probability calculus was the thing I should do next.[159]

21. *The Approaching War; The Jewish Problem*

It was in July, 1927, after the big shooting in Vienna, described below, that I began to expect the worst: that the democratic bastions of Central Europe would fall, and that a totalitarian Germany would start another world war. By about 1929 I realized that among the politicians of the West only Churchill in England, then an outsider whom nobody took seriously, understood the German menace. I then thought that the war would come in a few years. I was mistaken: everything developed much more slowly than I thought possible, considering the logic of the situation.

Obviously, I was an alarmist. But essentially I had judged the situation correctly. I realized that the social democrats (the only remaining political party with a strong democratic element) were powerless to resist the totalitarian parties in Austria and Germany. I expected, from 1929 on, the rise of Hitler; I expected the annexation, in some form or other, of Austria by Hitler; and I expected the War against the West. (*The War Against the West* is the title of an excellent book by Aurel Kolnai.) In these expectations my assessment of the Jewish problem played a considerable role.

My parents were both born in the Jewish faith, but were baptized into the Protestant (Lutheran) Church before any of their children arrived. After much thought my father had decided that living in an overwhelmingly Christian society imposed the obligation to give as little offence as possible— to become assimilated. This, however, meant giving offence to organized Judaism. It also meant being denounced as a coward, as a man who feared anti-Semitism. All this was understandable. But the answer was that anti-Semitism was an evil, to be feared by Jews and non-Jews alike, and that it was the task of all people of Jewish origin to do their best not to provoke it: moreover, many Jews did merge with the population: assimilation worked. Admittedly it is understandable that people who were despised for their racial origin should react by saying that they were proud of it. But racial pride is not only stupid but wrong, even if provoked by racial hatred. All nationalism or racialism is evil, and Jewish nationalism is no exception.

I believe that before the First World War Austria, and even Germany, treated the Jews quite well. They were given almost all rights, although there were some barriers established by tradition, especially in the army. In a perfect society, no doubt, they would have been treated in every respect as equals. But like all societies this was far from perfect: although Jews, and people of Jewish origin, were equal before the law, they were not treated as equals in every respect. Yet I believe that the Jews were treated as well as one could reasonably expect. A member of a Jewish family converted to Roman Catholicism had even become an Archbishop (Archbishop Kohn of Olmütz); though because of an intrigue in which use was made of popular anti-Semitism, he had to resign his seat in 1903. The proportion of Jews or men of Jewish origin among University professors, medical men, and lawyers was very high, and open resentment was aroused by this only after the First World War. Baptized Jews could rise to the highest positions in the civil service.

Journalism was one profession which attracted many Jews,

and quite a few of them certainly did little to raise professional standards. The kind of sensational journalism provided by some of these people was for many years strongly criticized—mainly by other Jews, such as Karl Kraus, anxious to defend civilized standards. The dust raised by these quarrels did not make the contestants popular. There were also Jews prominent among the leaders of the Social Democratic Party, and since they were, as leaders, targets of vile attacks, they contributed to the increasing tension.

Clearly, here was a problem. Many Jews looked conspicuously different from the "autochthonous" population. There were many more poor Jews than rich ones; but some of the rich ones were typically *nouveaux riches*.

Incidentally, while in England anti-Semitism is linked with the idea that Jews are (or once were) "moneylenders"—as in *The Merchant of Venice,* or in Dickens or Trollope—I never heard this suggestion made in Austria, at least not prior to the rise of the Nazis. There were a few Jewish bankers, such as the Austrian Rothschilds, but I never heard it suggested that they had ever engaged in the kind of moneylending to private individuals of which one reads in English novels.

In Austria, anti-Semitism was basically an expression of hostility towards those who were felt to be strangers; a feeling exploited not only by the German Nationalist party of Austria, but also by the Roman Catholic party. And, characteristically, this reprehensible resistance to strangers (an attitude, it seems, which is almost universal) was shared by many of the families of Jewish origin. During the First World War there was an influx into Vienna of Jewish refugees from the old Austrian Empire, which had been invaded by Russia. These "Eastern Jews", as they were called, had come straight from virtual ghettos,[160] and they were resented by those Jews who had settled down in Vienna; by assimilationists, by many orthodox Jews, and even by Zionists, who were ashamed of those they regarded as their poor relations.

The situation improved legally with the dissolution of the Austrian Empire at the end of the First World War; but as anybody with a little sense could have predicted, it deteriorated socially: many Jews, feeling that freedom and full equality had now become a reality, understandably but not wisely entered politics and journalism. Most of them meant well; but the influx of Jews into the parties of the left contributed to the downfall of those parties. It seemed quite obvious that, with much latent popular anti-Semitism about, the best service which a good socialist who happened to be of Jewish origin could render to his party was *not* to try to play a role in it. Strangely enough, few seemed to think of this obvious rule.

As a result, the fight between the right and the left, which was almost from the start a kind of cold civil war, was fought by the right more and more under the flag of anti-Semitism. There were frequent anti-Semitic riots at the University, and constant protests against the excessive number of Jews among the professors. It became impossible for anybody of Jewish origin to become a University teacher. And the competing parties of the right were outbidding each other in their hostility towards the Jews.

Other reasons why I expected the defeat of the Social Democratic Party at least after 1929 can be found in some of the footnotes to my *Open Society*.[161] Essentially they were connected with Marxism—more especially with the policy (formulated by Engels) of using violence, at least as a threat. The threat of violence gave the police an excuse, in July, 1927, to shoot down scores of peaceful and unarmed social democratic workers and bystanders in Vienna. My wife and I (we were not yet married) were among the incredulous witnesses of the scene. It became clear to me that the policy of the social democratic leaders, though they acted with good intentions, was irresponsible *and* suicidal. (Incidentally I found that Fritz Adler—the son of the first-rate leader of the Vienna social democrats, a friend of Einstein's, and a translator of Duhem—when I met him in July, 1927, a few days after the massacre, was of the same opinion.) More than six years were to elapse, however, before the final suicide of the Social Democratic Party brought about the end of democracy in Austria.

22. Emigration: England and New Zealand

My *Logik der Forschung* was surprisingly successful, far beyond Vienna. There were more reviews, in more languages, than there were twenty-five years later of *The Logic of Scientific Discovery*, and fuller reviews even in English. As a consequence I received many letters from various countries in Europe and many invitations to lecture, including an invitation from Professor Susan Stebbing of Bedford College, London. I came to England in the autumn of 1935 to give two lectures at Bedford College. I had been invited to speak about my own ideas, but I was so deeply impressed by Tarski's achievements, then completely unknown in England, that I chose them as my topic instead. My first lecture was on "Syntax and Semantics" (Tarski's semantics) and the second on Tarski's theory of truth. I believe that it was on this occasion that I first aroused the interest of Professor Joseph Henry Woodger, the biologist and philosopher of biology, in Tarski's work.[162] Altogether I paid in 1935-36 two long visits to England with a very short stay in Vienna between them. I was on leave of absence without pay from my teaching job, while my wife continued to teach, and to earn.

During these visits I gave not only these two lectures at Bedford College, but also three lectures on probability at Imperial College, on an invitation arranged by Hyman Levy, professor of mathematics at Imperial College; and I read two papers in Cambridge (with G. E. Moore present, and on the second occasion C. H. Langford, the American philosopher, who was splendid in the discussion), and one in Oxford, where Freddie Ayer had earlier introduced me to Isaiah Berlin and to Gilbert Ryle. I also read a paper on "The Poverty of Historicism", in Professor Hayek's seminar at the London School of Economics and Political Science (L.S.E.). Although Hayek came from Vienna, where he had been a Professor and Director of the Institute for Trade Cycle Research (*Konjunkturforschung*), I met him first in the L.S.E.[163] Lionel Robbins (now Lord Robbins) was present at the seminar and so was Ernst Gombrich, the art historian. Years later G. L. S. Shackle, the economist, told me that he too had been present.

In Oxford I met Schrödinger, and had long conversations with him. He was very unhappy in Oxford. He had come there from Berlin where he had presided over a seminar for theoretical physics which was probably unique in the history of science: Einstein, von Laue, Planck, and Nernst had been among its regular members. In Oxford he had been very hospitably received. He could not of course expect a seminar of giants; but what he did miss was the passionate interest in theoretical physics, among students and teachers alike. We discussed my statistical interpretation of Heisenberg's indeterminacy formulae. He was interested, but sceptical, even about the status of quantum mechanics. He gave me some offprints of papers in which he expressed doubts about the Copenhagen interpretation; it is well known that he never became reconciled to it—that is, to Bohr's "complementarity". Schrödinger mentioned that he might return to Austria. I tried to dissuade him, because he had made no secret of his anti-Nazi attitude when he left Germany, and this would be held against him if the Nazis should gain power in Austria. But in the late autumn of 1936 he did return. A chair in Graz had become vacant and Hans Thirring, professor of theoretical physics in Vienna, made the suggestion that he should give up his chair in Vienna and go to Graz, so that Schrödinger could take over Thirring's chair in Vienna. But Schrödinger would have none of this; he went to Graz, where he stayed about eighteen months. After Hitler's invasion of Austria, Schrödinger and his wife, Anne-marie, had a hairbreadth's escape. She drove their car to a place near to the Italian border, where they abandoned it. Taking only hand luggage they crossed the border. From Rome, where they arrived almost penniless, they managed to telephone De Valera, the Irish Prime Minister (and a mathematician), who happened then to be in Geneva, and De Valera told them to join him there. On the Italian-Swiss border they became suspect to the Italian guards because they had hardly any luggage, and money equivalent to less than one pound. They were taken out of the train, which left the border station without them. In the end they were allowed to take the next train for Switzerland. And that is how Schrödinger became the Senior Professor of the Institute of Advanced Studies in Dublin, which then did not even exist. (There is still no such Institute in Britain.)

One of the experiences which I remember well from my visit in 1936 was when Ayer took me to a meeting of the Aristotelian Society at which Bertrand Russell spoke, perhaps the greatest philosopher since Kant.

Russell was reading a paper on "The Limits of Empiricism".[164] Assuming that empirical knowledge was obtained by induction, and at the same time much impressed by Hume's criticism of induction, Russell suggested that we had to adopt some *principle of induction* which in its turn could not be based on induction. Thus the adoption of this principle marked the limits of empiricism. Now I had in my *Grundprobleme*, and more briefly in *Logik der Forschung*, attributed to Kant precisely these arguments, and so it appeared to me that Russell's position was in this respect identical with Kant's apriorism.

After the lecture there was a discussion, and Ayer encouraged me to speak. So I said first that I did not believe in induction at all, even though I believed in learning from experience, and in an empiricism *without* those Kantian limits which Russell proposed. This statement, which I formulated as briefly and as pointedly as I could with the halting English at my disposal, was well received by the audience who, it appears, took it as a joke, and laughed. In my second attempt I suggested that the whole trouble was due to the mistaken assumption that *scientific knowledge* was a species of *knowledge*—knowledge in the ordinary sense in which if I know that it is raining it must be *true* that it is raining, so that knowledge implies truth. But, I said, what we call "scientific knowledge" was hypothetical, and often not true, let alone certainly or probably true (in the sense of the calculus of probability). Again the audience took this for a joke, or a paradox, and they laughed and clapped. I wonder whether there was anybody there who suspected that not only did I seriously hold these views, but that, in due course, they would widely be regarded as commonplace.

It was Woodger who suggested that I answer the advertisement for a teaching position in philosophy in the University of New Zealand (at Canterbury University College, as the present University of Canterbury was then called). Somebody —it may have been Hayek—introduced me to Dr Walter Adams (later Director of the London School of Economics) and to Miss Esther Simpson, who together were running the Academic Assistance Council, which was then trying to help the many refugee scientists from Germany, and had already begun to help some from Austria.

In July, 1936, I left London for Copenhagen—I was seen off by Ernst Gombrich—in order to attend a Congress,[165] and to meet Niels Bohr, a meeting I have described in section 18. From Copenhagen I returned to Vienna; travelling through Hitler's Germany. At the end of November I received a letter from Dr A. C. Ewing, offering me academic hospitality in the name of the Moral Sciences Faculty of Cambridge University, together with a letter of support from Walter Adams of the Academic Assistance Council; shortly after, on Christmas Eve,

1936, I received a cable offering me a lectureship in Canterbury University College, Christchurch, New Zealand. This was a normal position, while the hospitality offered by Cambridge was meant for a refugee. Both my wife and I would have preferred to go to Cambridge, but I thought that this offer of hospitality might be transferable to somebody else. So I accepted the invitation to New Zealand and asked the Academic Assistance Council and Cambridge to invite Fritz Waismann, of the Vienna Circle, in my stead. They agreed to this request.

My wife and I resigned from our schoolteaching positions, and within a month we left Vienna for London. After five days in London we sailed for New Zealand, arriving in Christchurch during the first week of March, 1937, just in time for the beginning of the New Zealand academic year.

I felt certain that my help would soon be needed for Austrian refugees from Hitler. But it was another year before Hitler invaded Austria and before the cries for help started. A committee in Christchurch was constituted to obtain permits for refugees to enter New Zealand; and some were rescued from concentration camps and from prison thanks to the energy of Dr R. M. Campbell, of the New Zealand High Commission in London.

23. *Early Work in New Zealand*

Before we went to New Zealand I had stayed in England, in all for about nine months, and it had been a revelation and an inspiration. The honesty and decency of the people and their strong feeling of political responsibility made the greatest possible impression on me. But even the university teachers I met were utterly misinformed about Hitler's Germany, and wishful thinking was universal. I was in England when popular loyalty to the ideas of the League of Nations destroyed the Hoare-Laval plan (which might well have prevented Mussolini from joining forces with Hitler); and I was there when Hitler entered the Rhineland, an act supported by an upsurge of English popular opinion. I also heard Neville Chamberlain speak in favour of a rearmament budget, and I tried to comfort myself with the idea that he was only Chancellor of the Exchequer, and that there was therefore no real need for him to understand what he was arming against, or how urgent it all was. I realized that democracy—even British democracy—was not an institution designed to fight totalitarianism; but it was very sad to find that there was apparently only one man— Winston Churchill—who understood what was happening, and that literally nobody had a good word for him.

In New Zealand the situation was similar but somewhat exaggerated. There was no harm in the people: like the British they were decent, friendly, and well disposed. But the continent of Europe was infinitely remote. In those days New Zealand had no contact with the world except through England, five weeks away. There was no air connection and one could not expect an answer to a letter in less than three months. In the First World War the country had suffered terrible losses, but all that was forgotten. The Germans were well liked and war was unthinkable.

I had the impression that New Zealand was the best-governed country in the world, and the most easily governed.

It was a wonderfully quiet and pleasant atmosphere for work, and I settled down quickly to continue work which had been interrupted for several months. I won a number of friends who were interested in my work and who greatly encouraged me. Hugh Parton, the physical chemist, Frederick White, the physicist, and Bob Allan, the geologist, came first. Then came Colin Simkin, the economist, Alan Reed, the lawyer, George Roth, the radiation physicist, and Margaret Dalziel, then a student of the Classics and of English. Further south, in Dunedin, Otago, were John Findlay, the philosopher, and John Eccles, the neurophysiologist. All these became lifelong friends.

I first concentrated—apart from teaching (I alone did the teaching in philosophy)[166]—on probability theory, especially on an axiomatic treatment of the probability calculus and on the relation between the probability calculus and Boolean algebra; and I soon finished a paper, which I compressed to minimum length. It was published later in *Mind*.[167] I continued this work for many years: it was a great standby whenever I had a cold. I also read some physics, and thought further about quantum theory. (I read, among other things, the exciting and disturbing letter[168] in *Nature* by Halban, Joliot, and Kowarski on the possibility of a uranium explosion, some letters on the same topic in *The Physical Review*, and an article by Karl K. Darrow in the *Annual Report of the Board of Regents of the Smithsonian Institution.*[169])

I had for a long time been thinking about the methods of the social sciences; after all, it had been in part a criticism of Marxism that had started me, in 1919, on my way to *Logik der Forschung*. I had lectured in Hayek's seminar on "The Poverty of Historicism", a lecture which contained (or so I thought) something like an application of the ideas of *Logik der Forschung* to the methods of the social sciences. I discussed these ideas with Hugh Parton, and with Dr H. Larsen, who was then teaching in the department of economics. However, I was most reluctant to publish anything against Marxism: where they still existed on the continent of Europe, the Social Democrats were after all the only political force still resisting tyranny. I felt that, in the situation then prevailing, nothing should be published against them. Even though I regarded their policy as suicidal, it was unrealistic to think that they could be reformed by a piece of writing: any published criticism could only weaken them.

Then came the news, in March, 1938, of Hitler's occupation of Austria. There was now an urgent need to help Austrians to escape. I also felt that I could no longer hold back whatever knowledge of political problems I had acquired since 1919; I decided to put "The Poverty of Historicism" in a publishable form. What came out of it were two more or less complementary pieces: *The Poverty of Historicism* and *The Open Society and Its Enemies* (which at first I had intended to call: "False Prophets: Plato—Hegel—Marx").

24. The Open Society *and* The Poverty of Historicism

Originally I simply intended to elaborate and to put into publishable English my talk in Hayek's seminar (first given in German in Brussels in the house of my friend Alfred Braunthal),[170] showing more closely how "historicism" inspired both Marxism and fascism. I saw the finished paper clearly before me: a fairly long paper, but of course easily publishable in one piece.

My main trouble was to write it in acceptable English. I had written a few things before, but they were linguistically very bad. My German style in *Logik der Forschung* had been reasonably light—for German readers; but I discovered that English standards of writing were utterly different, and far higher than German standards. For example, no German reader minds polysyllables. In English, one has to learn to be repelled by them. But if one is still fighting to avoid the simplest mistakes, such higher aims are far more distant, however much one may approve of them.

The Poverty of Historicism is, I think, one of my stodgiest pieces of writing. Besides, after I had written the ten sections which form the first chapter, my whole plan broke down: section 10, on essentialism, turned out to puzzle my friends so much that I began to elaborate it, and out of this elaboration and a few remarks I made on the totalitarian tendencies of Plato's *Republic*—remarks which were also thought obscure by my friends (especially Henry Dan Broadhead and Margaret Dalziel)—there grew, or exploded, without any plan and against all plans, a truly unintended consequence, *The Open Society*. After it had begun to take shape I cut it out of *The Poverty* and reduced *The Poverty* to what was more or less its originally intended content.

There was also a minor factor which contributed to *The Open Society*: I was incensed by the obscurantism of some examination questions about "the one and the many" in Greek philosophy, and I wanted to bring into the open the political tendencies linked with these metaphysical ideas.

After *The Open Society* had broken away from *The Poverty*, I next finished the first three chapters of the latter. The fourth chapter, which until then had existed only in a sketchy form (without any discussion of what I later called "situational logic"), was completed, I think, only after the first draft of the Plato volume of *The Open Society* had been written.

It was no doubt due partly to internal developments in my thought that these works proceeded in this somewhat confused way, but partly also, I suppose, to the Hitler-Stalin pact and the actual outbreak of the war, and to the strange course of the war. Like everybody else, I feared that after the fall of France, Hitler would invade England. I was relieved when he invaded Russia instead, but afraid that Russia would collapse. Yet, as Churchill says in his book on the First World War, wars are not won but lost; and the Second World War was lost by

Hitler's tanks in Russia and by Japan's bombers at Pearl Harbor.

The Poverty and *The Open Society* were my war effort. I thought that freedom might become a central problem again, especially under the renewed influence of Marxism and the idea of large-scale "planning" (or "dirigism"); and so these books were meant as a defence of freedom against totalitarian and authoritarian ideas, and as a warning against the dangers of historicist superstitions. Both books, and especially *The Open Society* (no doubt the more important one), may be described as books on the philosophy of politics.

Both grew out of the theory of knowledge of *Logik der Forschung* and out of my conviction that our often unconscious views on the theory of knowledge and its central problems ("What can we know?", "How certain is our knowledge?") are decisive for our attitude towards ourselves and towards politics.[171]

In *Logik der Forschung* I tried to show that our knowledge grows through trial and error-elimination, and that the main difference between its prescientific and its scientific growth is that on the scientific level we consciously search for our errors: *the conscious adoption of the critical method* becomes the main instrument of growth. It seems that already at that time I was well aware that the critical method—or the critical approach—consists, generally, in the search for difficulties or contradictions and their tentative resolution, and that this approach could be carried far beyond science, for which *critical tests* are characteristic. For I wrote: "In the present work I have relegated the critical—or, if you will, the 'dialectical'—method of resolving contradictions to second place, since I have been concerned with the attempts to develop the practical methodological aspects of my views. In an as yet unpublished work I have tried to take the critical path. . . ."[172] (The allusion was to *Die beiden Grundprobleme*.)

In *The Open Society* I stressed that the critical method, though it will use tests wherever possible, and preferably practical tests, can be generalized into what I described as the critical or rational attitude.[173] I argued that one of the best senses of "reason" and "reasonableness" was openness to criticism—readiness to be criticized, and eagerness to criticize oneself; and I tried to argue that this critical attitude of reason-

ableness should be extended as far as possible.[174] I suggested
that the demand that we extend the critical attitude as far as
possible might be called "critical rationalism", a suggestion
which was later endorsed by Adrienne Koch,[175] and by Hans
Albert.[176]

Implicit in this attitude is the realization that we shall
always have to live in an imperfect society. This is so not only
because even very good people are very imperfect; nor is it
because, obviously, we often make mistakes because we do not
know enough. Even more important than either of these reasons is the fact that there always exist irresolvable clashes of
values: there are many moral problems which are insoluble
because moral principles may conflict.

There can be no human society without conflict: such a
society would be a society not of friends but of ants. Even if
it were attainable, there are human values of the greatest
importance which would be destroyed by its attainment,
and which therefore should prevent us from attempting
to bring it about. On the other hand, we certainly ought to
bring about a reduction of conflict. So already we have here
an example of a clash of values or principles. This example
also shows that clashes of values and principles may be valuable, and indeed essential for an open society.

One of the main arguments of *The Open Society* is directed
against moral relativism. The fact that moral values or principles may clash does not invalidate them. Moral values or
principles may be discovered, and even invented. They may be
relevant to a certain situation, and irrelevant to other situations. They may be accessible to some people and inaccessible
to others. But all this is quite distinct from relativism; that is,
from the doctrine that any set of values can be defended.[177]

In this, my intellectual autobiography, a number of the
other philosophical ideas of *The Open Society* (some of them
pertaining to the history of philosophy, others to the philosophy of history) ought really to be mentioned—more, indeed,
than can be discussed here. Among them is what was the first
fairly extensive exposition of my anti-essentialist position and,
I suspect, the first statement of an anti-essentialism which is
not nominalistic or observationalistic. In connection with this
exposition, *The Open Society* contained some criticisms of
Wittgenstein's *Tractatus*, criticisms which have been almost
completely neglected by Wittgenstein's commentators.

In a similar context I also wrote on the *logical paradoxes* and formulated some new paradoxes. I also discussed their relation to the *paradox of democracy* (a discussion which has given rise to a fairly extensive literature) and to the more general *paradoxes of sovereignty*.

A voluminous literature, which in my opinion has contributed little to the problem, has sprung from a mistaken criticism of my ideas on *historical explanation*. In section 12 of *Logik der Forschung* I discussed what I called "causal explanation",[178] or deductive explanation, a discussion which had been anticipated, without my being aware of it, by J. S. Mill, though perhaps a bit vaguely (because of his lack of distinction between an initial condition and a universal law).[179] When I first read "The Poverty of Historicism" in Brussels a former pupil of mine, Dr Karl Hilferding,[180] made an interesting contribution to the discussion, to which the philosophers Carl Hempel and Paul Oppenheim also contributed: Hilferding pointed out the relation that some of my remarks on historical explanation had to section 12 of *Logik der Forschung*. (These remarks eventually became pages 143-46 of the book edition [1957(g)] of *The Poverty*. Hilferding's discussion, based on *Logik der Forschung,* brought out some of the points now on pages 122-24 and 133 of [1957(g)];[181] points connected partly with the logical relation between explanation and prediction, and partly with the triviality of the universal laws much used in historical explanations: these laws are usually uninteresting simply because they are in the context unproblematic.)

I did not, however, regard this particular analysis as especially important for *historical* explanation, and what I did regard as important needed some further years in which to mature. It was the problem of rationality (or the "rationality principle" or the "zero method" or the "logic of the situation").[182] But for years the unimportant thesis—in a misinterpreted form—has, under the name "the deductive model", helped to generate a voluminous literature.

The much more important aspect of the problem, the method of situational analysis, which I first added to *The Poverty*[183] in 1938, and later explained a little more fully in Chapter 14 of *The Open Society*,[184] was developed from what I had previously called the "zero method". The main point here was an attempt *to generalize the method of economic*

*theory (marginal utility theory) so as to become applicable to
the other theoretical social sciences.* In my later formulations,
this method consists of constructing a *model of the social
situation*, including especially the institutional situation, in
which an agent is acting, in such a manner as to explain the
rationality (the zero-character) of his action. Such models, then,
are the testable hypotheses of the social sciences; and those
models that are "singular", more especially, are the (in principle testable) singular hypotheses of history.

In this connection I may perhaps also refer to the theory
of the abstract society, which was first added in the American
edition of *The Open Society*.[185]

For myself *The Open Society* marks a turning point, for it
made me write history (somewhat speculative history) which,
to some extent, gave me an excuse to write about methods of
historical research.[186] I had done some unpublished research in
the history of philosophy before, but this was my first published contribution. I think it has, to say the least, raised a
number of new historical problems—in fact, a wasps' nest of
them.

The first volume of *The Open Society*, which I called *The
Spell of Plato*, originated, as already mentioned, from an extension of section 10 of *The Poverty*. In the first draft of this
extension there were a few paragraphs on Plato's totalitarianism, on its connection with his historicist theory of decline or
degeneration, and on Aristotle. These were based on my earlier
reading of the *Republic*, the *Statesman, Gorgias*, and some
books of the *Laws*, and on Theodor Gomperz's *Greek Thinkers*, a book much beloved since my days in secondary school.
The adverse reactions of my New Zealand friends to these
paragraphs produced in the end *The Spell of Plato*, and with
it *The Open Society*. For it turned me back to the study of the
sources, because I wanted to give full evidence for my views.
I reread Plato most intensively; I read Diels, Grote (whose
view, I found, was essentially the same as mine), and many
other commentators and historians of the period. (Full references will be found in *The Open Society*.) What I read was
determined largely by what books I could get in New Zealand:
during the war there was no possibility of getting books from
overseas for my purposes. For some reason or other I could
not get, for example, the Loeb edition of the *Republic*

(Shorey's translation), though the second volume, I found after the war, had been published in 1935. This was a great pity, since it is by far the best translation, as I was to discover later. The translations which were available were so unsatisfactory that, with the help of Adam's marvellous edition, I began to do translations myself, in spite of my very scanty Greek, which I tried to improve with the help of a school grammar which I had brought from Austria. Nothing would have come of this but for the great amount of time I spent on these translations: I had found before that I had to rewrite again and again translations from Latin, and even from German, if I wanted to make an interesting idea clear, in reasonably forceful English. I have been accused of bias in my translations; and indeed they are biased. But there are no unbiased translations of Plato and, I suggest, there can be none. Shorey's is one of the few which has no liberal bias, because he accepted Plato's politics, in the same sense, approximately, in which I rejected them.

I sent *The Poverty* to *Mind,* but it was rejected; and immediately after completing *The Open Society* in February, 1943 (it had been rewritten many times), I sent it to America for publication. The book had been written in trying circumstances; libraries were severely limited, and I had had to adjust myself to whatever books were available. I had a desperately heavy teaching load, and the University authorities not only were unhelpful, but tried actively to make difficulties for me. I was told that I should be well advised not to publish anything while in New Zealand, and that any time spent on research was a theft from the working time as a lecturer for which I was being paid.[187] The situation was such that without the moral support of my friends in New Zealand I could hardly have survived. Under these circumstances the reaction of those friends in the United States to whom I sent the manuscript was a terrible blow. They did not react at all for many months; and later, instead of submitting the manuscript to a publisher, they solicited an opinion from a famous authority, who decided that the book, because of its irreverence towards Aristotle (not Plato), was not fit to be submitted to a publisher.

After almost a year, when I was at my wit's end and in terribly low spirits, I obtained, by chance, the English address of my friend Ernst Gombrich, with whom I had lost contact during the war. Together with Hayek, who most generously offered his help (I had not dared to trouble him since I had seen him only a few times in my life), he found a publisher. Both wrote most encouragingly about the book. The relief was immense. I felt that these two had saved my life, and I still feel so.

25. Other Work in New Zealand

This was not the only work I did in New Zealand. I also did some work in logic—in fact, I invented for myself something now called "natural deduction"[188]—and I did much work, and much lecturing, on the logic of scientific discovery, including work in the history of science. This latter work consisted in the main in applications of my logical ideas on discovery to actual discoveries; but I also tried to make clear to myself the immense historical importance of erroneous theories, such as the Parmenidean theory of the full world.

In New Zealand I gave courses of lectures on noninductivist methods of science to the Christchurch branch of the Royal Society of New Zealand and the Medical School in Dunedin. These were initiated by Professor (later Sir John) Eccles. During my last two years at Christchurch I gave lunchtime lectures to the teachers and students of the science departments of Canterbury University College. All this was hard work (today I cannot imagine how I did it) but extremely enjoyable. In later years I have met former participants in these courses the world over, scientists who assured me that I had opened their eyes—and there were some highly successful scientists among them.

I liked New Zealand very much, in spite of the hostility shown by some of the University authorities to my work, and I was ready to stay there for good. Early in 1945 I received an invitation from the University of Sydney. There followed some newspaper criticism in Australia about the appointment of a foreigner, and some questions were asked in Parliament. So I cabled my thanks and declined. Shortly afterwards—the war in Europe was in its last stages—I received a cable, signed by Hayek, offering me a readership at the University of London, tenable at the London School of Economics, and thanking me for sending *The Poverty* to *Economica*, of which he was the acting editor. I felt that Hayek had saved my life once more. From that moment I was impatient to leave New Zealand.

26. England: At the London School of Economics and Political Science

Wartime conditions were still prevailing when we left New Zealand, and our boat was ordered to sail round Cape Horn. This was a fantastically and unforgettably beautiful sight. We arrived in England early in January, 1946, and I started work at the London School of Economics.

The L.S.E. was in those days, just after the war, a marvellous institution. It was small enough for everybody on the staff to know everybody else. The staff, though few, were outstanding, and so were the students. There were lots of them—larger classes than I had later at the L.S.E.—eager, mature, and extremely appreciative; and they presented a challenge to the teacher. Among these students was a former regular officer of the Royal Navy, John Watkins, now my successor at the L.S.E.

I had come back from New Zealand with lots of open problems, in part purely logical, in part matters of method, including the method of the social sciences; and being now in a school of the social sciences, I felt that those latter problems had—for a time—a claim on me prior to problems of method in the natural sciences. Yet the social sciences never had for me the same attraction as the theoretical natural sciences. In fact, the only theoretical social science which appealed to me was economics. But like many before me I was interested to compare the natural and the social sciences from the point of view of their methods, which was to some extent a continuation of work I had done in *The Poverty*.

One of the ideas I had discussed in *The Poverty* was the influence of a prediction upon the event predicted. I had called this the "Oedipus effect", because the oracle played a most important role in the sequence of events which led to the fulfilment of its prophecy. (It was also an allusion to the psychoanalysts, who had been strangely blind to this interesting fact, even though Freud himself admitted that the very dreams dreamt by patients were often coloured by the theories of their analysts; Freud called them "obliging dreams".) For a time I thought that the existence of the Oedipus effect distinguished the social from the natural sciences. But in biology too—even in molecular biology—expectations often play a role in bringing about what has been expected. At any rate, my refutation of the idea that this could serve as a distinguishing mark between social and natural science provided the germ of my paper "Indeterminism in Quantum Physics and in Classical Physics".[189]

This, however, took some time. My first paper after my return to Europe arose out of a very kind invitation to contribute to a symposium, "Why are the Calculuses of Logic and Arithmetic Applicable to Reality?",[190] at the Joint Session of the Aristotelian Society and the Mind Association in Manchester in July, 1946. It was an interesting meeting, and I was received by the English philosophers with the utmost friendliness and, especially by Ryle, with considerable interest. In fact, my *Open Society* had been well received in England, far beyond my expectations; even a Platonist who hated the book commented on its "fertility of ideas", saying that "almost every sentence gives us something to think about"—which of course pleased me more than any facile agreement.

And yet there could be no doubt that my ways of thinking, my interests, and my problems were utterly uncongenial to many English philosophers. Why this was so I do not know. In some cases it might have been my interest in science. In others it might have been my critical attitude towards positivism, and towards language philosophy. This brings me to my encounter with Wittgenstein, of which I have heard the most varied and absurd reports.

Early in the academic year 1946-47 I received an invitation from the Secretary of the Moral Sciences Club at Cambridge to read a paper about some "philosophical puzzle". It was of course clear that this was Wittgenstein's formulation, and that behind it was Wittgenstein's philosophical thesis that there are no genuine problems in philosophy, only linguistic puzzles. Since this thesis was among my pet aversions, I decided to speak on "Are there Philosophical Problems?". I began my paper (read on October 26, 1946, in R. B. Braithwaite's room in King's College) by expressing my surprise at being invited by the Secretary to read a paper "stating some philosophical puzzle"; and I pointed out that, by implicitly denying that philosophical problems exist, whoever wrote the invitation took sides, perhaps unwittingly, in an issue created by a genuine philosophical problem.

I need hardly say that this was meant merely as a challenging and somewhat lighthearted introduction to my topic. But at this very point, Wittgenstein jumped up and said loudly and, it seemed to me, angrily: "The Secretary did exactly as he was told to do. He acted on my own instruction." I did not take any notice of this and went on; but as it turned out, at least some of Wittgenstein's admirers in the audience did take notice of it, and as a consequence took my remark, meant as a joke, for a serious complaint against the Secretary. And so did the poor Secretary himself, as emerges from the minutes, in which he reports the incident, adding a footnote: "This is the Club's form of invitation."[191]

However, I went on to say that if I thought that there were no genuine philosophical problems, I would certainly not be a philosopher; and that the fact that many people, or perhaps all people, thoughtlessly adopt untenable solutions to many, or perhaps all, philosophical problems provided the only justification for being a philosopher. Wittgenstein jumped up again, interrupting me, and spoke at length about puzzles and the nonexistence of philosophical problems. At a moment which appeared to me appropriate, I interrupted him, giving a list I had prepared of philosophical problems, such as: Do we know things through our senses?, Do we obtain our knowledge by induction? These Wittgenstein dismissed as being logical rather than philosophical. I then referred to the problem whether potential or perhaps even actual infinities exist, a problem he dismissed as mathematical. (This dismissal got into the minutes.) I then mentioned moral problems and the problem of the validity of moral rules. At that point Wittgenstein, who was sitting near the fire and had been nervously playing with the poker, which he sometimes used like a conductor's baton to emphasize his assertions, challenged me: "Give an example of a moral rule!" I replied: "Not to threaten visiting lecturers with pokers." Whereupon Wittgenstein, in a rage, threw the poker down and stormed out of the room, banging the door behind him.

I really was very sorry. I admit that I went to Cambridge hoping to provoke Wittgenstein into defending the view that there are no genuine philosophical problems, and to fight him on this issue. But I had never intended to make him angry; and it was a surprise to find him unable to see a joke. I realized only later that he probably did indeed feel that I was joking, and that it was this that offended him. But though I had

wanted to treat my problem lightheartedly, I was in earnest—
perhaps more so than was Wittgenstein himself, since, after all,
he did not believe in genuine philosophical problems.

After Wittgenstein left us we had a very pleasant discussion,
in which Bertrand Russell was one of the main speakers. And
Braithwaite afterwards paid me a compliment (perhaps a
doubtful compliment) by saying that I was the only man who
had managed to interrupt Wittgenstein in the way in which
Wittgenstein interrupted everyone else.

Next day in the train to London there were, in my com-
partment, two students sitting opposite each other, a boy reading a book and a girl reading a leftish journal. Suddenly she
asked: "Who is this man Karl Popper?" He replied: "Never
heard of him." Such is fame. (As I later found out, the journal
contained an attack on *The Open Society*.)

The meeting of the Moral Sciences Club became almost
immediately the subject of wild stories. In a surprisingly short
time I received a letter from New Zealand asking whether it
was true that Wittgenstein and I had come to blows, both
armed with pokers. Nearer home the stories were less exaggerated, but not much.

The incident was, in part, attributable to my custom,
whenever I am invited to speak in some place, of trying to
develop some consequences of my views which I expect to be
unacceptable to the particular audience. For I believe that there
is only one excuse for a lecture: to challenge. It is the only
way in which speech can be better than print. This is why I
chose my topic as I did. Besides, this controversy with Wittgenstein touched on fundamentals.

I claim that there are philosophical problems; and even
that I have solved some. Yet, as I have written elsewhere
"nothing seems less wanted than a simple solution to an age-
old philosophical problem".[192] The view of many philosophers
and, especially, it seems, of Wittgensteinians, is that if a problem is soluble, it cannot have been philosophical. There are of
course other ways of getting over the scandal of a solved
problem. One can say that all this is old hat; or that it leaves
the real problem untouched. And, after all, surely, this solution
must be all wrong, must it not? (I am ready to admit that quite
often an attitude like this is more valuable than one of excessive agreement.)

One of the things which in those days I found difficult to

understand was the tendency of English philosophers to flirt with nonrealistic epistemologies: phenomenalism, positivism, Berkeleyan or Humean, or Machian idealism ("neutral monism"), sensationalism, pragmatism—these playthings of philosophers were in those days still more popular than realism. After a cruel war lasting for six years this attitude was surprising, and I admit that I felt that it was a bit "out of date" (to use a historicist phrase). Thus, being invited in 1946-47 to read a paper in Oxford, I read one under the title "A Refutation of Phenomenalism, Positivism, Idealism, and Subjectivism". In the discussion, the defence of the views which I had attacked was so feeble that it made little impression. However, the fruits of this victory (if any) were gathered by the philosophers of ordinary language, since language philosophy soon came to support common sense. Indeed, its attempts to adhere to common sense and realism are in my opinion by far the best aspect of ordinary-language philosophy. But common sense, though often right (and especially in its realism), is not always right. And things get really interesting just when it is wrong. These are precisely the occasions which show that we are badly in need of enlightenment. They are also the occasions on which the usages of ordinary language cannot help us. To put it in another way, ordinary language, and with it the philosophy of ordinary language, is conservative. But in matters of the *intellect* (as opposed, perhaps, to art, or to politics) nothing is less creative and more commonplace than conservatism.

All this seems to me very well formulated by Gilbert Ryle: "The rationality of man consists not in his being unquestioning in matters of principle but in never being unquestioning; not in cleaving to reputed axioms, but in taking nothing for granted."[193]

27. Early Work in England

Although I have known sorrow and great sadness, as is everybody's lot, I do not think that I have had an unhappy hour as a philosopher since we returned to England. I have worked hard, and I have often got deep into insoluble difficulties. But I have been most happy in finding new problems, in wrestling with them, and in making some progress. This, or so I feel, is the best life. It seems to me infinitely better than the life of mere contemplation (to say nothing of divine self-contemplation) which Aristotle recommends as the best. It is a completely restless life, but it is highly self-contained— *autark* in Plato's sense, although no life, of course, can be fully *autark*. Neither my wife nor I liked living in London; but ever since we moved to Penn in Buckinghamshire, in 1950, I have been, I suspect, the happiest philosopher I have met,

This is far from irrelevant to my intellectual development since it has helped me immensely in my work. But there is also some feedback here: one of the many great sources of happiness is to get a glimpse, here and there, of a new aspect of the incredible world we live in, and of our incredible role in it.

Before our move to Buckinghamshire my main work was on "natural deduction". I had started it in New Zealand, where one of the students in my logic class, Peter Munz (now Professor of History at Victoria University), encouraged me much by his understanding and his excellent and independent development of an argument.[194] (He cannot remember the incident.) After my return to England I talked about it to Paul Bernays, the set theoretician, and once to Bertrand Russell. (Tarski was not interested, which I could well understand, as he had more important ideas on his mind; but Evert Beth took some real interest in it.) It is a very elementary but also strangely beautiful theory—much more beautiful and symmetrical than the logical theories I had known before.

The general interest which inspired these investigations came from Tarski's paper "On the Concept of Logical Consequence",[195] which I had heard him read at a Congress in Paris in the autumn of 1935. This paper, and especially certain doubts expressed in it,[196] led me to two problems: (1) how far is it possible to formulate logic in terms of truth or deducibility, that is, transmission of truth and retransmission of falsity? And (2) how far is it possible to characterize the logical constants of an object language as symbols whose functioning can be fully described in terms of deducibility (truth transmission)? Many other problems sprang from these problems, and from my many attempts to solve them.[197] Yet in the end, after several years of effort, I gave up when I discovered a mistake I had made, although the mistake was not serious and although in repairing it I was led to some interesting results. These, however, I have never published.[198]

With Fritz Waismann I travelled to Holland in 1946, invited to a Congress of the International Society for Significs. This was the beginning of a close connection with Holland which lasted for several years. (Earlier I had been visited in England by the physicist J. Clay, who had read my *Logik der Forschung* and with whom I shared many views.) It was on this occasion that I first met Brouwer, the founder of the intuitionist interpretation of mathematics, and also Heyting, his foremost disciple, A. D. De Groot, the psychologist and methodologist, and the brothers Justus and Herman Meijer. Justus became very interested in my *Open Society*, and started almost at once on the first translation of the book, into the Dutch language.[199]

In 1949 I was made a professor of logic and scientific method in the University of London. Perhaps in acknowledgement of this I often began my lectures on scientific method with an explanation of why this subject is nonexistent—even more so than some other nonexistent subjects. (However, I did not repeat myself very much in my lectures: I have never used a set of lecture notes for a second time.)

The people from whom I learned most in those early days in England were Gombrich, Hayek, Medawar, and Robbins—none of them philosophers; there was also Terence Hutchinson, who had written with great understanding about the methods of economics. But what I missed most in those days was to be able to talk at length to a physicist, although I had met Schrödinger again in London, and had a good innings with Arthur March in Alpbach, Tyrol, and another with Pauli in Zurich.

28. *First Visit to the United States. Meeting Einstein*

In 1949 I received an invitation to give the William James Lectures at Harvard. This led to my first visit to America, and it made a tremendous difference to my life. When I read Professor Donald Williams's most unexpected letter of invitation I thought a mistake had been made: I thought I had been invited in the belief that I was Joseph Popper-Lynkeus.

I was at that time working on three things: a series of papers on natural deduction; various axiomatizations of probability; and the methodology of social science. The only topic which seemed to fit a course of eight or ten public lectures was the last of these, and so I chose as the title of the lectures "The Study of Nature and of Society".

We sailed in February, 1950. Of the members of the department of philosophy at Harvard I had met only Quine before. Now I also met C. I. Lewis, Donald Williams, and Morton White. I also met again, for the first time since 1936, a number of old friends: the mathematician Paul Boschan, Herbert Feigl, Philipp Frank (who introduced me to the great physicist Percy Bridgman, with whom I quickly became friends), Julius Kraft, Richard von Mises, Franz Urbach, Abraham Wald, and Victor Weisskopf. I also met, for the first time, Gottfried von Haberler who, as I later heard from Hayek, had apparently been the first economist to become interested in my theory of method; George Sarton and I. Bernard Cohen, the historians of science; and James Bryant Conant, the President of Harvard.

I liked America from the first, perhaps because I had been somewhat prejudiced against it. There was in 1950 a feeling of freedom, of personal independence, which did not exist in Europe and which, I thought, was even stronger than in New Zealand, the freest country I knew. These were the early days of McCarthyism—of the by now partly forgotten anti-communist crusader, Senator Joseph McCarthy—but judging by the general atmosphere I thought that this movement, which was thriving on fear, would in the end defeat itself. On my return to England I had an argument about this with Bertrand Russell.

I admit that things might have developed in a very different way. "It cannot happen here" is always wrong: a dictatorship can happen anywhere.

The greatest and most lasting impact of our visit was made by Einstein. I had been invited to Princeton, and read in a seminar a paper on "Indeterminism in Quantum Physics and in Classical Physics", an outline of a much longer paper.[200] In the discussion Einstein said a few words of agreement, and Bohr spoke at length (going on until we were the only two left), arguing with the help of the famous two-slit experiment that the situation in quantum physics was completely new, and altogether incomparable with that in classical physics. The fact that Einstein and Bohr came to my lecture I regard as the greatest compliment I have ever received.

I had met Einstein before my talk, first through Paul Oppenheim, in whose house we were staying. And although I was most reluctant to take up Einstein's time, he made me come again. Altogether I met him three times. The main topic of our conversation was indeterminism. I tried to persuade him to give up his determinism, which amounted to the view that the world was a four-dimensional Parmenidean block universe in which change was a human illusion, or very nearly so. (He agreed that this had been his view, and while discussing it I called him "Parmenides".) I argued that if men, or other organisms, could experience change and genuine succession in time, then this was real. It could not be explained away by a theory of the successive rising into our consciousness of time slices which in some sense coexist; for this kind of "rising into consciousness" would have precisely the same character as that succession of changes which the theory tries to explain away. I also brought in the somewhat obvious biological arguments: that the evolution of life, and the way organisms behave, especially higher animals, cannot really be understood on the basis of any theory which interprets time as if it were something like another (anisotropic) space coordinate. After all, we do *not* experience space coordinates. And this is because they are simply nonexistent: we must beware of hypostatizing them; they are constructions which are almost wholly arbitrary. Why should we then experience the time coordinate—to be sure, the one appropriate to our inertial system—not only as real but also as absolute, that is, as unalterable and independent of anything we can do (except changing our state of motion)?

The *reality of time and change* seemed to me the crux of realism. (I still so regard it, and it has been so regarded by some idealistic opponents of realism, such as Schrödinger and Gödel.)

When I visited Einstein, Schilpp's *Einstein* volume in *The Library of Living Philosophers* had just been published; this volume contained a now famous contribution of Gödel's which employed, against the reality of time and change, arguments from Einstein's two relativity theories.[201] Einstein had come out in that volume strongly in favour of realism. And he clearly disagreed with Gödel's idealism: he suggested in his reply that Gödel's solutions of the cosmological equations might have "to be excluded on physical grounds".[202]

Now I tried to present to Einstein-Parmenides as strongly as I could my conviction that a clear stand must be made against any idealistic view of time. And I also tried to show that, though the idealistic view was compatible with both determinism and indeterminism, a clear stand should be made in favour of an "open" universe—one in which the future was in no sense contained in the past or the present, even though they do impose severe restrictions on it. I argued that we should not be swayed by our theories to give up common sense too easily. Einstein clearly did not want to give up realism (for which the strongest arguments were based on common sense), though I think that he was ready to admit, as I was, that we might be forced one day to give it up if very powerful arguments (of Gödel's type, say) were to be brought against it. I therefore argued that with regard to time, and also to indeterminism (that is, the incompleteness of physics), the situation was precisely similar to the situation with regard to realism. Appealing to his own way of expressing things in theological terms, I said: if God had wanted to put everything into the world from the beginning, He would have created a universe without change, without organisms and evolution, and without man and man's experience of change. But He seems to have thought that a live universe with events unexpected even by Himself would be more interesting than a dead one.

I also tried to make plain to Einstein that such a position need not disturb his critical attitude towards Bohr's claim that quantum mechanics was complete; on the contrary, it was a position which suggested that we can *always* push our problems further, and that science in general was likely to turn out to be incomplete (in some sense or other).

For we can always continue asking why-questions. Although Newton believed in the truth of his theory, he did not believe that it gave an ultimate explanation, and he tried to give a theological explanation of action at a distance. Leibniz did not believe that mechanical push (action at vanishing distance) was ultimate, and he asked for an explanation in terms of repulsive forces; an explanation which was later given by the electrical theory of matter. Explanation is always incomplete:[203] we can always raise another why-question. And the new why-question may lead to a new theory which not only "explains" the old theory, but corrects it.[204]

This is why the evolution of physics is likely to be an endless process of correction and better approximation. And even if one day we should reach a stage where our theories were no longer open to correction, since they were simply true, they would still not be complete—and we would know it. For Gödel's famous incompleteness theorem would come into play: in view of the mathematical background of physics, at best an infinite sequence of such true theories would be needed in order to answer the problems which in any given (formalized) theory would be undecidable.

Such considerations do not prove that the objective physical world is incomplete, or undetermined: they only show the essential incompleteness of our efforts.[204a] But they also show that it is barely possible (if possible at all) for science to reach a stage in which it can provide genuine support for the view that the physical world is deterministic. Why, then, should we not accept the verdict of common sense—at least until these arguments have been refuted?[205]

This is the substance of the argument with which I tried to convert Einstein-Parmenides. Besides this, we also discussed more briefly such problems as operationalism,[206] positivism and the positivists and their strange fear of metaphysics, verification versus falsification, falsifiability, and simplicity. I learned to my surprise that Einstein thought my suggestions concerning simplicity (in *Logik der Forschung*) had been universally accepted, so that everybody now knew that the simpler theory was preferable because of its greater power of excluding possible states of affairs; that is, its better testability.[207]

Another topic we discussed was Bohr and complementarity —an unavoidable topic after Bohr's contribution to the discussion the night before; and Einstein repeated in the strongest possible terms what he had indicated in the Schilpp volume: that, in spite of the greatest efforts, he could not understand what Bohr meant by complementarity.[208]

I also remember some scathing remarks of Einstein's on the triviality, from a physicist's point of view, of the theory of the atom bomb, which seemed to me to go just a little too far, considering that Rutherford had thought it impossible to utilize atomic energy. Perhaps these remarks were slightly coloured by his dislike of the bomb and all it involved, but no doubt he meant what he said, and no doubt he was essentially right.

It is difficult to convey the impression made by Einstein's personality. Perhaps it may be described by saying that one felt immediately at home with him. It was impossible not to trust him, not to rely implicitly on his straightforwardness, his kindliness, his good sense, his wisdom, and his almost child-like simplicity. It says something for our world, and for America, that so unworldly a man not only survived, but was appreciated and so greatly honoured.

During my visit to Princeton I also met Kurt Gödel again, and I discussed with him both his contribution to the Einstein volume and some aspects of the possible significance of his incompleteness theorem for physics.

It was after our first visit to America that we moved to Penn in Buckinghamshire, which was then a quiet and beautiful little place. Here I could do more work than I had ever done before.

29. Problems and Theories

Already in 1937, when trying to make sense of the famous "dialectic triad" (*thesis: antithesis: synthesis*) by interpreting it as a form of the method of trial and error-elimination, I suggested that all scientific discussions start with a problem (P_1), to which we offer some sort of tentative solution—a *tentative theory* (TT); this theory is then criticized, in an attempt at *error elimination* (EE); and as in the case of dialectic, this process renews itself: the theory and its critical revision give rise to new *problems* (P_2).[209]

Later, I condensed this into the following schema:

$$P_1 \rightarrow TT \rightarrow EE \rightarrow P_2,$$

a schema which I often used in lectures.

I liked to sum up this schema by saying that *science begins with problems, and ends with problems*. But I was always a little worried about this summary, for every scientific problem arises, in its turn, in a theoretical context. It is soaked in theory. So I used to say that we may begin the schema at any place: we may begin with TT_1 and end with TT_2; or we may begin with EE_1 and end with EE_2. However, I used to add that it is often from some *practical problem* that a theoretical development starts; and although any formulation of a practical problem unavoidably brings in theory, the practical problem itself may be just "felt": it may be "prelinguistic"; we— or an amoeba—may *feel* cold or some other irritation, and this may induce us, or the amoeba, to make tentative moves —perhaps theoretical moves—in order to get rid of the irritation.

But the problem "Which comes first, the problem or the theory?" is not so easily solved.[210] In fact, I found it unexpectedly fruitful and difficult.

For *practical problems* arise because something has gone wrong, because of some unexpected event. But this means that the organism, whether man or amoeba, has previously adjusted itself (perhaps ineptly) to its environment, by evolving some expectation, or some other structure (say, an organ). Yet such an adjustment is the preconscious form of developing a theory; and since any practical problem arises relative to some adjustment of this kind, practical problems are, essentially, imbued with theories.

In fact, we arrive at a result which has unexpectedly interesting consequences: *the first theories—that is, the first tentative solutions of problems—and the first problems must somehow have arisen together.*

But this has some further consequences:

Organic structures and problems arise together. Or in other words, *organic structures are theory-incorporating as well as problem-solving structures.*

Later (especially in section 37 of this *Autobiography*, below) I will return to biology and evolutionary theory. Here I will only point out that there are some subtle issues surrounding the various distinctions between formulated and theoretical problems on the one hand, and problems which are merely "felt", and also practical problems, on the other.

Amongst these issues are the following.

(1) The relationship between a formulated problem and a formulated (tentative) solution may be regarded as, essentially, a *logical* relationship.

(2) The relationship between a "felt" problem (or a practical problem) and a solution, however, is a fundamental relationship of *biology*. It may be important in the description of the behaviour of individual organisms, or in the theory of

the evolution of a species or a phylum. (Most problems—perhaps all—are more than "survival problems", they are very concrete problems posed by very specific situations.)

(3) The relationship between problems and solutions clearly plays an important role in the *histories* of individual organisms, especially of human organisms; and it plays a particularly important role in the history of intellectual endeavours, such as the history of science. All history should be, I suggest, a history of problem situations.

(4) On the other hand this relationship seems to play *no* role in the history of the *inorganic* evolution of the universe, or of inorganic parts of it (say, of the evolution of stars, or of the "survival" of stable elements, or stable compounds, and the consequent rarity of unstable ones).

A very different point is also of some importance.

(5) Whenever we say that an organism has tried to solve a problem, P_1 say, we are offering a more or less risky *historical conjecture*. Though it is a historical conjecture, it is proposed in the light of historical or biological theories. The conjecture is an attempt to solve a historical problem, $P(P_1)$ say, which is quite distinct from the problem P_1 attributed by the conjecture to the organism in question.[211] Thus it is possible that a scientist like Kepler may have thought that he had solved a problem P_1, while the historian of science may try to solve the problem $P(P_1)$: "Did Kepler solve P_1 or another problem? What was the actual *problem situation*?". And the solution of $P(P_1)$ may indeed be (as I think it is) that Kepler solved a problem quite different from the one he believed he had solved.

On the animal level it is of course *always* conjectural—in fact, it is a highly theoretical construction—if a scientist conjectures of an individual animal or species (say, some microbe treated with penicillin) that it has reached a solution (say, becoming penicillin resistant) to a problem facing it. Such an ascription sounds metaphorical, even anthropomorphic, but it may not be so: it may simply state the conjecture that such was the environmental situation that unless the species (or population of organisms) changed in a certain way (perhaps by an alteration in the distribution of its gene population), it would get into trouble.

One may say that all this is obvious: most of us know that it is a difficult task to formulate our problems clearly, and that we often fail in this task. Problems are not easily identified or described, unless, indeed, some ready-made problem has been set us, as in an examination; but even then we may find that the examiner did not formulate his problem well, and that we can do better. Thus there is only too often the problem of formulating the problem—and the problem whether this was really the problem to be formulated.

Thus problems, even practical problems, are always theoretical. Theories, on the other hand, can only be understood as tentative solutions of problems, and in relation to problem situations.

In order to avoid misunderstandings, I want to stress that the relations here discussed between problems and theories are not relations between the words "problem" and "theory": I have discussed neither usages nor concepts. What I have discussed are relations between problems and theories—especially those theories which precede the problems; those problems which arise from theories, or with them; and those theories which are tentative solutions of certain problems.

30. Debates with Schrödinger

It was in 1947 or 1948 that Schrödinger let me know that he was coming to London, and I met him in the mews house of one of his friends. From then on we were in fairly regular contact by way of letters, and by personal meetings in London, and later in Dublin, in Alpbach, Tyrol, and in Vienna.

In 1960 I was in hospital in Vienna, and as he was too ill to come to the hospital, his wife, Annemarie Schrödinger, came to see me every day. Before I returned to England I visited them in their apartment in the Pasteurgasse. It was the last time I saw him.

Our relations had been somewhat stormy. Nobody who knew him will be surprised at this. We disagreed violently on many things. Originally I had taken it almost for granted that he, with his admiration for Boltzmann, would not hold a positivist epistemology, but our most violent clash was sparked off when I criticized one day (in 1954 or 1955 approximately) the Machian view now usually called "neutral monism"—even though we both agreed that, contrary to Mach's intentions, this doctrine was a form of idealism.[212]

Schrödinger had absorbed his idealism from Schopenhauer.

But I had expected him to see the weakness of this philosophy, a philosophy about which Boltzmann had said harsh things, and against which for example Churchill, who never claimed to be a philosopher, had produced excellent arguments.[213] I was even more surprised when Schrödinger expressed such sensualist and positivist opinions as that ("all our knowledge . . . rests entirely on immediate sense perception").[214]

We had another violent clash over my paper "The Arrow of Time",[215] in which I asserted the existence of physical processes which are irreversible whether or not any entropy increase may be connected with them. The typical case is an expanding spherical light wave, or a process (like an explosion) that sends particles to infinity (of Newtonian space). The opposite—a coherent spherical wave contracting from infinity (or an implosion from infinity) cannot occur—not because such a thing is ruled out by the universal laws of light propagation or of motion, but because it would be physically impossible to realize the initial conditions.[216]

Schrödinger had written some interesting papers trying to rescue Boltzmann's theory, according to which the direction of entropy increase fully determined the direction of time (or "defined" this direction—but let us forget about this). He had insisted that this theory would collapse if there were a method, such as the one I had suggested, by which we could decide the arrow of time independently of entropy increase.[217]

So far we agreed. But when I asked him to tell me where I was wrong, Schrödinger accused me of unfeelingly destroying the most beautiful theory in physics—a theory with deep philosophical content; a theory which no physicist would dare to harm. For a nonphysicist to attack such a theory was, he felt, presumptuous if not sacrilegious. He followed this up by inserting (in parentheses) a new passage into *Mind and Matter*: "This has a momentous consequence for the methodology of the physicist. He must never introduce anything that decides independently upon the arrow of time, else Boltzmann's beautiful building collapses."[218] I still feel that Schrödinger was carried away by enthusiasm: if the physicist or anybody else *can* independently decide upon the arrow of time, and if this *has* the consequence which Schrödinger (I think correctly) attributes to it, then, like it or not, he must accept the collapse of the Boltzmann-Schrödinger theory, and the argument for idealism based on it. Schrödinger's refusal to do so was wrong

—unless he could find another way out. But he believed that no other way existed.

Another clash was over a thesis of his—an unimportant one I think, but he thought it very important—in his beautiful book *What is Life?*. This is a work of genius, especially the short section entitled "The Hereditary Code-Script", which in its very title contains one of the most important of biological theories. Indeed, the book is a marvel: written for the educated nonscientist it contains new and pioneering scientific ideas.

Yet it also contains, in response to its main question "What is Life?", a suggestion which seems to me quite obviously mistaken. In Chapter 6 there is a section which begins with the words "What is the characteristic feature of life? When is a piece of matter said to be alive?". To this question Schrödinger gives a reply in the title of the next section: "*It Feeds on 'Negative Entropy'*".[219] The first sentence of this section reads, "It is by avoiding the rapid decay into the inert state of 'equilibrium' that an organism appears so enigmatic. . .". After briefly discussing the statistical theory of entropy, Schrödinger asks: "How would we express in terms of the statistical theory the marvellous faculty of a living organism, by which it delays the decay into thermodynamical equilibrium (death)? We said before: 'It feeds upon negative entropy', attracting, as it were, a stream of negative entropy upon itself. . . ."[220] And he adds: "Thus the device by which an organism maintains itself stationary at a fairly high level of orderliness (=fairly low level of entropy) really consists in continually sucking orderliness from its environment."[221]

Now admittedly organisms do all this. But I denied, and I still deny,[222] Schrödinger's thesis that it is this which is *characteristic* of life, or of organisms; for it holds for every steam engine. In fact every oil-fired boiler and every self-winding watch may be said to be "continually sucking orderliness from its environment". Thus Schrödinger's answer to his question cannot be right: feeding on negative entropy is not "the characteristic feature of life".

I have written here about some of my disagreements with Schrödinger, but I owe him an immense personal debt: in spite of all our quarrels, which more than once looked like a final parting of our ways, he always came back to renew our discussions—discussions which were more interesting, and certainly more exciting, than any I had with any other physicist. The topics we discussed were topics on which I tried to do some work. And the very fact that he raised the question *What is Life?* in that marvellous book of his gave me courage to raise it again for myself (although I tried to avoid the *what-is?* form of the question).

In the remainder of this *Autobiography* I intend to report on ideas rather than on events, though I may make historical remarks where it seems relevant. What I am aiming at is a survey of the various ideas and problems on which I have worked during my later years, and on which I am still working. Some of them will be seen to be connected with the problems I had the great good fortune to discuss with Schrödinger.

31. Objectivity and Criticism

Much of my work in recent years has been in defence of objectivity, attacking or counterattacking subjectivist positions.

To start with, I must make it quite clear that I am not a behaviourist, and my defence of objectivity has nothing to do with any denial of "introspective methods" in psychology. I do not deny the existence of subjective experiences, of mental states, of intelligences, and of minds; I even believe these to be of the utmost importance. But I think that our theories about these subjective experiences, or about these minds, should be as objective as other theories. And by an objective theory I mean a theory which is arguable, which can be exposed to rational criticism, preferably a theory which can be tested: one which does not merely appeal to our subjective intuitions.

As an example of some simple testable laws about subjective experiences I might mention optical illusions such as the Müller-Lyer illusion. An interesting optical illusion was recently shown to me by my friend Edgar Tranekjaer Rasmussen: if a swinging pendulum—a weight suspended from a string—is observed by placing a dark glass before *one* eye it appears, in binocular vision, to move round a horizontal circle rather than in a vertical plane; and if the dark glass is placed before the other eye, it appears to move round the same circle in the opposite direction.

These experiences can be tested by using independent subjects (who, incidentally, *know,* and have *seen,* that the pendulum swings in a plane). They can also be tested by using subjects who habitually (and testably) use monocular vision only: they fail to report the horizontal movement.

An effect like this may give rise to all sorts of theories. For example, that binocular vision is used by our central decoding system to *interpret* spatial distances, and that these interpretations may work in some cases independently of our "better knowledge". Such interpretations seem to play a subtle biological role. No doubt they work very well, and quite unconsciously, under normal conditions; but our decoding system may be misled by abnormal ones.

All of this suggests that our sense organs have many subtle decoding and interpreting devices built into them—that is, adaptations, or theories. They are not of the nature of "valid" theories ("valid", say, because they necessarily impose themselves upon all our experiences) but rather of conjectures, since, especially under unusual conditions, they may produce mistakes. A consequence of this is that there are no uninterpreted visual sense data, no sensations or "elements" in the sense of Mach: whatever is "given" to us is already interpreted, decoded.

In this sense, an objective theory of subjective perception may be constructed. It will be a biological theory which describes normal perception not as the subjective source or the subjective epistemological basis of our subjective knowledge, but rather as an objective achievement of the organism by which the organism solves certain *problems* of adaptation. And these problems may, conjecturally, be specified.

It will be seen how very far the approach here suggested is removed from behaviourism. And as for subjectivism, although the approach here suggested may make subjective experiences (and subjective experiences of "knowing" or "believing") its *object,* the theories or conjectures with which it works can be perfectly objective and testable.

This is just one example of the *objectivist* approach, for which I have been fighting in epistemology, quantum physics, statistical mechanics, probability theory, biology, psychology, and history.[223]

Perhaps most important to the objectivist approach is the recognition of (1) objective problems, (2) objective achievements, that is, solutions of problems, (3) knowledge in the objective sense, (4) criticism, which presupposes objective knowledge in the form of linguistically formulated theories.

(1) Although we may feel disturbed by a problem, and may ardently wish to solve it, the problem itself is something objective—as is the fly by which we are disturbed, and which we may ardently wish to get rid of. That it is an objective problem, that it is present, and the role it may play in some events, are conjectures (just as the presence of the fly is a conjecture).

(2) The solution of a problem, usually found by trial and error, is an achievement, a success, in the objective sense. That something *is* an achievement is a conjecture, and it may be an arguable conjecture. The argument will have to refer to the (conjectured) problem, since achievement or success is, like a solution, always relative to a problem.

(3) We must distinguish achievements or solutions in the objective sense from subjective feelings of achievement, or of knowing, or of belief. Any achievement may be regarded as a solution of a problem, and thus as a *theory* in a generalized sense; and as such it belongs to the world of *knowledge in the objective sense*—which, precisely, is the world of problems and their tentative solutions, and of the critical arguments which bear on them. Geometrical theories and physical theories, for example, belong to this world of knowledge in the objective sense ("world 3"). They are, as a rule, conjectures, in various states of their critical discussion.

(4) Criticism may be said to continue the work of natural selection on a nongenetic (exosomatic) level: it presupposes the existence of objective knowledge, in the form of *formulated theories*. Thus it is only through language that conscious criticism becomes possible. This, I conjecture, is the main reason for the importance of language; and I conjecture that it is human language which is responsible for the peculiarities of man (including even his achievements in the nonlinguistic arts such as music).

32. Induction; Deduction; Objective Truth

There is perhaps a need here for a few words about the myth of induction, and about some of my arguments against induction. And since at present the most fashionable forms of the myth connect induction with an untenable subjectivist philosophy of deduction, I must first say a little more about the objective theory of deductive inference, and about the objective theory of truth.

I did not originally intend to explain Tarski's theory of objective truth in this *Autobiography;* but after writing briefly about it in section 20 I happened to come across some evidence showing that certain logicians have not understood the theory in the sense in which I think it should be understood. As the theory is needed to explain the fundamental difference between deductive inference and the mythical inductive inference, I will explain it briefly. I shall begin with the following problem.

How can one ever hope to understand what is meant by saying that a statement (or a *"meaningful* sentence", as Tarski calls it)[224] corresponds to the facts? Indeed, it seems that unless one accepts something like a picture theory of language (as did Wittgenstein in the *Tractatus*) one cannot speak of anything like correspondence between a statement and a fact. But the picture theory is hopelessly and indeed outrageously mistaken, and so there seems to be no prospect of explaining the correspondence of a statement to a fact.

This may be said to be the fundamental problem encountered by the so-called "correspondence theory of truth"; that is, by the theory which explains truth as correspondence to the facts. Understandably enough, the difficulty has led philosophers to suspect that the correspondence theory must be false or—even worse—meaningless. Tarski's philosophical achievement in this field was, I suggest, that he reversed this decision. He did this very simply by reflecting that a theory which deals with any relation between a statement and a fact must be able to speak about (a) statements and (b) facts. In order to be able to speak about statements, it must use names of statements, or descriptions of statements, and perhaps words such as "statement"; that is, the theory must be in a metalanguage, a language in which one can speak about language. And in order to be able to speak about facts and purported facts, it must use names of facts, or descriptions of facts, and perhaps words like "fact". Once we have a metalanguage, a language like this in which we can speak about statements *and* facts, it becomes easy to make assertions about the correspondence between a statement and a fact; for we can say:

The statement in the German language that consists of the three words, "Gras", "ist", and "grün", in that order, corresponds to the facts if, and only if, grass is green.

The first part of this is a description of a German statement (the description is given in *English*, which here serves as our metalanguage, and consists *in part* of English quotation names of German words); and the second part contains a description (also in English) of a (purported) fact, of a (possible) state of affairs. And the whole statement asserts the correspondence. More generally, we can put it like this. Let "*X*" abbreviate some English name, or some English description, of a statement belonging to the language *L*, and let "*x*" indicate the translation of *X* into English (which serves as a metalanguage of *L*); then we can say (in English, that is in the metalanguage of *L*) quite generally:

(+) *The statement X in the language L corresponds to the facts if and only if x.*

Thus it is possible, even trivially possible, to speak in an *appropriate metalanguage* about the correspondence between a statement and a (purported) fact. And so the riddle is solved: correspondence does not involve structural similarity between a statement and a fact, or anything like the relation between a picture and the scene pictured. For once we have a suitable metalanguage it is easy to explain, with the help of (+), what we mean by correspondence to the facts.

Once we have thus explained correspondence to the facts, we can replace "corresponds to the facts" by "is true (in *L*)". Note that *"is true"* is a metalinguistic predicate, predicable of statements. It is to be preceded by metalinguistic *names* of statements—for example quotation names—and it can therefore be clearly distinguished from a phrase like "*It is true that*". For example "It is true that snow is red" does not contain a metalinguistic predicate of statements; it belongs to the same language as does "Snow is red", and not to the metalanguage of that language. The unexpected triviality of Tarski's result seems to be one of the reasons why it is difficult to understand. On the other hand, the triviality might reasonably have been expected, since after all everybody understands what "truth" means as long as he does not begin to think (wrongly) about it.

The most significant application of the correspondence theory is not to specific statements like "Grass is red" or "Grass is green", but to the descriptions of general logical situations. For example, we wish to say things like this. If an inference is valid then if the premises are all true, the conclusion must be true; that is, the truth of the premises (if they are all true) is invariably transmitted to the conclusion; and the falsity of the conclusion (if it is false) is invariably retransmitted to at least one of the premises. (I have christened these laws respectively "the law of the transmission of truth" and "the law of the retransmission of falsity".)

These laws are fundamental for the theory of deduction, and the use here of the words "truth" and "are true" (which are replaceable by the words "correspondence to the facts" and "correspond to the facts") is obviously far from redundant.

The correspondence theory of truth which Tarski rescued is a theory which regards truth as *objective*: as a property of theories, rather than as an experience or belief or something subjective like that. It is also *absolute*, rather than relative to some set of assumptions (or beliefs); for we may ask of any set of assumptions whether these assumptions are true.

Now I turn to deduction. A deductive inference may be said to be valid if and only if it invariably transmits truth from the premises to the conclusion; that is to say, if and only if all inferences of the same logical form transmit truth. One can also explain this by saying: a deductive inference is valid if and only if no *counterexample exists*. Here a counterexample is an inference of the same form with true premises and a false conclusion, as in:

All men are mortal. Socrates is mortal. ∴ Socrates is a man.

Let "Socrates" be here the name of a dog. Then the premises are true and the conclusion is false. Thus we have a counterexample and the inference is invalid.

Thus deductive inference is, like truth, *objective*, and even *absolute*. Objectivity does not mean, of course, that we can always ascertain whether or not a given statement is true. Nor can we always ascertain whether a given inference is valid. If we agree to use the term "true" only in the objective sense, then there are many statements which we can *prove* to be true; yet *we cannot have a general criterion of truth*. If we had such a criterion, we would be omniscient, at least potentially, which we are not. According to the work of Gödel and Tarski, we cannot even have a general criterion of truth for arithmetical statements, although we can of course describe infinite sets of arithmetical statements which are true. In the same way, we may agree to use the term "valid inference" in the objective sense, in which case we can prove of many inferences that they are valid (that is, they unfailingly transmit truth); yet we have no general criterion of validity—not even if we confine ourselves to purely arithmetical statements. As a consequence, we have no general criterion for deciding whether or not some given arithmetical statement follows validly from the axioms of arithmetic. Nevertheless, we can describe infinitely many rules of inference (of many degrees of complexity) for which it is possible to *prove* validity; that is, the nonexistence of a counterexample. *Thus it is false to say that deductive inference rests upon our intuition.* Admittedly, if we have not established the validity of an inference, then we may allow ourselves to be led by guesses—that is, by intuition; intuition cannot be done without, but more often than not it leads us astray. (This is obvious; we know from the history of science that there have been many more bad theories than good ones.) And thinking intuitively is something totally different from appealing to intuition as if this was as good as appealing to an argument.

As I have often said in lectures, such things as intuition, or the feeling that something is self-evident, may *perhaps* be partially explained by truth, or by validity, but never vice versa. No statement is true, and no inference is valid, just because we feel (however strongly) that it is. It can be admitted, of course, that our intellect, or our faculty of reasoning or judging (or whatever we may call it), is so adjusted that, under fairly ordinary circumstances, we accept, or judge, or believe, what is true; largely no doubt because there are some dispositions built into us for checking things critically. However, optical illusions, to take a comparatively simple example, show that we cannot rely too much on our intuition, even if it takes a form somewhat akin to compulsion.

That we may explain such subjective feelings or intuitions

as the result of being presented with truth or validity and of having run through some of our normal critical checks does not allow us to turn the matter round and say: this statement is true or this inference is valid because I believe it, or because I feel compelled to believe it, or because it is self-evident, or because the opposite is inconceivable. Nevertheless, for hundreds of years this kind of talk has served subjectivist philosophers in place of arguments.

The view is still widely held that in logic we have to appeal to intuition because without circularity there cannot be arguments for or against the rules of deductive logic: all arguments must presuppose logic. Admittedly, all arguments make use of logic and, if you like, "presuppose" it, though much may be said against this way of putting things. Yet it is a fact that we can establish the validity of some rules of inference without making use of them.[225] To sum up, deduction or deductive validity is objective, as is objective truth. Intuition, or a feeling of belief or of compulsion, may perhaps be sometimes due to the fact that certain inferences are valid; but the validity is objective, and explicable neither in psychological nor in behaviourist nor in pragmatist terms.

I have often expressed this attitude by saying: "I am not a belief philosopher." Indeed, beliefs are quite insignificant for a theory of truth, or of deduction, or of "knowledge" in the objective sense. A so-called "true belief" is a belief in a theory which is true; and whether or not it is true is not a question of belief, but a question of fact. Similarly, "rational belief", if there can be said to be such a thing, consists in giving preference to what is preferable in the light of critical arguments. So this again is not a question of belief, but a question of argument, and of the objective state of the critical debate.[226]

As for induction (or inductive logic, or inductive behaviour, or learning by induction or by repetition or by "instruction") I assert that there is no such thing. If I am right then this solves, of course, the problem of induction.[227] (There are other problems left which may also be called problems of induction, such as whether the future will be like the past. But this problem, which in my opinion is far from stirring can also be solved: the future will in part be like the past and in part not at all like the past.)

What is the present most fashionable reply to Hume? It is that induction is, of course, not "valid", because the word "valid" means "deductively valid"; thus the invalidity (in the *deductive* sense) of inductive arguments creates no problem: we have deductive reasoning and inductive reasoning; and although the two have a lot in common—both consist of arguing in accordance with well-tried, habitual, and fairly intuitive rules—there is also a lot of difference.[228]

What deduction and induction are supposed to have in common, especially, can be put like this. The validity of deduction cannot be validly proved, for this would be proving logic by logic, which would be circular. Yet such a circular argument, it is said, may in fact clarify our views and strengthen our confidence. *The same is true for induction.* Induction may perhaps be beyond inductive justification, yet inductive reasoning about induction is useful and helpful, if not indispensable.[229] Moreover, in both the theory of deduction and the theory of induction, such things as intuition or habit or convention or practical success *may* be appealed to; and sometimes they *must* be appealed to.

To criticize this fashionable view I repeat what I said earlier in this section: a deductive inference is *valid if no counterexample exists.* Thus we have a method of objective critical testing at our disposal: to any proposed rule of deduction, we can try to construct a counterexample. If we succeed, then the inference, or the rule of inference, is invalid, whether or not it is held to be intuitively valid by some people or even by everybody. (Brouwer thought that he had done just this—that he had given a counterexample for indirect proofs—explaining that these were mistakenly imagined to be valid because only *infinite* counterexamples exist, so that indirect proofs are valid in all finite cases.) As we have objective tests and in many cases even objective proofs at our disposal, psychological considerations, subjective convictions, habits, and conventions become completely irrelevant to the issue.

Now what is the situation with regard to induction? When is an inductive inference inductively "unsound" (to use a word other than "invalid")? The only answer which has been suggested is: when it leads to frequent practical mistakes in inductive behaviour. But I assert that every rule of inductive inference ever proposed by anybody would, if anyone were to use it, lead to such frequent practical mistakes.

The point is that there is no rule of inductive inference—inference leading to theories or universal laws—ever proposed which can be taken seriously for even a minute. Carnap seems to agree; for he writes:[230]

> By the way, Popper finds it "interesting" that I give in my lecture an example of deductive inference, but no example of inductive inference. Since in my conception probabilistic ("inductive") reasoning consists essentially not in making inferences, but rather in assigning probabilities, he should instead have required examples of principles for probability assignments. And this request, not made but reasonable, was anticipated and satisfied.

But Carnap developed only a system that assigns the probability zero to all universal laws:[231] and although Hintikka (and others) have since developed systems which do attribute an inductive probability other than zero to universal statements, there is no doubt that these systems seem to be essentially confined to very poor languages, in which even a primitive natural science could not be formulated. Moreover, they are restricted to cases in which only *finitely* many theories are available at any time.[232] (This does not stop the systems from being frighteningly complicated.) Anyway, to my mind such laws—of which there are, in practice, always infinitely many—*ought* to be given "probability" zero (in the sense of the calculus of probability) though their degree of corroboration may be greater than zero. And even if we do adopt a new system—one that assigns to some laws the probability, let us say, of 0.7—what do we gain? Does it tell us whether or not the law has good inductive support? By no means; all it tells us is that according to some (largely arbitrary) new system—no matter whose—*we ought to believe* in the law with a degree of belief equal to 0.7, provided we want our feelings of belief to conform to this system. What difference such a rule would make and, if it makes a difference, how it is to be criticized—what it excludes, and why it is to be preferred to Carnap's and my own arguments for assigning zero probabilities to universal laws—is difficult to say.[233]

Sensible rules of inductive inference do not exist. (This seems to be recognized by the inductivist Nelson Goodman.)[234] The best rule I can extract from all my reading of the inductivist literature would be something like this:

"The future is likely to be not so very different from the past."

This, of course, is a rule which everybody accepts in practice; and something like it we must accept also in theory if we are realists (as I believe we all are, whatever some may say). The rule is, however, so vague that it is hardly interesting. And in spite of its vagueness, the rule assumes too much, and certainly much more than we (and thus any inductive rule) should assume *prior* to all theory formation; for it assumes a *theory of time*.

But this was to be expected. Since there can be no theory-free observation, and no theory-free language, there can of course be no theory-free rule or principle of induction; no rule or principle on which all theories should be based.

Thus induction is a myth. No "inductive logic" exists. And although there exists a "logical" interpretation of the probability calculus, there is no good reason to assume that this "generalized logic" (as it *may* be called) is a system of "inductive logic".[235]

Nor is it to be regretted that induction does not exist: we seem to do quite well without it—with theories which are bold guesses, and which we criticize and test as severely as we can, and with as much ingenuity as we possess.

Of course, *if* this is good practice—successful practice—then Goodman and others may say that it is an "inductively valid" rule of induction. But my whole point is that it is good practice *not* because it is successful, or reliable, or what not, but because it tells us that it is bound to lead to error and so keeps us conscious of the need to look out for these errors, and to try to eliminate them.

33. *Metaphysical Research Programmes*

After the publication of *The Open Society* in 1945 my wife pointed out to me that this book did not represent my central philosophical interests, for I was not primarily a political philosopher. I had in fact said so in the Introduction; but she was satisfied neither by this disclaimer, nor by my subsequent return to my old interests, to the theory of scientific knowledge. She pointed out to me that my *Logik der Forschung* had long been unobtainable and by then was very nearly forgotten; and that, since I was assuming its results in my new writings, it had become urgent that it should be translated into English. I quite agreed with her, but without her insistent reminders, through many years, I should have let it rest; even so it took another fourteen years for *The Logic of Scientific Discovery* to be published (in 1959) and another seven years for the second German edition of *Logik der Forschung*.

During these years I did more and more work which I intended to use in a companion volume to *The Logic of Scientific Discovery*; and in approximately 1952 I decided to call this volume *Postscript: After Twenty Years,* hoping that it would come out in 1954.

It was sent to the printers in 1956, together with the (English) manuscript of *The Logic of Scientific Discovery,* and I received the proofs of both volumes early in 1957. Proof-reading turned into a nightmare. I could complete only the first volume, which was published in 1959, and I then had to have operations on both eyes. After this I could not start proofreading again for some time, and as a result the *Postscript* is still unpublished, with the exception of one or two extracts.[236] It was of course read by several of my colleagues and students.

In this *Postscript* I reviewed and developed the main problems and solutions discussed in *Logik der Forschung*. For example, I stressed that I had *rejected all attempts at the justification of theories, and that I had replaced justification by criticism*:[237] we can never justify a theory. But we can sometimes "justify" (in a different sense) our *preference* for a theory, considering the state of the critical debate; for a theory may stand up to criticism better than its competitors. To this the objection may be made that a critic must always justify his own theoretical position. My answer is: he need not, for he may significantly criticize a theory if he can show an unexpected contradiction to exist either within a theory, or between it and some other interesting theory, though of course the latter criticism would not as a rule be decisive.[238] Previously, most philosophers had thought that any claim to rationality meant rational *justification* (of one's beliefs); my thesis was, at least since my *Open Society,* that rationality meant rational *criticism* (of one's own theory and of competing theories). Thus the old philosophy linked the ideal of rationality with final, demonstrable knowledge (either proreligious or anti-religious: religion was the main issue) while I linked it with the *growth of conjectural knowledge*. This itself I linked with the idea of a better and better approximation to truth, or of *increasing truthlikeness or verisimilitude*.[239] According to this view, finding theories which are better approximations to truth is what the scientist aims at; the aim of science is knowing more and more. This involves *the growth of the content of our theories,* the growth of our knowledge of the world.

Apart from a restatement of my theory of knowledge, one of my aims in the *Postscript* was to show that the realism of my *Logik der Forschung* was a criticizable or arguable position. I stressed that *Logik der Forschung* was the book of a realist but that at that time I did not dare to say much about realism. The reason was that I had not then realized that a metaphysical position, though not testable, might be rationally criticizable or arguable. I had confessed to being a realist, but I had thought that this was no more than a confession of faith. Thus I had written about a realist argument of mine that it "expresses the metaphysical faith in the existence of regularities in our world (a faith which I share, and without which practical action is hardly conceivable)".[240]

In 1958 I published two talks, partly based on the *Postscript*, under the title "On the Status of Science and of Metaphysics" (now in *Conjectures and Refutations*[241]). In the second of these talks I tried to show that metaphysical theories may be susceptible to criticism and argument, because they may be attempts to solve *problems*—problems perhaps open to better or less good solutions. This idea I applied in the second talk to five metaphysical theories: determinism, idealism (and subjectivism), irrationalism, voluntarism (Schopenhauer's), and nihilism (Heidegger's philosophy of nothingness). And I gave reasons for rejecting these as unsuccessful attempts to solve their problems.

In the last chapter of the *Postscript* I argued in a similar way for indeterminism, realism, and objectivism. I tried to show that these three metaphysical theories are compatible and, in order to show the compatibility by a kind of model, I proposed that we conjecture *the reality of dispositions* (such as potentials or fields) *and especially of propensities*. (This is one way of arguing in favour of the propensity interpretation of probability. Another way will be mentioned in the next section.)

But one of the main points of that chapter was a description and appreciation of the role played by *metaphysical re-*

search programmes;[242] I showed, with the help of a brief historical sketch, that *there had been changes down the ages in our ideas of what a satisfactory explanation ought to be like.* These ideas changed under the pressure of criticism. Thus they were criticizable, though not testable. They were metaphysical ideas—in fact, metaphysical ideas of the greatest importance.

I illustrated this with some historical remarks on the different "metaphysical research programmes that have influenced the development of physics since the days of Pythagoras"; and I proposed a new metaphysical view of the world, and with it a new research programme, based on the idea of the reality of dispositions and on the propensity interpretation of probability. (This view, I now think, is also helpful in connection with evolution.)

I have reported here on these developments for two reasons.

(1) Because metaphysical realism—the view that there is a real world to be discovered—solves some of the problems which are left open by my solution of the problem of induction.

(2) Because I intend to argue that the theory of natural selection is not a testable scientific theory, but a metaphysical research programme; and although it is no doubt the best at present available, it can perhaps be slightly improved.

I will not say more about point (1) than that, when we think we have found an approximation to the truth in the form of a scientific theory which has stood up to criticism and to tests better than its competitors, we shall, as realists, accept it as a basis for practical action, simply because we have nothing better (or nearer to the truth). But we need not accept it as true: we need not believe in it (which would mean believing in its truth).[243]

About (2) I will say more when I come to discuss the theory of evolution in section 37.

34. Fighting Subjectivism in Physics: Quantum Mechanics and Propensity

Few great men have had an intellectual impact upon the twentieth century comparable to that of Ernst Mach. He influenced physics, physiology, psychology, the philosophy of science, and pure (or speculative) philosophy. He influenced

Einstein, Bohr, Heisenberg, William James, Bertrand Russell—
to mention just a few names. Mach was not a great physicist;
but he was a great personality and a great historian and philosopher of science. As a physiologist, psychologist, and philosopher of science, he held many important and original views
to which I subscribe. He was, for instance, an evolutionist in
the theory of knowledge, and in the field of psychology and
physiology, especially in the study of the senses. He was critical
of metaphysics, but he was sufficiently tolerant to admit, and
even to stress, the necessity of metaphysical ideas as guiding
lights for the physicist, even the experimental physicist. Thus
he wrote, in his *Principles of the Theory of Heat*, about
Joule: [244]

> When it comes to general (philosophical) questions [which
> Mach calls "metaphysical" on the previous page], Joule is
> almost silent. But where he speaks, his utterances closely re-
> semble those of Mayer. And indeed, one cannot doubt that such
> comprehensive experimental investigations, all with the same
> aim, can be carried out only by a man who is inspired by a
> great and philosophically most profound view of the world.

A passage like this is the more remarkable as Mach had
previously published a book, *The Analysis of Sensations*, in
which he wrote that "my approach *eliminates all metaphysical
questions*", and that "all we can know of the world expresses
itself necessarily in sensations" (or in sense data, "*Sinnesem-
pfindungen*").

Unfortunately, neither his biological approach nor his
tolerance made much impact on the thought of our century;
what was so influential—especially upon atomic physics—was
his antimetaphysical intolerance, combined with his theory of
sensations. That Mach's influence on the new generation of
atomic physicists became so persuasive is indeed one of the
ironies of history. For he was a vehement opponent of atomism and the "corpuscular" theory of matter, which he, like
Berkeley, [245] regarded as metaphysical.

The philosophical impact of Mach's positivism was largely
transmitted by the young Einstein. But Einstein turned away
from Machian positivism, partly because he realized with a
shock some of its consequences; consequences which the next
generation of brilliant physicists, among them Bohr, Pauli, and
Heisenberg, not only discovered but enthusiastically embraced:

they became *subjectivists*. But Einstein's withdrawal came too late. Physics had become a stronghold of subjectivist philosophy, and it has remained so ever since.

Behind this development there were, however, two serious problems, connected with quantum mechanics and the theory of time; and one problem which is, I think, not so serious, the subjectivist theory of entropy.

With the rise of quantum mechanics, most of the younger physicists became convinced that quantum mechanics, unlike statistical mechanics, was not a theory of ensembles, but of the mechanics of single fundamental particles. (After some wavering I too accepted this view.) On the other hand, they were also convinced that quantum mechanics, like statistical mechanics, was a probabilistic theory. As a mechanical theory of fundamental particles, it had an objective aspect. As a probabilistic theory, it had (or so they thought) a subjective aspect. Thus it was an utterly new type of fundamental theory, combining objective and subjective aspects. Such was its revolutionary character.

Einstein's view diverged somewhat from this. For him, probabilistic theories such as statistical mechanics were extremely interesting and important and beautiful. (In his early days he had made some crucial contributions to them.) But they were neither fundamental physical theories, nor objective: they were, rather, subjectivist theories, theories which we have to introduce *because of the fragmentary character of our knowledge.* From this it follows that quantum mechanics, in spite of its excellence, is not a fundamental theory, but incomplete (because its statistical character shows that it works with incomplete knowledge), and that the objective or complete theory we must search for would not be a probabilistic but a deterministic theory.

It will be seen that the two positions have an element in common: both assume that a probabilistic or statistical theory somehow makes use of our subjective knowledge, or lack of knowledge.

This can be well understood if we consider that the only objectivist interpretation of probability discussed at that time (the late 1920s) was the frequency interpretation. (This had been developed in various versions by Venn, von Mises,

Reichenbach; and later by myself.) Now frequency theorists hold that there are objective questions concerning mass phenomena, and corresponding objective answers. But they have to admit that whenever we speak to the probability of a *single* event, *qua* element of a mass phenomenon, the objectivity becomes problematic; so that it may well be asserted that with respect to single events, such as the emission of one photon, probabilities merely evaluate our ignorance. For the objective probability tells us only what happens on the average if this sort of event is repeated many times: about the single event itself the objective statistical probability says nothing.

It was here that subjectivism entered quantum mechanics, according to both Einstein's view and to that of his opponents. And it was here that I tried to fight subjectivism by introducing the propensity interpretation of probability. This was not an *ad hoc* introduction. It was, rather, the result of a careful revision of the arguments underlying the frequency interpretation of probability.

The main idea was that propensities could be regarded as *physical realities*. They were measures of dispositions. Measurable physical dispositions ("potentials") had been introduced into physics by the theory of fields. Thus there was a precedent here for regarding dispositions as physically real; and so the suggestion that we should regard propensities as physically real was not so very strange. It also left room, of course, for indeterminism.

To show the kind of problem of interpretation which the introduction of propensities was intended to solve, I will discuss a letter which Einstein wrote to Schrödinger.[246] In this letter, Einstein refers to a well-known thought experiment which Schrödinger had published in 1935.[247] Schrödinger had pointed out the possibility of arranging some radioactive material so as to trigger a bomb, with the help of a Geiger counter. The arrangement can be made in such a way that either the bomb explodes within a certain time interval or else the fuse is disconnected. Let the probability of an explosion equal 1/2. Schrödinger argued that if a cat is placed next to the bomb, the probability that it will be killed will also be 1/2. The whole arrangement might be described in terms of quantum mechanics, and in this description, there will be a superposition of two states of the cat—a live and a dead state.

Thus the quantum-mechanical description—the ψ-function —does not describe anything real: for the real cat will be either alive or dead.

Einstein argues in his letter to Schrödinger that this means that quantum mechanics is subjective and incomplete:

> If one tries to interpret the ψ-function as a complete description [of the real physical process described by it] . . . then this would mean that at the moment in question, the cat is neither alive nor blown to bits. Yet one condition or the other would be realized by an observation.
>
> If one rejects this view [of the completeness of the ψ-function] then one has to assume that the ψ-function does not describe a real state of affairs, but the totality of *our knowledge with respect to the state of affairs*. This is Born's interpretation which, it seems, is today accepted by most theoretical physicists.[248]

Upon acceptance of my propensity interpretation, however, this dilemma disappears, and quantum mechanics, that is the ψ-function, *does* describe a real state of affairs—a real disposition—though not a deterministic state of affairs. And although the fact that the state of affairs is not deterministic may well be said to indicate an incompleteness, this incompleteness may be not a fault of the theory—of the description —but a reflection of the indeterminateness of reality, of the state of affairs itself.

Schrödinger had always felt that $|\,\psi\;\psi^*\,|$ must describe something physically *real*, such as a real density. And he also was aware of the possibility[249] that reality itself may be indeterminate. According to the propensity interpretation these intuitions were quite correct.

I will not discuss here any further the propensity theory of probability and the role it can play in clarifying quantum mechanics, because I have dealt with these matters fairly extensively elsewhere.[250] I remember that the theory was not well received to start with, which neither surprised nor depressed me. Things have changed very much since then, and some of the same critics (and defenders of Bohr) who at first dismissed my theory contemptuously as incompatible with quantum mechanics now say that it is all old hat, and in fact identical with Bohr's view.

I regarded myself as more than rewarded for almost forty years of heartsearching when I received a letter from B. L. van der Waerden, the mathematician and historian of quantum mechanics, about my paper of 1967, "Quantum Mechanics without 'The Observer' ", in which he said that he fully agreed with all the thirteen theses of my paper, and also with my propensity interpretation of probability.[251]

35. Boltzmann and the Arrow of Time

The irruption of subjectivism into physics—and especially into the theory of time and entropy—began long before the rise of quantum mechanics. It was closely connected with the tragedy of Ludwig Boltzmann, one of the great physicists of the nineteenth century, and at the same time an ardent and almost militant realist and objectivist.

Boltzmann and Mach were colleagues at the University of Vienna. Boltzmann was professor of physics there when Mach was called, in 1895, to a chair in the philosophy of science, established especially for him. It must have been the first chair of its kind in the world. Later Moritz Schlick occupied the chair, and after him Victor Kraft.[252] In 1901, when Mach resigned, Boltzmann succeeded him, keeping his chair of physics. Mach, who was Boltzmann's senior by six years, stayed in Vienna approximately until Boltzmann's death in 1906; and during this period, and for many years after, Mach's influence was constantly increasing. Both were physicists, Boltzmann by far the more brilliant and creative of the two;[253] and both were philosophers. Mach was called to Vienna as a philosopher, on the initiative of two philosophers. (After Boltzmann had been called to succeed Stefan in a chair of physics—a chair of which Mach had had some hopes—the idea of calling Mach instead to a chair of philosophy originated with Heinrich Gomperz, then only twenty-one, who took action through his father.)[254] On the philosophical merits of Boltzmann and Mach my judgement is frankly partisan. Boltzmann is little known as a philosopher; until quite recently I too knew next to nothing about his philosophy, and I still know much less about it than I should. Yet with what I know I agree; more closely perhaps than with any other philosophy. Thus I greatly prefer Boltzmann to Mach—not only as a physicist and a philosopher but also, I admit, as a person. But I also find Mach's personality extremely attractive; and although I am utterly opposed to his "analysis of sensations", I agree with his biological approach to the problem of (subjective) knowledge.

Boltzmann and Mach both had a great following among physicists, and they were involved in an almost deadly struggle. It was a struggle over the research programme of physics, and over the "corpuscular" hypothesis; that is, over atomism and the molecular or kinetic theory of gases and of heat. Boltzmann was an atomist, and he defended both atomism and Maxwell's kinetic theory of heat and of gases. Mach was opposed to these "metaphysical" hypotheses. He favoured a "phenomenological thermodynamics" from which he hoped to exclude all "explanatory hypotheses"; and he hoped to extend the "phenomenological" or "purely descriptive" method to the whole of physics.

In all these issues my sympathies are entirely on Boltzmann's side. But I have to admit that, in spite of his superior mastery of physics and his (in my opinion) superior philosophy, Boltzmann lost the battle. He was beaten on an issue of fundamental importance—his bold probabilistic derivation of the second law of thermodynamics, the law of entropy increase, from the kinetic theory (Boltzmann's H-theorem). He was beaten, I think, because he had been too bold.

His derivation is intuitively most convincing: he associates entropy with disorder; he shows, convincingly and correctly, that disordered states of a gas in a box are more "probable" (in a perfectly good and objective sense of "probable") than ordered states. And then he concludes (and this conclusion turned out to be invalid[255]) that there is *a general mechanical law* according to which closed systems (enclosed gases) tend to assume more and more probable states; which means that ordered systems tend to become more and more disordered the older they get, or that the entropy of a gas *tends to increase with time.*

All this is highly convincing; but in this form it is unfortunately wrong. Boltzmann at first interpreted his H-theorem as proving a *one-directional increase of disorder with time.* But as Zermelo pointed out,[256] Poincaré had proved previously (and Boltzmann never challenged this proof) that every closed system (gas) returns, after some finite time, to the neighbourhood of any state in which it was before. Thus all states are (approximately) recurring for ever; and if the gas was once in an ordered state, it will after some time return to it. Accordingly there can be no such thing as a preferred direction of time—an "arrow of time"—which is associated with entropy increase.

Zermelo's objection was, I think, decisive: it revolutionized Boltzmann's own view, and statistical mechanics and thermodynamics became, especially after 1907 (the date of the article of the Ehrenfests[257]), strictly symmetrical with respect to the direction of time; and so far they have remained so. The situation looks like this: every closed system (a gas, say) spends almost all its time in disordered states (equilibrium states). There will be fluctuations from the equilibrium, but the frequency of their occurrence rapidly decreases with their increasing size. Thus if we find that a gas is in some state of fluctuation (that is, a state of better *order* than the equilibrium state), we can conclude that it was *probably* preceded, and will *just as probably* be succeeded, by a state nearer to equilibrium (*disorder*). Accordingly, if we want to predict its future, we can predict (with high probability) an entropy increase; and a precisely analogous retrodiction of its past can also be made. It is strange that it is rarely seen that with Zermelo a revolution occurred in thermodynamics: Zermelo often gets a dishonourable mention or none at all.[258]

Unfortunately, Boltzmann did not see at once the seriousness of Zermelo's objection; thus his first reply was unsatisfactory, as Zermelo pointed out. And with Boltzmann's second reply to Zermelo there started what I regard as the great tragedy: Boltzmann's lapse into subjectivism. For in this second reply,

(a) Boltzmann gave up his theory of an objective arrow of time, and also his theory that entropy tends to increase in the direction of this arrow; that is, he gave up what had been one of his central points;

(b) he introduced *ad hoc* a beautiful but wild cosmological hypothesis;

(c) he introduced a subjectivist theory of the arrow of time, and a theory which reduced the law of entropy increase to a tautology.

The connection between these three points of Boltzmann's second reply can best be expounded as follows.[259]

(a) Let us start by assuming that time has objectively no arrow, no direction, that it is in this respect just like a space coordinate; and that the objective *"universe"* is completely symmetrical with respect to the two directions of time.

(b) Let us further assume that the whole universe is a system (like a gas) in thermal equilibrium (maximal disorder). In such a universe, there will be *fluctuations* of entropy (disorder); regions in space and time, that is, in which there is some order. These regions of low entropy will be very rare—the rarer the lower the entropy valley; and on our symmetry assumption, the valley will rise in a similar way in both time directions, and flatten out towards maximum entropy. Let us in addition assume that life is only possible on the sides of deeply cut entropy valleys; and let us call these regions of changing entropy "worlds".

(c) Now we need only assume that, subjectively, we (and probably all animals) *experience* the time coordinate as having a direction—an arrow—pointing towards the entropy increase; this means that the time coordinate becomes successively or serially conscious to us as, in the "world" (the region in which we live), the entropy increases.

If (a) to (c) hold then, clearly, entropy will always increase with increasing time; that is, with the time of our consciousness. On the biological hypothesis that time gets an arrow only within the experience of animals, and only in the direction in which entropy increases, the law of entropy increase becomes a necessary law—but only subjectively valid.

The following diagram may help. (See Fig. 1.)

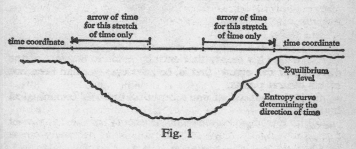

Fig. 1

The upper line is the time coordinate; the lower line indicates an entropy fluctuation. The arrows indicate regions in which life may occur, and in which time may be experienced as having the indicated direction.

Boltzmann—and also Schrödinger—suggest that the direction towards the "future" can be fixed by a definition, as the following quotation from Boltzmann's second reply to Zermelo shows: [260]

We have the choice of two kinds of picture. Either we assume that the whole universe is at the present moment in a very improbable state. Or else we assume that the aeons during which this improbable state lasts, and the distance from here to Sirius, are *minute* if compared with the age and size of the whole universe. In such a universe, which is in thermal equilibrium as a whole and therefore dead, relatively small regions of the size of our galaxy will be found here and there; regions (which we may call "worlds") which deviate significantly from thermal equilibrium for relatively short stretches of those "aeons" of time. Among these worlds the probabilities of their state [i.e. the entropy] will increase as often as they decrease. In the universe as a whole the two directions of time are indistinguishable, just as in space there is no up or down. However, just as at a certain place on the earth's surface we can call "down" the direction towards the centre of the earth, so a living organism that finds itself in such a world at a certain period of time can define the "direction" of time as going from the less probable state to the more probable one (the former will be the "past" and the latter the "future"), and by virtue of this definition [*sic*] he will find that his own small region, isolated from the rest of the universe, is "initially" always in an improbable state. It seems to me that this way of looking at things is the only one which allows us to understand the validity of the second law, and the heat death of each individual world, without invoking a unidirectional change of the entire universe from a definite initial state to a final state.

I think that Boltzmann's idea is staggering in its boldness and beauty. But I also think that it is quite untenable, at least for a realist. It brands unidirectional change as an illusion. This makes the catastrophe of Hiroshima an illusion. Thus it makes our world an illusion, and with it *all our attempts to find out more about our world*. It is therefore self-defeating (like every idealism). Boltzmann's idealistic *ad hoc* hypothesis clashes with his own realistic and almost passionately maintained anti-idealistic philosophy, and with his passionate wish to know.

But Boltzmann's *ad hoc* hypothesis also destroys, to a considerable extent, the physical theory which it was intended to save. For his great and bold attempt to derive the law of entropy increase ($dS/dt \geq 0$) from mechanical and statistical assumptions—his *H*-theorem—fails completely. It fails for his objective time (that is, his directionless time) since for it entropy decreases as often as it increases.[261] And it fails for his subjective time (time with an arrow) since here only a definition or an illusion makes the entropy increase, and no kinetic, no dynamic, no statistical or mechanical proof could (or could be required to) establish this fact. Thus it destroyed the physical theory—the kinetic theory of entropy—which Boltzmann tried to defend against Zermelo. The sacrifice of his realistic philosophy for the sake of his *H*-theorem was in vain.

I think that, in time, he must have realized all this, and that his depression and suicide in 1906 may have been connected with it.

Although I admire the beauty and the intellectual boldness of Boltzmann's idealistic *ad hoc* hypothesis, it now turns out that it was not "bold" in the sense of my methodology: it did not add to our knowledge, it was not content-increasing. On the contrary, it was destructive of all content. (Of course, the theory of equilibrium and fluctuations was unaffected; see note 256.)

This was why I did not feel any regret (though I was very sad for Boltzmann) when I realized that my example of a nonentropic physical process which had an arrow of time[262] destroyed Boltzmann's idealistic *ad hoc* hypothesis. I admit that it destroyed something remarkable—an argument for idealism which seemed to belong to pure physics. But unlike Schrödinger, I was not prone to look for such arguments; and since I was, like Schrödinger, opposed to the use of quantum theory in support of subjectivism, I was glad that I had been able to attack an even older stronghold of subjectivism in physics.[263] And I felt that Boltzmann would have approved of the attempt (though perhaps not of the results).

The story of Mach and Boltzmann is one of the strangest in the history of science; and it is one which shows the historical power of fashions. But fashions are stupid and blind, especially philosophical fashions; and that includes the belief that history will be our judge.

In the light of history—or in the darkness of history—Boltzmann was defeated, according to all accepted standards, though everybody admits his eminence as a physicist. For he never succeeded in clearing up the status of his H-theorem; nor did he explain entropy increase. (Instead, he created a new problem—or, as I think, a pseudoproblem: is the arrow of time a consequence of entropy increase?) He was also defeated as a philosopher. During his later life, Mach's positivism and Ostwald's "energetics", both of them antiatomist, waxed so influential that Boltzmann became disheartened (as his *Lectures on Gas Theory* show). Such was the pressure that he lost faith in himself and in the reality of atoms: he suggested that the corpuscular hypothesis may perhaps be only a heuristic device (rather than a hypothesis about a physical reality); a suggestion to which Mach reacted with the remark that it was "not a wholly chivalrous countermove in the debate" (*"ein nicht ganz ritterlicher polemischer Zug"*[264]).

To this day Boltzmann's realism and objectivism have been vindicated neither by himself nor by history. (The worse for history.) Even though the atomism he had defended won its first great victory with the help of his idea of statistical fluctuations (I am alluding to Einstein's paper on Brownian movement of 1905), it was the philosophy of Mach—the philosophy of the arch-opponent of atomism—that became the accepted creed of the young Einstein and probably thereby of the founders of quantum mechanics. Nobody denied Boltzmann's greatness as a physicist, of course, and especially as one of the two founders of statistical mechanics. But whatever there is in the way of a renaissance of his ideas seems to be linked either with his subjectivist theory of the arrow of time (Schrödinger, Reichenbach, Grünbaum), or with a subjectivist interpretation of statistics and of his H-theorem (Born, Jaynes). The goddess of history—venerated as our judge—still plays her tricks.

I have told this story here because it throws some light on the idealistic theory that the arrow of time is a subjective illusion, and because the fight against this theory has taken up much of my thought in recent years.

36. The Subjectivist Theory of Entropy

What I mean here by the subjectivist theory of entropy[265] is not Boltzmann's theory, in which the arrow of time is subjective but entropy objective. I mean rather a theory, originally due to Leo Szilard,[266] according to which the entropy of a system increases whenever our information about it decreases, and *vice versa*. According to Szilard's theory, any gain of information or knowledge must be interpreted as a decrease in entropy: in accordance with the second law it must somehow be paid for by an at least equal increase in entropy.[267]

I admit that there is something intuitively satisfying in this thesis—especially, of course, for a subjectivist. Undoubtedly, information (or "informative content") can be measured by improbability, as in fact I pointed out in 1934 in my *Logik der Forschung*.[268] Entropy, on the other hand, can be equated with the *probability* of the state of the system in question. Thus the following equations *appear* to be valid:

$$\text{information} = \text{negentropy};$$
$$\text{entropy} = \text{lack of information} = \text{nescience}.$$

These equations, however, should be used with the greatest caution: all that has been shown is that entropy and lack of information can be measured by *probabilities*, or interpreted as probabilities. It has not been shown that they are probabilities of the same attributes of the same system.

Let us consider one of the simplest possible cases of entropy increase, the expansion of a gas in driving a piston. Let there be a cylinder with a piston in the middle. (See Fig. 2.) Let the cylinder be kept at constant high temperature by a heat bath,

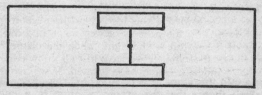

Fig. 2

so that any loss of heat is at once replaced. If there is a gas on the left which drives the piston to the right, thus enabling us to obtain work (lifting a weight), then we pay for this by an increase in the entropy of the gas.

Let us assume, for simplicity's sake, that the gas consists of one molecule only, the molecule M. (This assumption is standard among my opponents—Szilard, or Brillouin—so it is permissible[269] to adopt it; it will, however, be critically discussed later on.) Then we *can* say that the increase of entropy corresponds to a loss of information. For before the expansion of the gas, we knew of the gas (that is, of our molecule M) that it was in the left half of the cylinder. After the expansion, and when it has done its work, we do not know whether it is in the left half or in the right half, because the piston is now at the far right of the cylinder: the informative content of our knowledge is clearly much reduced.[270]

I am of course ready to accept this. What I am *not* ready to accept is Szilard's more general argument by which he tries to establish the theorem that knowledge, or information, about the position of the molecule M can be converted into negentropy, and *vice versa*. This alleged theorem I regard, I am afraid, as sheer subjectivist nonsense.

Szilard's argument consists of an idealized thought experiment; it may be put—with some improvement, I think—as follows.[271]

Assume we *know* at the moment t_0 that the gas—that is to say, the one molecule M—is in the left half of our cylinder. Then we can at this moment slide a piston into the middle of the cylinder (for example, from a slit in the side of the cylinder)[272] and wait until the expansion of the gas, or the momentum of M, has pushed the piston to the right, lifting a weight. The energy needed was, obviously, supplied by the heat bath. The negentropy needed, and lost, was supplied by our knowledge; the knowledge was lost when the negentropy was consumed, that is, in the process of expansion and during the movement of the piston to the right; when the piston reaches the right end of the cylinder we have lost all knowledge of the part of the cylinder in which M is located. If we reverse the procedure by *pushing* back the piston, the same amount of energy will be needed (and added to the heat bath) and the same amount of negentropy must come from somewhere; for we end up with the situation from which we started, including the knowledge that the gas—or M—is in the left half of the cylinder.

Thus, Szilard suggests, knowledge and negentropy can be converted one into the other. (He supports this by an analysis —in my opinion a spurious one—of a direct measurement of the position of M; yet as he merely suggests, but does not claim, that this analysis is generally valid, I will not argue against it. I think, moreover, that the presentation here given strengthens his case somewhat—at any rate it makes it more plausible.)

I now come to my criticism. It is essential for Szilard's purposes to operate with one single molecule *M* rather than with a gas of many molecules.[273] If we have a gas of several molecules, the knowledge of the positions of these molecules does not help us in the least (it is thus *not sufficient*), unless indeed the gas happens to be in a very negentropic state; say, with most of the molecules on the left side. But then *it will obviously be this objective negentropic state* (rather than our subjective knowledge of it) which we can exploit; and should we, without knowing it, slide in the piston at the right moment, then again we can exploit this objective state (knowledge is thus *not necessary*).

So let us first operate, as Szilard suggests, with *one* molecule, *M*. But in this case, I assert, *we do not need any knowledge* regarding the location of *M*: all we need is to slide our piston into the cylinder. If *M* happens to be on the left, the piston will be driven to the right, and we can lift the weight. And if *M* is on the right, the piston will be driven to the left, and we can also lift a weight: nothing is easier than to fit the apparatus with some gear so that it lifts a weight in *either case*, without our having to know which of the two possible directions the impending movement will take.

Thus no knowledge is needed here for the balancing of the entropy increase; and Szilard's analysis turns out to be a mistake: he has offered no valid argument whatever for the intrusion of knowledge into physics.

It seems to me necessary, however, to say a little more about Szilard's thought experiment and also about mine. For the question arises: *can this particular experiment of mine be used to refute the second law of thermodynamics* (the law of entropy increase)?

I do not think so, even though I *do* believe that the second law is actually refuted by Brownian movement.[274]

The reason is this: the assumption of a gas represented by *one* molecule, *M*, is not only an idealization (which would not matter) but amounts to the assumption that the gas is, *objectively*, constantly in a state of minimum entropy. It is a gas which even if expanded takes up, we must assume, no appreciable subspace of the cylinder: this is why it will be found always only on one side of the piston. For example, we can turn a flap in the piston into, say, a horizontal position (see Fig. 3), so that the piston can be pushed back without resistance to the centre, where the flap is turned back to its working

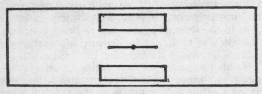

Fig. 3

position; if we do this, we can be quite sure that the whole gas —the whole *M*—is on *one* side of the piston only; and so it will push the piston. But assume we have in fact *two* molecules in the gas; then these may be on different sides, and the piston may not be pushed by them. This shows that *the use of one molecule M only* plays an essential role in my answer to Szilard (just as it did in Szilard's argument) and it also shows that *if* we could have a gas consisting of one powerful molecule *M*, it would indeed violate the second law. But this is not surprising since the second law describes an essentially statistical effect.

Let us look more closely at this second thought experiment —the case of *two molecules*. The information that both are in the left half of the cylinder would indeed enable us to close the flap and thus put the piston into its working position. But what drives the piston to the right is not our knowledge of the fact that both molecules are on the left. It is, rather, the momenta of the two molecules—or, if you like, the fact that the gas is in a state of low entropy.

Thus these particular thought experiments of mine do *not* show that a perpetual motion machine of the second order is possible;[275] but since, as we have seen, the use of *one* molecule is essential to Szilard's own thought experiment, my thought experiments show the invalidity of Szilard's argument, and thus of the attempt to base the subjectivist interpretation of the second law upon thought experiments of this type.

The edifice that has been built on Szilard's (in my opinion invalid) argument, and on similar arguments by others, will continue, I fear, to grow; and we will continue to hear that "entropy—like probability—measures the lack of information", and that machines can be driven by knowledge, like Szilard's machine. Hot air and entropy, I imagine, will continue to be produced for as long as there are some subjectivists about to provide an equivalent amount of nescience.

37. *Darwinism as a Metaphysical Research Programme*

I have always been extremely interested in the theory of evolution, and very ready to accept evolution as a fact. I have also been fascinated by Darwin as well as by Darwinism—though somewhat unimpressed by most of the evolutionary philosophers; with the one great exception, that is, of Samuel Butler.[276]

My *Logik der Forschung* contained a theory of the growth of knowledge by trial and error-elimination, that is, by Darwinian *selection* rather than Lamarckian *instruction;* this point (at which I hinted in that book) increased, of course, my interest in the theory of evolution. Some of the things I shall have to say spring from an attempt to utilize my methodology and its resemblance to Darwinism to throw light on Darwin's theory of evolution.

The Poverty of Historicism[277] contains my first brief attempt to deal with some epistemological questions connected with the theory of evolution. I continued to work on such problems, and I was greatly encouraged when I later found that I had come to results very similar to some of Schrödinger's.[278]

In 1961 I gave the Herbert Spencer Memorial Lecture in Oxford, under the title "Evolution and the Tree of Knowledge".[279] In this lecture I went, I believe, a little beyond Schrödinger's ideas; and I have since developed further what I regard as a slight improvement on Darwinian theory,[280] while keeping strictly within the bounds of Darwinism as opposed to Lamarckism—within natural selection, as opposed to instruction.

I tried also in my Compton lecture (1966)[280a] to clarify several connected questions; for example, the question of the *scientific status* of Darwinism. It seems to me that Darwinism stands in just the same relation to Lamarckism as does:

Deductivism   *to* Inductivism,
Selection   *to* Instruction by Repetition,
Critical Error Elimination *to* Justification.

The logical untenability of the ideas on the right-hand side of this table establishes a kind of logical explanation of Darwinism (i.e. of the left-hand side). Thus it could be described as "almost tautological"; or it could be described as applied logic—at any rate, as applied *situational logic* (as we shall see).

From this point of view the question of the scientific status of Darwinian theory—in the widest sense, the theory of trial and error-elimination—becomes an interesting one. I have come to the conclusion that Darwinism is not a testable scientific theory, but a *metaphysical research programme*—a possible framework for testable scientific theories.[281]

Yet there is more to it: I also regard Darwinism as an application of what I call "situational logic". Darwinism as situational logic can be understood as follows.

Let there be a world, a framework of limited constancy, in which there are entities of limited variability. Then some of the entities produced by variation (those which "fit" into the conditions of the framework) may "survive", while others (those which clash with the conditions) may be eliminated.

Add to this the assumption of the existence of a special framework—a set of perhaps rare and highly individual conditions—in which there can be life or, more especially, self-reproducing but nevertheless variable bodies. Then a situation is given in which the idea of trial and error-elimination, or of Darwinism, becomes not merely applicable, but almost logically necessary. This does not mean that either the framework or the origin of life is necessary. There may be a framework in which life would be possible, but in which the trial which leads to life has not occurred, or in which all those trials which led to life were eliminated. (The latter is not a mere possibility but may happen at any moment: there is more than one way in which all life on earth might be destroyed.) What is meant is that if a life-permitting situation occurs, and if life originates, then this total situation makes the Darwinian idea one of situational logic.

To avoid any misunderstanding: it is not in every possible situation that Darwinian theory would be successful; rather, it is a very special, perhaps even a unique situation. But even in a situation without life Darwinian selection can apply to some extent: atomic nuclei which are relatively stable (in the situation in question) will tend to be more abundant than unstable ones; and the same may hold for chemical compounds.

I do not think that Darwinism can explain the origin of life. I think it quite possible that life is so extremely improbable that nothing can "explain" why it originated; for statistical explanation must operate, *in the last instance*, with very high probabilities. But if our high probabilities are merely low probabilities which have become high because of the immensity of the available time (as in Boltzmann's "explanation"; see text to note 260 in section 35), then we must not forget that in this way it is possible to "explain" almost everything.[282] Even so, we have little enough reason to conjecture that any explanation of this sort is applicable to the origin of life. But this does not affect the view of Darwinism as situational logic, once life and its framework are assumed to constitute our "situation".

I think that there is more to say for Darwinism than that it is just one metaphysical research programme among others. Indeed, its close resemblance to situational logic may account for its great success, in spite of the almost tautological character inherent in the Darwinian formulation of it, and for the fact that so far no serious competitor has come forward.

Should the view of Darwinian theory as situational logic be acceptable, then we could explain the strange similarity between my theory of the growth of knowledge and Darwinism: both would be cases of situational logic. The new and special element in the *conscious scientific approach to knowledge*—conscious criticism of tentative conjectures, and a conscious building up of selection pressure on these conjectures (by criticizing them)—would be a consequence of the emergence of a descriptive and argumentative language; that is, of a descriptive language whose descriptions can be criticized.

The emergence of such a language would face us here again with a highly improbable and possibly unique situation, perhaps as improbable as life itself. But given this situation, the theory of the growth of exosomatic knowledge through a conscious procedure of conjecture and refutation follows "almost" logically: it becomes part of the situation as well as part of Darwinism.

As for Darwinian theory itself, I must now explain that I

am using the term "Darwinism" for the modern forms of this theory, called by various names, such as "neo-Darwinism" or (by Julian Huxley) "The New Synthesis". It consists essentially of the following assumptions or conjectures, to which I will refer later.

(1) The great variety of the forms of life on earth originate from very few forms, perhaps even from a single organism: there is an evolutionary tree, an evolutionary history.

(2) There is an evolutionary theory which explains this. It consists in the main of the following hypotheses.

(a) Heredity: the offspring reproduce the parent organisms fairly faithfully.

(b) Variation: there are (perhaps among others) "small" variations. The most important of these are the "accidental" and hereditary mutations.

(c) Natural selection: there are various mechanisms by which not only the variations but the whole hereditary material is controlled by elimination. Among them are mechanisms which allow only "small" mutations to spread; "big" mutations ("hopeful monsters") are as a rule lethal, and thus eliminated.

(d) Variability: although *variations* in some sense—the presence of different competitors—are for obvious reasons prior to selection, it may well be the case that *variability*—the scope of variation—is controlled by natural selection; for example, with respect to the frequency as well as the size of variations. A gene theory of heredity and variation may even admit special genes controlling the variability of other genes. Thus we may arrive at a hierarchy, or perhaps at even more complicated interaction structures. (We must not be afraid of complications; for they are known to be there. For example, from a selectionist point of view we are bound to assume that something like the genetic code method of controlling heredity is itself an early product of selection, and that it is a highly sophisticated product.)

Assumptions (1) and (2) are, I think, essential to Darwinism (together with some assumptions about a changing environment endowed with some regularities). The following point (3) is a reflection of mine on point (2).

(3) It will be seen that there is a close analogy between the "conservative" principles (a) and (d) and what I have called dogmatic thinking; and likewise between (b) and (c), and what I have called critical thinking.

I now wish to give some reasons why I regard Darwinism as metaphysical, and as a research programme.

It is metaphysical because it is not testable. One might think that it is. It seems to assert that, if ever on some planet we find life which satisfies conditions (a) and (b), then (c) will come into play and bring about in time a rich variety of distinct forms. Darwinism, however, does not assert as much as this. For assume that we find life on Mars consisting of exactly three species of bacteria with a genetic outfit similar to that of three terrestrial species. Is Darwinism refuted? By no means. We shall say that these three species were the only forms among the many mutants which were sufficiently well adjusted to survive. And we shall say the same if there is only one species (or none). Thus Darwinism does not really *predict* the evolution of variety. It therefore cannot really *explain* it. At best, it can predict the evolution of variety under "favourable conditions". But it is hardly possible to describe in general terms what favourable conditions are—except that, in their presence, a variety of forms will emerge.

And yet I believe I have taken the theory almost at its best —almost in its most testable form. One might say that it "almost predicts" a great variety of forms of life.[283] In other fields, its predictive or explanatory power is still more disappointing. Take "adaptation". At first sight natural selection appears to explain it, and in a way it does; but hardly in a scientific way. To say that a species now living is adapted to its environment is, in fact, almost tautological. Indeed we use the terms "adaptation" and "selection" in such a way that we can say that, if the species were not adapted, it would have been eliminated by natural selection. Similarly, if a species has been eliminated it must have been ill adapted to the conditions. Adaptation or fitness is *defined* by modern evolutionists as survival value, and can be measured by actual success in survival: there is hardly any possibility of testing a theory as feeble as this.[284]

And yet, the theory is invaluable. I do not see how, without it, our knowledge could have grown as it has done since Darwin. In trying to explain experiments with bacteria which become adapted to, say, penicillin, it is quite clear that we are greatly helped by the theory of natural selection. Although it is metaphysical, it sheds much light upon very concrete and very practical researches. It allows us to study adaptation to a new environment (such as a penicillin-infested environment) in a rational way: it suggests the existence of a mechanism of adaptation, and it allows us even to study in detail the mechanism at work. And it is the only theory so far which does all that.

This is, of course, the reason why Darwinism has been almost universally accepted. Its theory of adaptation was the first nontheistic one that was convincing; and theism was worse than an open admission of failure, for it created the impression that an ultimate explanation had been reached.

Now to the degree that Darwinism creates the same impression, it is not so very much better than the theistic view of adaptation; it is therefore important to show that Darwinism is not a scientific theory, but metaphysical. But its value for science as a metaphysical research programme is very great, especially if it is admitted that it may be criticized, and improved upon.

Let us now look a little more deeply into the research programme of Darwinism, as formulated above under points (1) and (2).

First, though (2), that is, Darwin's theory of evolution, does not have sufficient explanatory power to *explain* the terrestrial evolution of a great variety of forms of life, it certainly *suggests* it, and thereby draws attention to it. And it certainly does *predict* that *if* such an evolution takes place, it will be *gradual*.

The nontrivial *prediction of gradualness* is important, and it follows immediately from (2)(a)-(2)(c); and (a) and (b) and at least the smallness of the mutations predicted by (c) are not only experimentally well supported, but known to us in great detail.

Gradualness is thus, from a logical point of view, the central prediction of the theory. (It seems to me that it is its only prediction.) Moreover, as long as changes in the genetic base of the living forms are gradual, they are—at least "in principle"—explained by the theory; for the theory does predict the occurrence of small changes, each due to mutation. However, "explanation in principle"[285] is something very different from the type of explanation which we demand in physics. While we can explain a particular eclipse by predicting it, we cannot predict or explain any particular evolutionary change (except perhaps certain changes in the gene population *within* one species); all we can say is that if it is not a small change, there must have been some intermediate steps—an important suggestion for research: a research programme.

Moreover, the theory predicts *accidental* mutations, and thus *accidental* changes. If any "direction" is indicated by the theory, it is that throwback mutations will be comparatively frequent. Thus we should expect evolutionary sequences of the random-walk type. (A random walk is, for example, the track described by a man who at every step consults a roulette wheel to determine the direction of his next step.)

Here an important question arises. How is it that random walks do not seem to be prominent in the evolutionary tree? The question would be answered if Darwinism could explain "orthogenetic trends", as they are sometimes called; that is, sequences of evolutionary changes in the same "direction" (nonrandom walks). Various thinkers such as Schrödinger and Waddington, and especially Sir Alister Hardy, have tried to give a Darwinian explanation of orthogenetic trends, and I also have tried to do so, for example, in my Spencer lecture.

My suggestions for an enrichment of Darwinism which might explain orthogenesis are briefly as follows.

(A) I distinguish external or environmental selection pressure from internal selection pressure. Internal selection pressure comes from the organism itself and, I conjecture, ultimately from its *preferences* (or "aims") though these may of course change in response to external changes.

(B) I assume that there are different classes of genes: those which mainly control the *anatomy*, which I will call *a*-genes; those which mainly control *behaviour*, which I will call *b*-genes. Intermediate genes (including those with mixed functions) I will here leave out of account (though it seems that they exist). The *b*-genes in their turn may be similarly subdivided into *p*-genes (controlling *preferences* or "aims") and *s*-genes (controlling *skills*).

I further assume that some organisms, under external selection pressure, have developed genes, and especially *b*-genes, which allow the organism a certain variability. The *scope* of behavioural variation will somehow be controlled by the genetic *b*-structure. But since external circumstances vary, a not too rigid determination of the behaviour by the *b*-structure may turn out to be as successful as a not too rigid genetic determination of heredity, that is to say of the scope of gene variability. (See (2)(d) above.) Thus we may speak of "purely behavioural" changes of behaviour, or variations of behaviour, meaning nonhereditary changes within the genetically determined scope or repertoire; and we may contrast them with genetically fixed or determined behavioural changes.

We can now say that certain environmental changes may lead to new problems and so to the adoption of new preferences or aims (for example, because certain types of food have disappeared). The new preferences or aims may at first appear in the form of new tentative behaviour (permitted but not fixed by the b-genes). In this way the animal may tentatively adjust itself to the new situation without genetic change. But this *purely behavioural* and tentative change, if successful, will amount to the adoption, or discovery, of a new ecological niche. Thus it will favour individuals whose *genetic p-structure* (that is, their instinctive preferences or "aims") more or less anticipates or fixes the new behavioural pattern of preferences. This step will prove decisive; for now those changes in the skill structure (s-structure) will be favoured which conform to the new preferences: skills for getting the preferred food, for example.

I now suggest that *only after the s-structure has been changed will certain changes in the a-structure be favoured; that is, those changes in the anatomical structure which favour the new skills*. The internal selection pressure in these cases will be "directed", and so lead to a kind of orthogenesis.

My suggestion for this internal selection mechanism can be put schematically as follows:

$$p \to s \to a.$$

That is, the preference structure and its variations control the selection of the skill structure and its variations; and this in turn controls the selection of the purely anatomical structure and its variations.

This sequence, however, may be cyclical: the new anatomy may in its turn favour changes of preference, and so on.

What Darwin called "sexual selection" would, from the point of view expounded here, be a special case of the internal selection pressure which I have described; that is, of a cycle starting with new *preferences*. It is characteristic that internal selection pressure may lead to comparatively bad adjustment to the environment. Since Darwin this has often been noted, and the hope of explaining certain striking maladjustments (maladjustments from a survival point of view, such as the display of the peacock's tail) was one of the main motives for Darwin's introduction of his theory of "sexual selection". The original preference may have been well adjusted, but the internal selection pressure and the feedback from the changed anatomy to changed preferences (a to p) may lead to exaggerated forms, both behavioural forms (rites) and anatomical ones.

As an example of nonsexual selection I may mention the woodpecker. A reasonable assumption seems to be that this specialization started with a *change in taste* (preferences) for new foods which led to genetic behavioural changes, and then to new skills, in accordance with the schema

$$p \rightarrow s;$$

and that the anatomical changes came last.[286] A bird undergoing anatomical changes in its beak and tongue without undergoing changes in its taste and skill can be expected to be eliminated quickly by natural selection, *but not the other way round.* (Similarly, and not less obviously: a bird with a new skill but without the new preferences which the new skill can serve would have no advantages.)

Of course there will be a lot of feedback at every stage: $p \rightarrow s$ will lead to feedback (that is, s will favour further changes, including genetic changes, in the same direction as p), just as a will act back on both s and p, as indicated. It is, one may conjecture, this feedback which is mainly responsible for the more exaggerated forms and rituals.[287]

To explain the matter with another example, assume that in a certain situation external selection pressure favours bigness. Then the same pressure will also favour sexual *preference* for bigness: preferences can be, as in the case of food, the result of external pressure. But once there are new p-genes a whole new cycle will be set up: it is the p-mutations which trigger off the orthogenesis.

This leads to a general principle of mutual reinforcement: we have on the one hand a primary *hierarchical control* in the preference or aim structure, over the skill structure, and further over the anatomical structure; but we also have a kind of secondary interaction or feedback between those structures. I suggest that this hierarchical system of mutual reinforcement works in such a way that in most cases the control in the preference or aim structure largely dominates the lower controls throughout the entire hierarchy.[288]

Examples may illustrate both these ideas. If we distinguish genetic changes (mutations) in what I call the "preference structure" or the "aim structure" from genetic changes in the "skill structure" and genetic changes in the "anatomical structure", then as regards the interplay between the aim structure and the anatomical structure there will be the following possibilities:

(a) Action of mutations of the aim structure on the anatomical structure: when a change takes place in taste, as in the case of the woodpecker, then the anatomical structure relevant for food acquisition may remain unchanged, in which case the species is most likely to be eliminated by natural selection (unless extraordinary skills are used); or the species may adjust itself by developing a new anatomical specialization, similar to an organ like the eye: a stronger interest in seeing (aim structure) in a species may lead to the selection of a favourable mutation for an improvement of the anatomy of the eye.

(b) Action of mutations of the anatomical structure on the aim structure: when the anatomy relevant for food acquisition changes, then the aim structure concerning food is in danger of becoming fixed or ossified by natural selection, which in its turn may lead to further anatomical specialization. It is similar in the case of the eye: a favourable mutation for an improvement of the anatomy will increase keenness of interest in seeing (this is similar to the opposite effect).

The theory sketched suggests something like a solution to the problem of how evolution leads towards what may be called "higher" forms of life. Darwinism as usually presented fails to give such an explanation. It can at best explain something like an improvement in the degree of adaptation. But bacteria must be adapted at least as well as men. At any rate, they have existed longer, and there is reason to fear that they will survive men. But what may perhaps be identified with the higher forms of life is a behaviourally richer preference structure—one of greater scope; and if the preference structure should have (by and large) the leading role I ascribe to it, then evolution towards higher forms may become understandable.[289] My theory may also be presented like this: higher forms arise through the primary hierarchy of $p \rightarrow s \rightarrow a$, that is, whenever and as long as the preference structure is in the lead. Stagnation and reversion, including overspecialization, are the result of an inversion due to feedback within this primary hierarchy.

The theory also suggests a possible solution (perhaps one among many) to the problem of the separation of species. The problem is this: mutations on their own may be expected to lead only to a change in the gene pool of the species, not to a new species. Thus local separation has to be called in to explain the emergence of new species. Usually one thinks of geographic separation.[290] But I suggest that geographic separation is merely a special case of separation due to the adoption of new behaviour and consequently of a new ecological niche; if a *preference* for an ecological niche—a certain *type* of location—becomes hereditary, then this could lead to sufficient local separation for interbreeding to discontinue, even though it was still physiologically possible. Thus two species might separate while living in the same geographical region—even if this region is only of the size of a mangrove tree, as seems to be the case with certain African molluscs. Sexual selection may have similar consequences.

The description of the possible genetic mechanisms behind orthogenetic trends, as outlined above, is a typical situational analysis. That is to say, only if the developed structures are of the sort that can simulate the methods of situational logic will they have any survival value.

Another suggestion concerning evolutionary theory which may be worth mentioning is connected with the idea of "survival value", and also with teleology. I think that these ideas may be made a lot clearer in terms of problem solving.

Every organism and every species is faced constantly by the threat of extinction; but this threat takes the form of concrete problems which it has to solve. Many of these concrete problems are not as such survival problems. The problem of finding a good nesting place may be a concrete problem for a pair of birds without being a survival problem for these birds, although it may turn into one for their offspring; and the species may be very little affected by the success of these particular birds in solving the problem here and now. Thus I conjecture that most problems are posed not so much by survival, but by *preferences*, especially *instinctive preferences*; and even if the instincts in question (*p*-genes) should have evolved under external selection pressure, the problems posed by them are not as a rule survival problems.

It is for reasons such as these that I think it is better to look upon organisms as problem-solving rather than as end-pursuing: as I have tried to show in "Of Clouds and Clocks",[291] we may in this way give a rational account—"in principle", of course—of *emergent evolution*.

I conjecture that the origin of *life* and the origin of *problems* coincide. This is not irrelevant to the question whether we can expect biology to turn out to be reducible to chemistry and further to physics. I think it not only possible but likely that we shall one day be able to recreate living things from nonliving ones. Although this would, of course, be extremely exciting in itself[292] (as well as from the reductionist point of view), it would not *establish* that biology can be "reduced" to physics or chemistry. For it would not establish a physical explanation of the emergence of problems—any more than our ability to produce chemical compounds by physical means establishes a physical theory of the chemical bond or even the existence of such a theory.

My position may thus be described as one that upholds a theory of *irreducibility and emergence*, and it can perhaps best be summarized in this way:

(1) I conjecture that there is no biological process which cannot be regarded as correlated in detail with a physical process or cannot be progressively analysed in physicochemical terms. But no physicochemical theory can explain the emergence of a new problem, and no physicochemical process can as such solve a *problem*. (Variational principles in physics, like the principle of least action or Fermat's principle, are perhaps similar but they are not solutions to problems. Einstein's theistic method tries to use God for similar purposes.)

(2) If this conjecture is tenable it leads to a number of distinctions. We must distinguish from each other:

a physical problem = a physicist's problem;

a biological problem = a biologist's problem;

an organism's problem = a problem like: How am I to survive? How am I to propagate? How am I to change? How am I to adapt?

a man-made problem = a problem like: How do we control waste?

From these distinctions we are led to the following thesis:
*the problems of organisms are not physical: they are neither
physical things, nor physical laws, nor physical facts. They are
specific biological realities; they are "real" in the sense that
their existence may be the cause of biological effects.*

(3) Assume that certain physical bodies have "solved"
their problem of reproduction: that they can reproduce themselves; either exactly, or, like crystals, with minor faults which
may be chemically (or even functionally) *inessential*. Still, they
might not be "living" (in the full sense) if they cannot adjust
themselves: they need reproduction *plus* genuine variability
to achieve this.

(4) The "essence" of the matter is, I propose, *problem
solving*. (But we should not talk about "essence"; and the term
is not used here seriously.) Life as we know it consists of
physical "bodies" (more precisely, structures) which are problem solving. This the various species have "learned" by natural
selection, that is to say by the method of reproduction plus
variation, which itself has been learned by the same method.
This regress is not necessarily infinite—indeed, it may go back
to some fairly definite moment of emergence.

Thus men like Butler and Bergson, though I suppose
utterly wrong in their theories, were right in their intuition.
Vital force ("cunning") does, of course, exist—but it is in its
turn a product of life, *of selection*, rather than anything like
the "essence" of life. It is indeed the preferences *which lead
the way*. Yet the way is not Lamarckian but Darwinian.

This emphasis on *preferences* (which, being dispositions,
are not so very far removed from propensities) in my theory
is, clearly, a purely "objective" affair: we *need not* assume
that these preferences are conscious. But they *may* become
conscious; at first, I conjecture, in the form of states of well-
being and of suffering (pleasure and pain).

My approach, therefore, leads almost necessarily to a research programme that asks for an explanation, in objective
biological terms, of the emergence of states of consciousness.

Reading this section again after six years,[202a] I feel the need
for another summary to bring out more simply and more

clearly how a purely selectionist theory (the theory of "organic selection" of Baldwin and Lloyd Morgan) can be used to justify certain intuitive aspects of evolution, stressed by Lamarck or Butler or Bergson, without making any concession to the Lamarckian doctrine of the inheritance of acquired characteristics. (For the history of organic selection see especially Sir Alister Hardy's great book, *The Living Stream.*[292b])

At first sight Darwinism (as opposed to Lamarckism) does not seem to attribute any evolutionary effect to the adaptive behavioural innovations (preferences, wishes, choices) of the individual organism. This impression, however, is superficial. Every behavioural innovation by the individual organism changes the relation between that organism and its environment: it amounts to the adoption of or even to the creation by the organism of a new ecological niche. But a new ecological niche means a new set of selection pressures, selecting for the chosen niche. Thus the organism, by its actions and preferences, partly *selects the selection pressures* which will act upon it and its descendants. Thus it may actively influence the course which evolution will adopt. The adoption of a new way of acting, or of a new expectation (or "theory"), is like breaking a new evolutionary path. And the difference between Darwinism and Lamarckism is not one between luck and cunning, as Samuel Butler suggested: we do not reject cunning in opting for Darwin and selection.

38. World 3 or the Third World

In his *Wissenschaftslehre*, Bolzano spoke of "truths in themselves" and, more generally, of "statements in themselves", in contradistinction to those (subjective) thought processes by which a man may think, or grasp truths; or, more generally, grasp statements, either true or false.

Bolzano's distinction between statements in themselves and subjective thought processes has always seemed to me of the greatest importance. Statements in themselves can stand in logical relations to each other: one statement can follow from another, and statements can be logically compatible or incompatible. Subjective thought processes, on the other hand, can only stand in psychological relations. They can disquieten us, or comfort us, can remind us of some experiences or suggest to us certain expectations; they can induce us to take some action, or to leave some planned action undone.

The two kinds of relations are utterly different. One man's thought processes can neither contradict those of another man, nor his own thought processes at some other time; but the *contents* of his thoughts—that is, the statements in themselves —can of course contradict the contents of another man's thoughts. On the other hand, contents, or statements in themselves, cannot stand in psychological relations: *thoughts in the sense of contents* or statements in themselves and *thoughts in the sense of thought processes* belong to *two entirely different "worlds"*.

If we call the world of "things"—of physical objects—the *first world,* and the world of subjective experiences (such as thought processes) the *second world*, we may call the world of statements in themselves the *third world*. (I now[293] prefer to call these three worlds "world 1", "world 2", and "world 3"; Frege sometimes called the latter the "third realm".)

Whatever one may think about the status of these three worlds—I have in mind such "questions" as whether they "really exist" or not, and whether world 3 may be in some sense "reduced" to world 2, and perhaps world 2 to world 1— it seems of the utmost importance first of all to distinguish them as sharply and clearly as possible. (If our distinctions are too sharp, this may be brought out by subsequent criticism.)

At the moment it is the distinction between world 2 and 3 which has to be made clear; and in this connection, we will come up against, and must face, arguments like the following.

When I think of a picture I know well, there may be a certain effort needed to recall it and "put it before my mind's eye". I can distinguish between (a) the real picture, (b) the process of imagining, which involves an effort, and (c) the more or less successful result, that is, the *imagined* picture. Clearly, the imagined picture (c) belongs exactly like (b) to world 2 rather than to world 3. Yet I may say things about it which are quite analogous to the logical relations between statements. For example, I may say that my image of the picture at time t_1 is incompatible with my image at time t_2 and even perhaps with a *statement* such as: "In the picture only the head and shoulders of the painted man are visible." Moreover, the imagined picture may be said to be the content of the process of imagining. All this is analogous to the thought content and the process of thinking. But who would deny that the imagined image belongs to world 2; that it is mental, and indeed part of the process of imagining?

This argument seems to me valid and quite important: I agree that within the thinking process some parts may be distinguished that may perhaps be called its content (or the thought, or the world 3 object) *as it has been grasped*. But it is precisely for this reason that I find it important to distinguish between the mental process and the thought content (as Frege called it) *in its logical or world 3 sense*.

I personally have only vague visual imaginings; it is usually only with difficulty that I can recall a clear, detailed, and vivid picture before my mind. (It is different with music.) Rather, I think in terms of schemata, of dispositions to follow up a certain "line" of thought, and very often in terms of words, especially when I am about to write down some ideas. And I often find myself mistaken in the belief that I "have got it", that I have grasped a thought clearly: when trying to write it down I may find that I have not got it yet. This "it", this something which I may not have got, which I cannot be quite certain that I *have* got before I have written it down, or at any rate formulated it in language so clearly *that I can look at it critically from various sides*, this "it" is the thought in the objective sense, the world 3 object which I am trying to grasp.

The decisive thing seems to me that we can put objective thoughts—that is, theories—before us in such a way that we can criticize them and argue about them. To do so, we must formulate them in some more or less permanent (especially linguistic) form. A written form will be preferable to a spoken form, and printing may be better still. And it is significant that we can distinguish between the criticism of a mere *formulation* of a thought—a thought can be formulated rather well, or not so well—and the logical aspects of the thought in itself; its truth; or its truthlikeness in comparison with some of its competitors; or its compatibility with certain other theories.

Once I had arrived at this stage I found that I had to people my world 3 with inmates other than statements; and I brought in, in addition to statements or theories, also problems, and arguments, especially critical arguments. For theories should be discussed always with an eye to the *problems* which they might solve.

Books and journals can be regarded as typical world 3

objects, especially if they develop and discuss a theory. Of course the physical shape of the book is insignificant, and even physical nonexistence does not detract from world 3 existence; think of all the "lost" books, their influence, and the search for them. And frequently even the formulation of an argument does not matter greatly. What do matter are *contents,* in the logical sense or world 3 sense. .

It is clear that everybody interested in science must be interested in world 3 objects. A physical scientist, to start with, may be interested mainly in world 1 objects—say, crystals and X-rays. But very soon he must realize how much depends on our interpretation of the facts, that is, on our theories, and so on world 3 objects. Similarly a historian of science, or a philosopher interested in science, must be largely a student of world 3 objects. Admittedly, he may also be interested in the relation between world 3 theories and world 2 thought processes; but the latter will interest him mainly in their relation to theories, that is, to objects belonging to world 3.

What is the ontological status of these world 3 objects? Or, to use less high-sounding language, are problems, theories, and arguments "real", like tables and chairs? When some forty-four years ago Heinrich Gomperz warned me that I was, potentially, not only a realist in the sense of believing in the reality of tables and chairs but also in the sense of Plato, who believed in the reality of Forms or Ideas—of concepts, and their meanings or essences—I did not like the suggestion, and I still do not include the left-hand side of the table of ideas (see section 7 above) among the denizens of my world 3. But I have become a realist with respect to the world 3 of *problems, theories, and critical arguments.*

Bolzano was, I think, doubtful about the ontological status of his statements in themselves, and Frege, it seems, was an idealist, or very nearly so. I too was, like Bolzano, doubtful for a long time, and I did not publish anything about world 3 until I arrived at the conclusion that its inmates were real; indeed, more or less as real as physical tables and chairs.

Nobody will doubt this as far as books are concerned, and other written matter. They are, like tables and chairs, made by us, though not in order to be sat upon, but in order to be read.

This seems easy enough; but what about the theories in

themselves? I agree that they are not quite as "real" as tables and chairs. I am prepared to accept something like a materialist starting point according to which, in the first place, only physical things like tables and chairs, stones and oranges, are to be called "real". But this is only a starting point: in the second place we are almost bound to extend the range of the term radically: gases and electric currents may kill us: should we not call them real? The field of a magnet may be made visible by iron filings. And who can doubt, with television such a familiar phenomenon, that some sort of reality has to be attributed to Hertz's (or Maxwell's) waves?

Should we call the pictures we see on television "real"? I think we should, for we can take photographs of them with the help of various cameras and they will agree, like independent witnesses.[294] But television pictures are the result of a process by which the set decodes highly complicated and "abstract" messages transmitted with the help of waves; and so we should, I think, call these "abstract" coded messages "real". They can be decoded, and the result of the decoding is "real".

We are now perhaps no longer quite so very far removed from the theory in itself—the abstract message coded in a book, say, and decoded by ourselves when we read the book. However, a more general argument may be needed.

All the examples given have one thing in common. We seem to be ready to call real anything which can *act upon physical things* such as tables and chairs (and photographic film, we may add), and which can be acted upon by physical things.[295] But our world of physical things has been greatly changed by the content of theories, like those of Maxwell and Hertz; that is by world 3 objects. Thus these objects should be called "real".

Two objections should be made. (1) Our physical world has been changed not by the theories in themselves but, rather, by their physical incorporation in books, and elsewhere; and books belong to world 1. (2) It has been changed not by the theories in themselves, but by our understanding of them, our grasp of them; that is, by mental states, by world 2 objects.

I admit both objections, but I reply to (1) that the change was brought about not by the physical aspects of the books but solely by the fact that they somehow "carried" a message, an informative content, a theory in itself. In response to (2), which I regard as a far more important objection, I admit even that *it is solely through world 2 as an intermediary between world 1 and world 3 that world 1 and world 3 can interact.*

This is an important point, as will be seen when I turn to the body-mind problem. It means that world 1 and world 2 can interact, and also world 2 and world 3; but world 1 and world 3 cannot interact directly, without some mediating interaction exerted by world 2. Thus although only world 2 can act immediately upon world 1, world 3 can act upon world 1 in an indirect way, owing to its influence upon world 2.

In fact, the "incorporation" of a theory in a book—and thus in a physical object—is an example of this. To be read, the book needs the intervention of a human mind, of world 2. But it also needs the theory in itself. For example, I may make a mistake: my mind may fail to grasp the theory correctly. But there is always the theory in itself, and somebody else may grasp it and correct me. It may easily be not a case of a difference of opinion, but a case of a real, unmistakable mistake—a failure to understand the theory in itself. And this may even happen to the originator of the theory. (It has happened more than once, even to Einstein.)[296]

I have touched here on an aspect which I have described in some of my papers on these and related subjects as the (partial) *autonomy of world 3.*[297]

By this I mean that although we may invent a theory, there may be (and in a good theory, there always will be) *unintended and unforeseen consequences.* For example, men may have invented the natural numbers or, say, the method of proceeding without end in the series of natural numbers. But the existence of prime numbers (and the validity of Euclid's theorem that there is no greatest prime) is something we *discover.* It is there, and we cannot change it. It is an unintended and unforeseen consequence of that invention of ours. And it is a necessary consequence: we cannot get around it. Things like prime numbers, or square numbers, and many others, are thus "produced" by world 3 itself, without further help from us. To this extent it may be described as "autonomous".

Somewhat related to the problem of autonomy but, I think, less important, is the problem of the timelessness of world 3. If an unambiguously formulated statement is true now, then it is true for ever, and always was true: truth is timeless (and

so is falsity). Logical relations such as contradictoriness or
compatibility are also timeless, and even more obviously so.

It would be easy for this reason to regard the whole of
world 3 as timeless, as Plato suggested of his world of Forms
or Ideas. We only need to assume that we never invent a theory
but always discover it. Thus we would have a timeless world
3, existing before life emerged and after all life will have disappeared, a world of which men discover here or there some
little bits.

This is a possible view; but I don't like it. Not only does it
fail to solve the problem of the ontological status of world 3,
but it makes this problem insoluble from a rational point of
view. For although it allows us to "discover" world 3 objects,
it fails to explain whether, in discovering these objects, we
interact with them, or whether they only act upon us; and how
they can act upon us—especially if we cannot act upon them.
It leads, I think, to a Platonic or neo-Platonic intuitionism, and
to a host of difficulties. For it is based, I think, upon the misunderstanding that the status of the *logical relations between
world 3 objects* must be shared by these objects.

I propose a different view—one which, I have found, is
surprisingly fruitful. *I regard world 3 as being essentially the
product of the human mind*. It is we who create world 3
objects. That these objects have their own inherent or autonomous laws which create unintended and unforeseeable consequences is only an instance (though a very interesting one)
of a more general rule, the rule that all our actions have such
consequences.

Thus I look at world 3 as a product of human activity, and
as one whose repercussions on us are as great as, or greater
than, those of our physical environment. There is a kind of
feedback in all human activities: in acting we always act,
indirectly, upon ourselves.

More precisely, I regard the world 3 of problems, theories,
and critical arguments as one of the results of the evolution of
human language, and as acting back on this evolution.

This is perfectly compatible with the timelessness of truth
and of logical relations; and it makes the reality of world 3
understandable. It is as real as other human products, as real
as a coding system—a language; as real as (or perhaps even
more real than) a social institution, such as a university or a
police force.

And world 3 has a history. It is the history of our ideas; not only a history of their discovery, but also a history of how we invented them: how we made them, and how they reacted upon us, and how we reacted to these products of our own making.

This way of looking at world 3 allows us also to bring it within the scope of an evolutionary theory which views man as an animal. There are animal products (such as nests) which we may regard as forerunners of the human world 3.

And ultimately it suggests a generalization in another direction. We may regard the world of problems, theories, and critical arguments as a special case, as a world 3 in the narrow sense, or the logical or intellectual province of world 3; and we may include in world 3 in a more general sense all the products of the human mind, such as tools, institutions, and works of art.

39. The Body-Mind Problem and World 3

I think that I was always a Cartesian dualist (although I never thought that we should talk about "substances"[298]); and if not a dualist, I was certainly more inclined to pluralism than to monism. I think it silly or at least high-handed to deny the existence of mental experiences or mental states or states of consciousness; or to deny that mental states are as a rule closely related to states of the body, especially physiological states. But it also seems clear that mental states are products of the evolution of life, and that little can be gained by linking them to physics rather than to biology.[299]

My earliest encounters with the body-mind problem made me feel, for many years, that it was a hopeless problem. Psychology, *qua* science of the self and its experiences, was almost nonexistent, *pace* Freud. Watson's behaviourism was a very understandable reaction to this state of affairs, and it had some methodological advantages—like so many other theories which deny what they cannot explain. As a philosophical thesis it was clearly wrong, even though irrefutable. That we do experience joy and sadness, hope and fear, not to mention a toothache, and that we do think, in words as well as by means of schemata; that we can read a book with more or less interest and attention—all this seemed to me obviously true, though easily denied; and extremely important, though obviously nondemonstrable. It also seemed to me quite obvious that we are embodied selves or minds or souls. *But how can the relation between our bodies (or physiological states) and our minds (or mental states) be rationally understood?* This question seemed to formulate the body-mind problem; and as far as I could see there was no hope of doing anything to bring it nearer to a solution.

In Schlick's *Erkenntnislehre* I found a discussion of the body-mind relation which was the first since those of Spinoza and Leibniz to fascinate me. It was beautifully clear, and it was worked out in considerable detail. It has been brilliantly discussed, and further developed, by Herbert Feigl. But although I found this theory fascinating, it did not satisfy me; and for many years I continued to think that nothing could be done about this problem, except perhaps by way of criticism; for example, by criticizing the views of those who thought that the whole problem was due to some "linguistic muddle".[300] (No doubt we sometimes create problems ourselves, through being muddled in speaking about the world; but why should not the world itself harbour some really difficult secrets, perhaps even insoluble ones? Riddles *may* exist;[301] and I think they do.)

I thought, however, that language does play a role: that although *consciousness* may be conjectured to be prelinguistic, what I call the *full consciousness of self* may be conjectured to be specifically human, and to depend on language. Yet this idea seemed to me of little importance until, as described in the previous section, I had developed certain views of Bolzano's (and, as I later found, also of Frege's) into a theory of what I called the "third world" or "world 3". It was only then that it dawned on me that the body-mind problem could be completely transformed if we call the theory of world 3 to our aid.[302] For it can help us to develop at least the rudiments of an *objective theory*—a biological theory—not only of subjective states of consciousness but also of selves.

Thus whatever new I might have to say on the body-mind problem is connected with my views on world 3.

It appears that the body-mind problem is still usually seen and discussed in terms of the various possible relationships (identity, parallelism, interaction) between states of consciousness and bodily states. As I am an interactionist myself, I think that a part of the problem may perhaps be discussed in this manner, but I am as doubtful as ever whether this discussion is worthwhile. In its stead I propose a biological and even evolutionist approach to the problem.

As I explained in section 37, I do not think highly of the theoretical or explanatory power of the theory of evolution. But I think that an evolutionist approach to biological problems is inescapable, and also that in so desperate a problem situation we must clutch gratefully even at a straw. So I propose, to start with, that we regard the human mind quite naively as if it were a highly developed bodily organ, and that we ask ourselves, as we might with respect to a sense organ, what it contributes to the household of the organism.

To this question there is at hand a typical answer which I propose to dismiss. It is that our consciousness enables us to see, or perceive, things. I dismiss this answer because for such purposes we have eyes and other sense organs. It is, I think, thanks to the observationalist approach to knowledge that consciousness is so widely identified with seeing or perceiving.

I propose instead that we regard the human mind first of all as *an organ that produces objects of the human world 3* (in the more general sense) and interacts with them. Thus I propose that we look upon the human mind, essentially, as the producer of human language, for which our basic aptitudes (as I have explained earlier[303]) are inborn; and as the producer of theories, of critical arguments, and many other things such as mistakes, myths, stories, witticisms, tools, and works of art.

It may perhaps be difficult to bring order into this medley, and perhaps not worth our while; but it is not difficult to offer a guess as to what came first. I propose that it was language, and that language is about the only exosomatic tool whose use is inborn or, rather, genetically based, in man.

This conjecture seems to me to have some explanatory power, even though it is of course difficult to test. I suggest that the emergence of descriptive language is at the root of the human power of imagination, of human inventiveness, and therefore of the emergence of world 3. For we may assume that the first (and almost human) function of descriptive language as a tool was to serve exclusively for *true* description, *true* reports. But then came the point when language could be used for lies, for "storytelling". This seems to me the decisive step, the step that made language truly descriptive and truly human. It led, I suggest, to storytelling of an explanatory kind, to myth making; to the critical scrutiny of reports and descriptions, and thus to science; to imaginative fiction and, I suggest, to art—to storytelling in the form of pictures.

However this may be, the physiological basis of the human mind, if I am right, might be looked for in the speech centre; and it may not be an accident that there seems to be only *one* centre of speech control in the two hemispheres of the brain; it may be the highest in the hierarchy of control centres.[304] (I am here consciously trying to revive Descartes's problem of the seat of consciousness, and even part of the argument which led him to the probably mistaken conjecture that it must be the pineal gland. The theory might perhaps become testable in experiments with the split brain.)[305]

I suggest that we distinguish states of "consciousness" in general from those highly organized states which seem to be characteristic of the human mind, the human world 2, the human self. I think animals are conscious. (This conjecture may become testable if we find, with the help of the electro-encephalograph, typical dreamlike sleeping in animals as well as in men.) But I also conjecture that animals do not have selves. About the "full consciousness of self", as it may be called, my central suggestion is that, just as world 3 is a product of world 2, so the specifically human world 2—the full consciousness of self—is a feedback product of *theory making*.

Consciousness as such (in its lower forms) seems to emerge and become organized before descriptive language does. Anyway, personalities emerge among animals, and a kind of knowledge or understanding of other personalities, especially in some higher social animals. (Dogs may even develop an intuitive understanding of human personalities.) But the full consciousness of self, I suggest, can emerge only through language: only after our knowledge of other persons has developed, and only after we have become conscious of our bodies' extensions in space and, especially, in time: only after we have become clear, in the abstract, about the regular interruptions to our consciousness in sleep, and have developed a *theory* of the continuity of our bodies—and thus of our selves —during sleep.

Thus the body-mind problem divides into at least two

quite distinct problems: the problem of the very close relationship between physiological states and certain states of consciousness, and the very different problem of the emergence
of the self, and its relation to its body. It is the problem of the
emergence of the self which, I suggest, can be solved only by
taking language and the objects of world 3 into account, and
the self's dependence on them. The consciousness of self involves, among other things, a distinction, however vague, between living and nonliving bodies, and thereby a rudimentary
theory of the main characteristics of life; also involved somehow is a distinction between bodies endowed with consciousness and others not so endowed. It involves too the projection
of the self into the future: the more or less conscious expectation of the child of growing up in time into an adult; and a
consciousness of having existed for some time in the past. Thus
it involves problems that assume the possession of a theory
of birth and perhaps even of death.

All this becomes possible only through a highly developed
descriptive language—a language which has not only led to the
production of this world 3, but which has been modified
through feedback from world 3.

But the body-mind problem seems to me not exhausted by
these two subproblems, the problem of states of consciousness, and the problem of the self. Although full consciousness
of self is, *in dispositional form,* always present in adults, these
dispositions are not always activated. On the contrary, we are
often in an intensely active mental state and, at the same time,
completely forgetful of ourselves, though always able to reflect
on ourselves at a moment's notice.

This state of intense mental activity which is not self-
conscious is reached, especially, in intellectual or artistic
work: in trying to understand a problem, or a theory; or in
enjoying an absorbing work of fiction, or perhaps in playing
the piano or playing a game of chess.[305a]

In such states, we may forget where we are—always an
indication that we have forgotten ourselves. What our mind is
engaged in, with the utmost concentration, is the attempt to
grasp a world 3 object, or to produce it.

I think that this is a far more interesting and characteristic state of mind than the perception of a round patch of
orange colour. And I think it important that, although only
the human mind achieves it, we find similar states of concen-

tration in hunting animals, for example, or in animals that try to escape from danger. The conjecture offers itself that it is in these stages of high concentration upon a task, or a problem, that both animal and human minds best serve their biological purposes. In more idle moments of consciousness, the mental organ may be, indeed, just idling, resting, recuperating, or, in a word, preparing itself, charging itself up, for the period of concentration. (No wonder that in self-observation we only too often catch ourselves idling rather than, say, thinking intensively.)

Now it seems clear to me that the achievements of the mind require an organ such as this, with its peculiar powers of concentration on a problem, with its linguistic power, its powers of anticipation, inventiveness, and imagination; and with its powers of tentative acceptance and rejection. There does not seem to be a physical organ which can do all this: it seems that something different, like consciousness, was needed, and had to be used as a *part* of the building material for the mind. No doubt, only as a part: many mental activities are unconscious; much is dispositional, and much is just physiological. But much of what is physiological and "automatic" (in playing the piano, say, or driving a car) at a certain period of time has *previously* been done by us with that conscious concentration which is so characteristic of the discovering mind—the mind faced with a difficult problem. Thus everything speaks in favour of the indispensability of the mind in the household of the higher organisms, and also for the need to let solved problems and "learned" situations sink back into the body, presumably to free the mind for new tasks.

A theory of this kind is clearly interactionist: there is interaction between the various organs of the body, and also between these organs and the mind. But beyond this I think that the interaction with world 3 always needs the mind in its relevant stages—although as the examples of learning to speak, to read, and to write show, a large part of the more mechanical work of coding and decoding can be taken over by the physiological system, which does similar work in the case of the sense organs.

It seems to me that the objectivist and biological approach sketched here allows us to see the body-mind problem in a new light. It appears too that it blends extremely well with some new work in the field of animal psychology, especially with the work of Konrad Lorenz. And there is also, it seems to me, a close kinship with some of D. T. Campbell's ideas on evolutionary epistemology and with some ideas of Schrödinger's.

40. The Place of Values in a World of Facts

The title of this section is close to that of a book by a great psychologist and a great man, Wolfgang Köhler.[306] I found his formulation of the problem in the first chapter of his book not only admirably put but very moving; and I think it will move not merely those who remember the times in which the book was written.[307] Yet I was disappointed by Köhler's own solution of his problem, What is the place of values in the world of facts; and how could they make their entry into this world of facts? I feel unconvinced by his thesis that *Gestalt* psychology can make an important contribution to the solution of this problem.

Köhler explains very clearly why few scientists, and few philosophers with scientific training, care to write about values. The reason is simply that so much of the talk about values is just hot air. So many of us fear that we too would only produce hot air or, if not that, something not easily distinguished from it. To me these fears seem to be well founded, in spite of Köhler's efforts to convince us that we should be bold and run the risk. At least in the field of ethical *theory* (I do not include the Sermon on the Mount) with its almost infinite literature, I cannot recall having read anything good and striking except Plato's *Apology of Socrates* (in which ethical theory plays a subsidiary role), some of Kant's works, especially his *Foundations of the Metaphysic of Morals* (which is not too successful) and Friedrich Schiller's elegiac couplets which wittily criticize Kant's rigorism.[308] Perhaps I might add to this list Schopenhauer's *Two Fundamental Problems of Ethics*. Except Plato's *Apology*, and Schiller's charming *reductio* of Kant, none of these come anywhere near to achieving their aim.

I shall therefore say nothing more than that values emerge together with problems; that values could not exist without problems; and that neither values nor problems can be derived or otherwise obtained from facts, though they often pertain to facts or are connected with facts. As far as problems are concerned we may, looking at some person (or some animal or plant), conjecture that he (or it) is trying to solve a certain problem, even though he (or it) may be quite unaware of that problem. Or else, a problem may have been described and discovered, critically or objectively, in its relations, say, to some other problem, or to some attempted solutions. In the first case only our historical conjecture belongs to world 3; in the second case the problem itself may be regarded as one of the inmates of world 3. It is like this with values. A thing, or an idea, or a theory, or an approach, may be conjectured to be objectively valuable in being of help in solving a problem, or as a solution of a problem, whether or not its value is consciously appreciated by those struggling to solve that problem. But if our conjecture is formulated and submitted to discussion, it will belong to world 3. Or else, a value (relative to a certain problem) may be created or discovered, and discussed, in its relations to other values and to other problems; in this quite different case it too may become an inmate of world 3.

Thus if we are right in assuming that once upon a time there was a physical world devoid of life, this world would have been, I think, a world without problems and thus without values. It has often been suggested that values enter the world only with consciousness. This is not my view. I think that values enter the world with life; and if there is life without consciousness (as I think there may well be, even in animals and men, for there appears to be such a thing as dreamless sleep) then, I suggest, there will also be objective values, even without consciousness.

There are thus two sorts of values: values created by life, by unconscious problems, and values created by the human mind, on the basis of previous solutions, in the attempt to solve problems which may be better or less well understood.

This is the place I see for values in a world of facts. It is a place in the world 3 of historically emergent problems and traditions, and this is part of the world of facts—though not of world 1 facts, but of facts partly produced by the human mind. The world of values transcends the valueless world of facts—the world of brute facts, as it were.

The innermost nucleus of world 3, as I see it, is the world of problems, theories, and criticism. Although values do not belong to this nucleus, it is dominated by values: the values of *objective truth, and of its growth.*[309] In a sense we can say that throughout this human intellectual world 3 this value remains the highest value of all, though we must admit other values into our world 3. For with every value proposed arises the problem: is it *true* that this is a value? And, is it *true* that it has its proper standing in the hierarchy of values: is it true that kindness is a higher value than justice, or even comparable with justice? (Thus I am utterly opposed to those who fear truth—who think it was a sin to eat from the tree of knowledge.)

We have generalized the idea of a human world 3 so that world 3 in the wider sense comprises not only the products of our intellect, together with the unintended consequences which emerge from them, but also the products of our mind in a much wider sense; for example, the products of our imagination. Even theories, products of our intellect, result from the criticism of myths, which are products of our imagination: they would not be possible without myths; nor would criticism be possible without the discovery of the distinction between fact and fiction, or truth and falsity. This is why myths and fictions should not be excluded from world 3. So we are led to include art and, in fact, all human products into which we have injected some of our ideas, and which incorporate the result of *criticism* (in a sense wider than merely intellectual criticism). We ourselves may be included, since we absorb and criticize the ideas of our predecessors, and try to form ourselves; and so may our children and pupils, our traditions and institutions, our ways of life, our purposes, and our aims.

It is one of the grave mistakes of contemporary philosophy not to see that these things—our offspring—though they are products of our minds, and though they bear upon our subjective experiences, have also an objective side. One way of life may be incompatible with another way of life in almost the same sense in which a theory may be logically incompatible with another. These incompatibilities are there, objectively, even if we are unaware of them. And so our purposes and our aims, like our theories, may compete, and may be critically compared and discussed.

Yet the subjective approach, especially the subjective theory of knowledge, treats of world 3 objects—even those in the narrower sense, such as problems, theories, and critical arguments—as if they were mere utterances or expressions of the knowing subject. This approach is closely similar to the expressionist theory of art. Generally, it regards a man's work only or mainly as the expression of his inner state; and it looks upon self-expression as an aim.

I am trying to replace this view of the relation of a man to his work by a very different one. Admitting that world 3 originates with us, I stress its considerable autonomy, and its immeasurable repercussions on us. Our minds, our selves, cannot exist without it; they are anchored in world 3. We owe to the interaction with world 3 our rationality, the practice of critical and self-critical thinking and acting. We owe to it our mental growth. And we owe to it our relation to our task, to our work, and its repercussions upon ourselves.

The expressionist view is that our talents, our gifts, and perhaps our upbringing, and thus "our whole personality", determine what we do. The result is good or bad, according to whether or not we are gifted and interesting personalities.

In opposition to this I suggest that everything depends upon the give-and-take between ourselves and our task, our work, our problems, our world 3; upon the repercussion upon us of this world; upon feedback, which can be amplified by our criticism of what we have done. It is through the attempt to see objectively the work we have done—that is to see it critically—and to do it better, through the interaction between our actions and their objective results, that we can transcend our talents, and ourselves.

As with our children, so with our theories, and ultimately with all the work we do: our products become largely independent of their makers. We may gain more knowledge from our children or from our theories than we ever imparted to them. This is how we can lift ourselves out of the morass of our ignorance; and how we can all contribute to world 3.

If I am right in my conjecture that we grow, and become ourselves, only in interaction with world 3, then the fact that we can all contribute to this world, if only a little, can give comfort to everyone; and especially to one who feels that in struggling with ideas he has found more happiness than he could ever deserve,

Notes

Abbreviations used in these Notes, such as *Replies*, or [1945 (c)], refer to the lists on pp. 239-47.

[1] The allusion is to Kierkegaard's conversation with Christian VIII in which the King asked him for his views on how a King should conduct himself. Kierkegaard said such things as: "First, it would be a good thing for the King to be ugly." (Christian VIII was very good-looking.) "Then he should be deaf and blind, or at least behave as if he were, for this solves many difficulties. . . . And then, he must not say much, but must have a little standard speech that can be used on all occasions, a speech therefore without content." (Francis Joseph used to say: "It was very nice, and it pleased me very much."—"Es war sehr schön, es hat mich sehr gefreut.")

[2] The case arose from my work with children. One of the boys for whom I was responsible had fallen from a climbing frame and had suffered a fractured skull. I was acquitted because I could prove that I had demanded for months that the authorities should remove the climbing frame, which I regarded as dangerous. (The authorities had tried to put the blame on me; a procedure about which the judge had some strong words to say.)

[3] See Otto Weininger, *Geschlecht und Charakter* (Vienna: Braumüller, 1903), p. 176: "All blockheads, from Bacon to Fritz Mauthner, have been critics of language." (Weininger adds that he should ask Bacon to forgive him for associating him in this way with Mauthner.) Compare this with *Tractatus*, 4.0031.

[4] Cp. n. 57 to Chap. 12 of *O.S.* [1945(c)], p. 297; [1950(a)], p. 653; [1962(c)], [1963(I)], and later editions, p. 312.

[5] Roger Martin du Gard, *L'Été 1914*; English translation by Stuart Gilbert, *Summer 1914* (London: John Lane, The Bodley Head, 1940).

[6] The problem has recently reached a new stage through Abraham Robinson's work on the infinitely small; see Abraham Robinson, *Non-Standard Analysis* (Amsterdam: North-Holland Publishing Company, 1966).

[7] The term *"essentialism"* (widely used now) and especially its application to *definitions* ("*essentialist definitions*") were, to my knowledge, first introduced in section 10 of *The Poverty* [1944(a)]; see esp. pp. 94-97; [1957(g)] and later editions, pp. 27-30; and in my

O.S., Vol. I [1945(b)], pp. 24-27; and Vol. II [1945(c)], pp. 8-20, 274-86; [1950(a)], pp. 206-18, 621-38; [1962(c)], [1963(1)], and later editions: Vol. I, pp. 29-32; Vol. II, pp. 9-21, 287-301. There is a reference on p. 202 of Richard Robinson's *Definition* (Oxford: Oxford University Press, 1950), to the 1945 edition of my *O.S.* [1945(c)], Vol. II, pp. 9-20; and what he says, for example, on pp. 153-57 (cp. the "utterances" on p. 158), and also on pp. 162-65, is in some respects very similar to what I say in the pages of my book to which he refers (though his remark on p. 71 about Einstein and simultaneity does not agree with what I say in [1945(c)], pp. 18f.; 108f.; [1950(a)], pp. 216f., 406; [1962(c)] and [1963(l)], Vol. II, pp. 20, 220). Compare also Paul Edwards, ed., *The Encyclopedia of Philosophy* (New York: Macmillan Company and Free Press, 1967; London: Collier Macmillan, 1967), Vol. II, pp. 314-17. "*Essentialism*" is there discussed at length under the main entry *Definition* (reference is made in the Bibliography to Robinson).

[7a] (Added in proofs.) I have recently made a change in terminology from the first, second and third worlds to world 1, world 2, and world 3, upon the suggestion of Sir John Eccles. For my older terminology, see [1968(r)] and [1968(s)]; for Sir John's suggestion, see his *Facing Reality* (New York, Heidelberg and Berlin: Springer-Verlag, 1970). The suggestion came too late to be incorporated into the original text of the present book except in one or two places. (Added 1975: I have now revised this to some extent.) See also n. 293 below.

[8] Annual Philosophical Lecture, British Academy, 1960 [1960(d)], [1961(f)]; republished in *C. & R.* [1963(a)]; see esp. pp. 19 f. and also p. 349 of my "Epistemology Without a Knowing Subject" [1968(s)], now Chap. 3 of my [1972(a)]. (The table reproduced here is a slight modification of the original one.)

[9] Cp. the 3d ed. of *C. & R.* [1969(h)], p. 28, the newly inserted point 9. (Point 9 of the earlier editions is now numbered 10.)

[10] Not even Gottlob Frege states it quite explicitly, though this doctrine is certainly implicit in his "Sinn und Bedeutung", and he even produces there arguments in its support. Cp. Peter Geach and Max Black, eds., *Translations from the Philosophical Writings of Gottlob Frege* (Oxford: Blackwell, 1952), pp. 56-78.

[11] Cp. my article "Quantum Mechanics without 'The Observer'" [1967(k)]; see esp. pp. 11-15, where the present problem is discussed. (This particular equivalence, incidentally, is questioned there.)

[12] One could hardly write in a prose translation (Parmenides, fragments 14-15):

Bright in the night with an alien light round the earth she is erring,
Always she wistfully looks round for the rays of the sun.

[13] Gottlob Frege suggests — mistakenly, I think — in "Der Gedanke", *Beiträg zur Philos. d. deutschen Idealismus*, 1 (1918-19), 58-77 (excellently translated by A. M. and Marcelle Quinton as "The Thought: A Logical Enquiry", *Mind*, n. s. 65 [1956], 289-311), that *only* of the emotional aspects of speech is a "perfect (*vollkommene*) translation almost impossible" (p. 63; p. 295 of the translation), and that "The more strictly scientific a presentation, the more easily is it translated" (*ibid.*). Ironically enough, Frege continues to say quite correctly that it makes no difference to any thought content which of the four German synonyms for "horse" (*Pferd, Ross, Gaul, Mähre*—they are different only in emotional content: *Mähre*, in particular, *need not* in every context be a female horse) is used in any formulation. Yet this very simple and unemotional thought of Frege's is, it appears, untranslatable into the English language, since English does not seem to have three good synonyms for "horse". The translator would, therefore, have to become a commentator by finding some common English word which has three good synonyms—preferably with strikingly different emotional or poetic associations.

[14] Cp., for example, section 37 of my *L.d.F.* [1934(b)], [1966(e)] and later editions; and also of *L.Sc.D.* [1959(a)] and later editions. The example I had in mind was gravitational redshift.

[15] For this idea, and the quotation, see section 6 of my *L.d.F.* [1934(b)], p. 13; [1966(e)], p. 15; "Sie sagen um so mehr, je mehr sie verbieten."; *L.Sc.D.* [1959(a)] and later editions, p. 41: "The more they prohibit the more they say." The idea was adopted by Rudolf Carnap in section 23 of his *Introduction to Semantics* (Cambridge, Mass.: Harvard University Press, 1942); see esp. p. 151. There Carnap attributes this idea to Wittgenstein "due to an error of memory", as he himself puts it in section 73 of his *Logical Foundations of Probability* (Chicago: University of Chicago Press, 1950), p. 406, where he attributes it to me. Carnap writes there: "The assertive power of a sentence consists in its excluding certain possible cases". I should now stress that these "cases" are, in science, *theories (hypotheses) of a higher or a lower degree of universality*. (Even what I called "basic statements" in *L.Sc.D.* are, as I stressed there, *hypotheses*, though of a low degree of universality.)

[16] The subset of the informative content which consists of basic statements (empirical statements) I called in *L.Sc.D.* the class of the theory's "potential falsifiers", or its "empirical content".

[17] For *non-a* belongs to the informative content of *a*, and *a* to the informative content of *non-a*, but *a* does not belong to its own informative content (unless it is a contradiction).

[18] The proof (which in the particular form given here was shown to me by David Miller) is quite straightforward. For the statement

"*b or t or both*" follows from "*a or t or both*" if and only if it follows from *a*; that is, if and only if the theory *t* follows from "*a and non-b*". But because *a* and *b* contradict one another (by hypothesis), this last statement says the same as *a*. Thus "*b or t or both*" follows from "*a or t or both*" if and only if *t* follows from *a;* and this, by assumption, it does not.

[19] J. W. N. Watkins, *Hobbes's System of Ideas* (London: Hutchinson, 1965), pp. 22 f.; second ed., 1973, pp. 8 f.

[20] (This note originally formed part of the text.)

All this can be stated even if we confine ourselves to just one of the two ideas of content so far discussed. It becomes even clearer in terms of a third idea of content, that is, the idea of the *problem content* of a theory.

Following a suggestion of Frege's, we may introduce the notion of a yes-or-no problem or, briefly, a *y*-problem: given any statement *a* (say, "Grass is green"), the corresponding *y*-problem ("Is grass green?") may be denoted by "*y(a)*". One sees at once that $y(a)=y(non\text{-}a)$: the problem whether grass is green is, *qua* problem, identical with the problem whether grass is not green, even though the two questions are differently formulated, and even though the answer "Yes" to one of them is equivalent to the answer "No" to the other.

We can define what I propose to call the problem content of a theory *t* in either of two equivalent ways: (1) it is the set of all those *y(a)* for which *a* is an element of the logical content of *t*; (2) it is the set of all those *y(a)* for which *a* is an element of the informative content of *t*. Thus the problem content is related to the two other contents in identical ways.

In our previous example of *N* (Newton's theory) and *E* (Einstein's), *y(E)* belongs to the problem content of *N*, and *y(N)* to that of *E*. If we denote by K ($=K_1$ and K_2 and K_3) the statement which formulates Kepler's three laws, restricted to the two-body problem, then K_1 and K_2 follow from *N* but contradict *E*, while K_3 and therefore *K* contradict both *N* and *E*. (See my paper [1957(i)], [1969 (k)], now Chap. 5 of [1972(a)]; and also [1963(a)], p. 62, n. 28.) Nevertheless, *y(K)*, and $y(K_1)$, $y(K_2)$, $y(K_3)$, all belong to the problem content both of *N* and of *E*, and *y(N)* and *y(E)* both belong to the problem contents of *K*, of K_1, of K_2, and of K_3.

That *y(E)*, the problem of the truth or falsity of Einstein's theory, belongs to the problem content of *K* and to that of *N* illustrates the fact that there can be no transitivity here. For the problem whether the theory of the optical Doppler effect is true—that is, *y(D)*—belongs to the problem content of *E*, but not to that of *N* or that of *K*.

Although there is no transitivity there may be a link: the problem contents of *a* and of *b* may be said to be linked by *y(c)* if *y(c)* belongs to that of *a* and also to that of *b*. Obviously, the problem contents of any *a* and *b* can always be linked by choosing some appropriate *c* (perhaps *c* = *a or b*); thus the bare fact that *a* and *b* are linked is trivial; but the fact that they are linked by some particular problem *y(c)* (which interests us for some reason or other) may not be trivial, and may add to the significance of *a*, of *b*, and of *c*. Most links are, of course, unknown at any given time.

²¹ Gottlob Frege, *Grundgesetze der Arithmetik* (Jena: H. Pohle, 1903), Vol. II, section 56.

²² Clifford A. Truesdell, "Foundations of Continuum Mechanics", in *Delaware Seminar in the Foundations of Physics*, ed. by Mario Bunge (Berlin, Heidelberg, New York: Springer-Verlag, 1967), pp. 35-48; see esp. p. 37.

²³ Gottlob Frege, "Über Begriff und Gegenstand", *Vierteljahrsschrift f. wissenschaftliche Philos.*, **16** (1892), 192-205. Cp. p. 43 of Geach and Black, eds., *Philosophical Writings of Gottlob Frege*, pp. 42-55 (see n. 10 above).

²⁴ See n. *1 to section 4; [1959(a)] and later editions, p. 35; [1966 (e)] and later editions p. 9; and also my two Prefaces.

²⁵ The problems dealt with here are discussed (though perhaps not fully enough) in the various Prefaces to *L.d.F.* and *L.Sc.D.* It is perhaps of some interest that the fact that I criticized there in some detail the whole approach of language analysis was not even mentioned when this book was reviewed in *Mind* (see also my reply to this review in n. 243 to section 33, below), though this journal was an obvious place in which to mention, and to answer, such a criticism; nor has the criticism been mentioned elsewhere. For other discussions of problems connected with the topic of this digression, see the references in n. 7 in the preceding section 6, and my various discussions of the descriptive and argumentative functions of language in *C.&R.*, [1963(a)] and later editions; and also [1966(f)], [1967(k)], [1968(r)], and [1968(s)] (the first of these now forms Chap. 6 and the last two Chaps. 3 and 4 of [1972(a)]).

An interesting example of a key word (*ephexēs* in Plato's *Timaeus* 55A) which has been misinterpreted (as "next in order of magnitude", instead of "next in order of time" or perhaps "in adjacent order") because the *theory* was not understood, and which can be interpreted in two different senses ("successively" in time, or "adjacent" applied to plane angles) without affecting Plato's *theory*, may be found in my paper "Plato, *Timaeus* 54E - 55A" [1970(d)]. For similar examples, see the 3d ed. of *C.&R.* [1969(h)], esp. pp. 165 and 408-12. In brief, one cannot translate without keeping the problem situation constantly in mind.

²⁶ See section IV to Chap. 19 of my *O.S.*, [1945(c)], [1950(a)], and

later editions, for the ambiguity of violence; and also the Index under "violence".

²⁷ See, for comments on all this, *The Poverty* [1944(a) and (b)] and [1945(a)], and [1957(g)], and esp. Chaps. 17 to 20 of my *O.S.* [1945(c)], [1966(a)]. The remarks on the workers of Vienna which follow here in the text repeat in the main what I said in my *O.S.*, in nn. 18 to 22 to Chap. 18, and n. 39 to Chap. 19. See also the references given in n. 26 above on *the ambiguity of violence*.

²⁸ G. E. R. Gedye, *Fallen Bastions* (London: Victor Gollancz, 1939).

²⁹ Cp. [1957(a)], reprinted as Chap. 1 of *C.&R.*, [1963(a)] and later editions.

³⁰ Cp. Ernst Mach, *The Science of Mechanics*, 6th English ed. with an Introduction by Karl Menger (La Salle, Ill.: Open Court Publishing Co., 1960), Chap. 2, section 6, subsection 9.

³¹ The formulation in italics was first suggested, and its significance discussed, in [1949(d)], now translated as the Appendix to [1972(a)]; see also [1957(i) & (j)], [1969(k)], now Chap. 5 of [1972 (a)].

³² Albert Einstein, *Über die spezielle und die allgemeine Relativitätstheorie* (Braunschweig: Vieweg, 1917); see esp. Chap. 22. I have used my own translation, but the corresponding passage occurs on p. 77 of the English translation referred to in the next footnote. It should be noted that Newton's theory lives on as a limiting case in Einstein's theory of gravitation. (This is particularly clear if Newton's theory is formulated in a "general relativistic" or "covariant" way, by taking the velocity of light as infinite [$c = \infty$]. This was shown by Peter Havas, "Four-Dimensional Formulations of Newtonian Mechanics and Their Relation to the Special and the General Theory of Relativity", *Reviews of Modern Physics*, 36 [1964], 938-65.)

³³ Albert Einstein, *Relativity: The Special and the General Theory. A Popular Exposition* (London: Methuen & Co., 1920), p. 132. (I have slightly improved upon the translation.)

³⁴ *L.d.F.* [1934(b)], p. 13; [1966(e)] and later editions, p. 15; and *L.Sc.D.* [1959(a)] and later editions, p. 41; see n. 15 to section 7 above.

³⁵ Cp. Hans Albert, *Marktsoziologie und Entscheidungslogik* (Neuwied and Berlin: Herman Luchterhand Verlag, 1967); see esp. pp. 149, 227 f., 309, 341 f. My very clumsy term, which Albert replaced by "immunization against criticism", was "conventionalist stratagem".

(Added in proofs.) David Miller has now drawn my attention to

n. 1 on p. 560 of Arthur Pap, "Reduction Sentences and Dispositional Concepts", in *The Philosophy of Rudolf Carnap*, ed. by Paul Arthur Schilpp (La Salle, Ill.: Open Court Publishing Co., 1963), pp. 559-97, which anticipates this use of "immunization".

[36] Cp. Chap. 1 of my *C.&R.*, [1963(a)] and later editions.

[37] For a much fuller discussion, see sections 2, 3, and 5 of my *Replies*.

[38] See *C.&R.*, [1963(a)] and later editions, Chap. 10, esp. the Appendix, pp. 248-50; Chap. 11, pp. 275-77; Chap. 8, pp. 193-200; and Chap. 17, p. 346. The problem was first discussed by me in section 15 of *L.d.F.* [1934(b)], pp. 33 f.; [1966(e)] and later editions, pp. 39-41; *L.Sc.D.*, [1959(a)] and later editions, pp. 69 f. A fairly full discussion of certain metaphysical theories (centred on metaphysical determinism and indeterminism) is to be found in my paper "Indeterminism in Quantum Physics and in Classical Physics" [1950(b)]; see esp. pp. 121-23.

[39] See pp. 37 f. of *C.&R.* [1963(a)] and later editions.

[40] See [1945(c)], pp. 101 f.; [1962(c)] and later editions, Vol. II, pp. 108 f.

[41] See Imre Lakatos, "Changes in the Problem of Inductive Logic", in *The Problem of Inductive Logic*, ed. by Imre Lakatos (Amsterdam: North-Holland Publishing Co., 1968), pp. 315-417, esp. p. 317.

[42] There does not seem to be any systematic time-dependence, as there is in the learning of meaningless syllables.

[43] Cp. C. Lloyd Morgan, *Introduction to Comparative Psychology* (London: Scott, 1894), and H. S. Jennings, *The Behaviour of the Lower Organisms* (New York: Columbia University Press, 1906).

[44] My view of habit formation may be illustrated by a report about the gosling Martina in Konrad Lorenz, *On Aggression* (London: Methuen & Co., 1966), pp. 57 f. Martina acquired a habit consisting of a certain detour towards a window before mounting the stairs to the first floor of Lorenz's house in Altenberg. This habit originated (*ibid.*, p. 57) with a typical escape reaction towards the light (the window). Although this first reaction was "repeated", "the habitual detour . . . became shorter and shorter". Thus repetition did not create this habit; and in this case it even tended to make it slowly disappear. (Perhaps this was something like an approach towards a critical phase.) Incidentally, many asides of Lorenz's seem to be in support of my view that scientists use the critical method—the method of conjectures and attempted refutations. For example he writes (*ibid.*, p. 8): "It is a very good morn-

ing exercise for a research scientist to discard a pet hypothesis every day before breakfast." Yet in spite of this insight he seems still to be influenced by inductivism. (See, for example, *ibid.*, p. 62: "But perhaps a whole series of countless repetitions . . . was necessary"; for another passage with clearly methodological intent see Konrad Lorenz, *Über tierisches und menschliches Verhalten* [Munich: R. Piper & Co., 1965], p. 388.) He does not always seem to realize that in science "repetitions" of observations are not inductive confirmations but critical attempts to check oneself—to catch oneself in a mistake. See also below, n. 95 to section 15, and text.

[45] According to *The Oxford English Dictionary,* the phrase "rule of trial and error" originated in arithmetic (see TRIAL 4). Note that neither Lloyd Morgan nor Jennings used the term in the sense of random trials. (This latter use seems to be due to Edward Thorndike.)

[46] Drawing a ball blindly from an urn does not ensure randomness unless the balls in the urn are well mixed. And blindness regarding the solution need not involve blindness regarding the problem: we may know that our problem is to win a game by drawing a white ball.

[47] D. Katz, *Animals and Men* (London: Longmans, 1937), p. 143.

[48] Jane Austen, *Emma* (London: John Murray, 1816), Vol. III, end of Chap. 3 (Chap. 39 of some later editions). Cp. p. 336 of R. W. Chapman, ed., *The Novels of Jane Austen,* 3d ed., (Oxford: Oxford University Press, 1933), Vol. IV.

[49] For the development of games, see Jean Piaget, *The Moral Judgment of the Child* (London: Routledge & Kegan Paul, 1932), esp. p. 18 for the dogmatic first two stages and the critical "third stage"; see also pp. 56-69. See further Jean Piaget, *Play, Dreams, and Imitation in Childhood* (London: Routledge & Kegan Paul, 1962).

[50] Something like this view may be found in Søren Kierkegaard, *Repetition* (Princeton: Princeton University Press; Oxford: Oxford University Press, 1942); cp., for example, pp. 77 f.

[51] Joseph Church, *Language and the Discovery of Reality* (New York: Random House, 1961), p. 36.

[52] *Ibid.*

[53] This seems to be the obvious explanation of the tragic incident of Helen Keller's alleged plagiarism when she was still a child, an incident which made a great impression on her, and perhaps helped her to sort out the different sources of the messages which all reached her in one and the same code.

⁵⁴ W. H. Thorpe writes in a passage (to which Arne Petersen has drawn my attention) in his interesting book *Learning and Instinct in Animals* (London: Methuen & Co., 1956), p. 122 (2d rev. ed., 1963, p. 135): "By true imitation is meant the copying of a novel or otherwise improbable act or utterance, or some act for which there is clearly no instinctive tendency." (Italicized in the original.) *There can be no imitation without elaborate instinctive tendencies for copying in general, and even for the specific kind of imitating act in particular.* No tape recorder can work without its built-in (as it were innate) ability for learning by imitation (imitation of vibrations) and if we do not provide it with a substitute for the need or drive to use its abilities (perhaps in the form of a human operator who *wants* the machine to do some recording *and* playing back), then it will not imitate. This seems to be true, then, of even the most *passive* forms of learning by imitation of which I can think. It is of course quite correct that we should speak of imitation only if the act to be imitated is not one which would be performed by animal *A* from instinct alone, without its having been first performed by another animal *B* in the presence of *A*. But there will be cases in which we have reason to suspect that *A may* have produced the act—perhaps at a somewhat later stage—without imitating *B*. Should we not call it a true imitation if *B*'s act led to *A*'s performing the act (much) earlier than it would have done otherwise?

⁵⁵ *C.&R.*, [1963(a)] and later editions, Chap. 1, esp. pp. 42-52. I refer there on p. 50, n. 16, to a thesis "Gewohnheit und Gesetzerlebnis" [On Habit and Belief in Laws] which I presented (in an unfinished state) in 1927, and in which I argued against Hume's idea that habit is merely the (passive) result of repetitive association.

⁵⁶ This is somewhat similar to Plato's theory of knowledge in *Meno* 80D-86C but of course also dissimilar.

⁵⁷ I feel that here is the place, more than anywhere else, to acknowledge the help I have received throughout this essay from my friends Ernst Gombrich and Bryan Magee. It was perhaps not so difficult for Ernst Gombrich for, although he does not agree with all I say about music, he at least sympathizes with my attitude. But Bryan Magee emphatically does not. He is an admirer of Wagner (on whom he has written a brilliant book, *Aspects of Wagner* [London: Alan Ross, 1968; New York: Stein & Day, 1969]). Thus he and I are here as completely at loggerheads as two people can possibly be. It is of lesser moment that in his judgement my sections 13 and 14 contain well-known muddles, and that some of the views I attack are Aunt Sallies. Of course, I do not quite agree with this; but the point I wish to make here is that our disagreement has not prevented him from helping me immensely, not only

with the rest of this autobiographical sketch but also with these two
sections that contain views on which we have seriously disagreed
for many years.

[58] It is a long time since I gave up these studies and I cannot now
remember the details. But it seems to me more than probable that
there was a certain amount of parallel singing, at the *organum* stage
which contained thirds *and* fifths (reckoned from the bass). I feel
that this should have preceded *fauxbourdon* singing.

[59] See D. Perkin Walker, "Kepler's Celestial Music", *Journal of
the Warburg and Courtauld Institutes*, 30 (1967), 228–50. I am
greatly indebted to Dr Walker for drawing my attention to the
passage which I quote in the text. It is from Kepler, *Gesammelte
Werke*, ed. by Max Caspar (Munich, 1940), Vol. VI, p. 328. The
passage is quoted in Latin by Walker, *Kepler's Celestial Music*, pp.
249 f., who also gives an English translation. The translation here
is my own. (I translate: *ut mirum amplius non sit*=there is no marvel greater or more sublime; *ut luderet* [=that he should enact] =
that he should conjure up a vision of; *ut quadamtenus degusterat*=
that he should almost [taste or touch or] reach.) Incidentally, I cannot agree that Plato's harmony of the spheres was monodic and
consisted "only of scales" (cp. Walker, *Kepler's Celestial Music*, n.
3 and text); on the contrary, Plato takes the greatest care to avoid
this interpretation of his words. (See for example *Republic* 617B,
where each of the eight Sirens sings one single tune, such that from
all the eight together "there came the concord of one single harmony". *Timaeus* 35B–36B and 90D should be interpreted in the light
of this passage. Relevant is also Aristotle, *De sensu* vii, 448 a 20 ff.
where the views of "some writers on concords" are examined who
"say that sounds do not arrive simultaneously but merely *seem* to
do so".) See also on singing in octaves Aristotle's *Problems* 918 b
40, 919 b 33–35 ("mixture"; "consonance") and 921 a 8–31 (see esp.
921 a 27 f.).

[60] I have alluded to this story in Chap. 1 of *C.&R.* [1963(a)] and
later editions, end of section vi, p. 50.

[61] It was only years later that I realized that in asking "How is
science possible?" Kant had Newton's theory in mind, augmented
by his own interesting form of atomism (which resembled that of
Boscovich); cp. *C.&R.*, Chaps. 2, 7, and 8, and my paper
"Philosophy and Physics" [1961(h)].

[62] For this distinction (and also for a more subtle one) see *C.&R.*
[1963(a)], Chap. 1, section v, pp. 47 f.

[63] Albert Schweitzer, *J. S. Bach* (Leipzig: Breitkopf und Härtel,
1908); first published in French in 1905; 7th ed., 1929; and new
English ed. (London: A. & C. Black, 1923), Vol. I, p. 1. Schweitzer
uses the term "objective" for Bach and "subjective" for Wagner.

would agree that Wagner is far more "subjective" than Beethoven. Yet I should perhaps say here that, though I greatly admire Schweitzer's book (especially his most excellent comments on the phrasing of Bach's themes) I cannot at all agree with an analysis of the contrast between "objective" and "subjective" musicians in terms of the musician's relation to his "time" or "period". It seems to me almost certain that in this Schweitzer is influenced by Hegel, whose appreciation of Bach impressed him. (See *ibid.*, pp. 225 f., and n. 56 on p. 230. On p. 225 [Vol. 1, p. 244 of the English ed.] Schweitzer recounts from Therese Devrient's memoirs a charming incident involving Hegel which is not very flattering to him.)

[64] The first of these [1968(s)] was an address delivered in 1967 and first published in *Logic, Methodology and Philosophy of Science*, Vol. III, pp. 333-73; the second [1968(r)] was first published in *Proceedings of the XIVth International Congress of Philosophy, Vienna: 2nd to 9th September 1968*, Vol. I, pp. 25-53. These two papers are now Chaps. 3 and 4 respectively of [1972(a)]. The third paper [1967(k)] cited in the text is in *Quantum Theory and Reality*. See also my *L.d.F.* and *L.Sc.D.*, sections 29 and 30 [1934(b)], pp. 60-67; [1966(e)] and later editions, pp. 69-76; [1959(a)] and later editions, pp. 104-11; my *C.&R.* [1963(a)], esp. pp. 224-31; and my paper "A Realist View of Logic, Physics, and History" [1970(l)] in *Physics, Logic and History*, now Chap. 8 of [1972(a)].

[65] See my *O.S.*, Vol. I [1945(b)], pp. 26, 96; Vol. II [1945(c)], pp. 12 f.; [1950(a)], pp. 35, 108, 210-12; [1962(c)], [1963(l)], and later editions, Vol. I, pp. 32, 109; Vol. II, pp. 13 f.

[65]a (Added 1975.) The same holds for expressionist or emotive theories of morals, and of moral judgements.

[66] See also the last section of my paper "Epistemology Without a Knowing Subject" [1968(s)], pp. 369-71; [1972(a)], pp. 146-50.

[67] Cited by Schweitzer, *J. S. Bach*, p. 153.

[68] Arthur Schopenhauer, *Die Welt als Wille und Vorstellung* [The World as Will and Idea], Vol. II (1844), Chap. 39; the second quotation is from Vol. I (1818 [1819]), section 52. Note that the German word *"Vorstellung"* is simply the translation into German of John Locke's term "idea".

[69] The German is: *"eine cantable Art im Spielen zu erlangen"*.

[70] Plato, *Ion;* cp. esp. 533D-536D.

[71] *Ibid.*, 534E.

[72] Plato, *Ion*, 535E; cp. 535C.

[73] See also my paper "Self-Reference and Meaning in Ordinary Language" [1954(c)], which now forms Chap. 14 of *C.&R.* [1963(a)];

and text to n. 163 of my *Replies* in P. A. Schilpp ed., *The Philosophy of Karl Popper* (La Salle: Open Court, 1974). Arguments purporting to show that self-referring jokes are impossible may be found in Gilbert Ryle, *The Concept of Mind* [London: Hutchinson, 1949], for example, on pp. 193–96; Peregrine Books ed. [Harmondsworth: Penguin Books, 1963], pp. 184–88. I think that Ion's remark is [or implies] "a criticism of itself" which according to Ryle, p. 196, should not be possible.

⁷⁴ Plato, *Ion* 541ᴇ–542ʙ.

⁷⁵ See my *O.S.* [1945(b) and (c)] and later editions, nn. 40 and 41 to Chap. 4, and text.

⁷⁶ Ernst Gombrich referred me to "In order to make me weep you yourself must suffer first" (Horace, *Ad Pisones*, 103 f.). Of course it is conceivable that what Horace intended to formulate was not an expressionist view but the view that only the artist who has suffered first is capable of critically judging the impact of his work. It seems to me probable that Horace was not conscious of the difference between these two interpretations.

⁷⁷ Plato, *Ion* 541ᴇ f.

⁷⁸ For much of this paragraph, and some criticism of the previous paragraphs, I am indebted to my friend Ernst Gombrich.
It will be seen that the secularized Platonic theories (of the work of art as subjective expression and communication, and as objective description) correspond to Karl Bühler's three functions of language; cp. my [1963(a)], pp. 134 f. and 295, and section 15.

⁷⁹ See E. H. Gombrich, *Art and Illusion* (London: Phaidon Press; New York: Pantheon Books, 1960; latest edition, 1972), *passim*.

⁸⁰ It will be seen that my attitude towards music resembles the theories of Eduard Hanslick (caricatured by Wagner as Beckmesser), a music critic of great influence in Vienna, who wrote a book against Wagner (*Vom Musikalisch-Schönen* [Leipzig: R. Weigel, 1854]; trans. by G. Cohen from the 7th rev. ed. as *The Beautiful in Music* [London: Novello and Co., 1891]). But I do not agree with Hanslick's rejection of Bruckner who, though venerating Wagner, was in his way as saintly a musician as Beethoven (who is now sometimes wrongly accused of dishonesty). It is an amusing fact that Wagner was greatly impressed by Schopenhauer—by *The World as Will and Idea*—and that Schopenhauer wrote in the *Parerga*, Vol. II, section 224 (first published in 1851, when Wagner was starting work on the music of *The Ring*), "One can say that Opera has been the bane of music". (He meant of course recent opera, although his arguments sound very general—much too general in fact.)

[81] Friedrich Nietzsche, *Der Fall Wagner* [The Case of Wagner] (Leipzig, 1888) and *Nietzsche contra Wagner*; both translated in *The Complete Works of Friedrich Nietzsche*, ed. by Oscar Levy (Edinburgh and London: T. N. Foulis, 1911), Vol. VIII.

[82] Arthur Schopenhauer, *Parerga*, Vol. II, section 224.

[83] Karl Bühler, *Die geistige Entwicklung des Kindes* (Jena: Fischer, 1918; 3d ed., 1922); English translation, *The Mental Development of the Child* (London: Kegan Paul, Trench, Trubner & Co., 1930). For the functions of language, see also his *Sprachtheorie* (Jena: Fischer, 1934); see esp. pp. 24-33.

[84] A word may perhaps be said here on Aristotle's hygienic theory of art. Art no doubt has some biological or psychological function like catharisis; I do not deny that great music may in some sense purify our minds. But is the greatness of a work of art summed up in the fact that it cleanses us more thoroughly than a lesser work? I do not think that even Aristotle would have said this.

[85] Cp. *C.&R.*, pp. 134 f., 295; *Of Clouds and Clocks* [1966 (f)], now Chap. 6 of [1972(a)], sections 14-17 and n. 47; "Epistemology Without a Knowing Subject" [1968(s)], esp. section 4, pp. 345 f. ([1972(a)], Chap. 3, pp. 119-22).

[86] Leonard Nelson was an outstanding personality, one of the small band of Kantians in Germany who had opposed the First World War, and who upheld the Kantian tradition of rationality.

[87] See my paper "Julius Kraft 1898-1960" [1962(f)].

[88] See Leonard Nelson, "Die Unmöglichkeit der Erkenntnis-theorie", *Proceedings of the IVth International Congress of Philosophy, Bologna; 5th to 11th April 1911* (Genoa: Formiggini, 1912), Vol. I, pp. 255-75; see also L. Nelson, *Über das sogenannte Erkenntnisproblem* (Göttingen: Vandenhoeck & Ruprecht, 1908).

[89] See Heinrich Gomperz, *Weltanschauungslehre* (Jena and Leipzig: Diederichs, 1905 and 1908), Vol. I, and Vol. II, part 1. Gomperz told me that he had completed the second part of the second volume but had decided not to publish it, and to abandon his plans for the later volumes. The published volumes were planned and executed on a truly magnificent scale, and I do not know the reason why Gomperz ceased to work on it, about eighteen years before I met him. Obviously it had been a tragic experience. In one of his later books, *Über Sinn und Sinngebilde—Verstehen und Erklären* (Tübingen: Mohr, 1929), he refers to his earlier theory of feelings, esp. on pp. 206 f. For his psychologistic approach—which he called "pathempiricism" (*Pathempirismus*) and which emphasized the role of feelings (*Gefühle*) in knowledge—

see esp. *Weltanschauungslehre*, sections 55-59 (Vol. II, pp. 220-93). Cp. also sections 36-39 (Vol. I, pp. 305-94).

⁹⁰ Karl Bühler, "Tatsachen und Probleme zu einer Psychologie der Denkvorgänge", *Archiv f. d. gesamte Psychologie*, 9 (1907), 297-365; 12 (1908), 1-23, 24-92, 93-123.

⁹¹ Otto Selz, *Über die Gesetze des geordneten Denkverlaufs* (Stuttgart: W. Spemann, 1913), Vol. I; (Bonn: F. Cohen, 1922), Vol. II.

⁹² Oswald Külpe, *Vorlesungen über Logik*, ed. by Otto Selz (Leipzig: S. Hirzel, 1923).

⁹³ A similar mistake can be found even in *Principia Mathematica*, since Russell failed, in places, to distinguish between an inference (logical implication) and a conditional statement (material implication). This confused me for years. Yet the main point—that an inference was an ordered set of statements—was sufficiently clear to me in 1928 to be mentioned to Bühler during my (public) Ph.D. examination. He admitted very charmingly that he had not considered the point.

⁹⁴ See *C.&R.* [1963(a)], pp. 134 f.

⁹⁵ I now find a similar argument in Konrad Lorenz: " . . . modifiability occurs . . . only in those . . . places where built-in learning mechanisms are phylogenetically programmed to perform just that function." (See Konrad Lorenz, *Evolution and Modification of Behaviour* [London: Methuen & Co., 1966], p. 47.) But he does not seem to draw from it the conclusion that the theories of reflexology and of the conditioned reflex are invalid: see especially *ibid.*, p. 66. See also section 10 above, esp. n. 44. One can state the main difference between association psychology or the theory of the conditioned reflex on the one hand, and discovery by trial and error on the other, by saying that the former is essentially Lamarckian (or "instructive") and the latter Darwinian (or "selective"). See now for example the investigations of Melvin Cohn, "Reflections on a Discussion with Karl Popper: The Molecular Biology of Expectation", *Bulletin of the All-India Institute of Medical Sciences*, 1 (1967), 8-16, and later works by the same author. For Darwinism, see section 37.

⁹⁶ W. von Bechterev, *Objektive Psychologie oder Psychoreflexologie* (originally published 1907-12), German ed. (Leipzig and Berlin: Teubner, 1913); and *Allgemeine Grundlagen der Reflexologie des Menschen* (originally published 1917), German ed. (Leipzig and Vienna: F. Deuticke, 1926); English ed., *General Principles of Human Reflexology* (London: Jarrolds, 1933).

⁹⁷ The title of my (unpublished) dissertation was "Zur Methoden-

frage der Denkpsychologie" [1928(a)].

⁹⁸ Compare with this paragraph some of my remarks against Reichenbach at a conference in 1934 ([1935(a)] reprinted in [1966(e)], [1969(e)], p. 257); there is a translation in *L.Sc.D.*, [1959(a)] and later editions, p. 315: "Scientific theories can never be 'justified', or verified. But . . . a hypothesis *A* can . . . achieve more than a hypothesis *B*. . . . The best we can say of a hypothesis is that up to now . . . it has been more successful than other hypotheses although, in principle, it can never be justified, verified, or even shown to be probable." See also the end of section 20 (text to nn. 156-58), and n. 243 to section 33, below.

⁹⁹ Rudolf Carnap, *Der logische Aufbau der Welt*, and *Scheinprobleme in der Philosophie: das Fremdpsychische und der Realismusstreit*, both first published (Berlin: Weltkreis-Verlag, 1928); second printing, both books in one (Hamburg: Felix Meiner, 1961). Now translated as *The Logical Structure of the World and Pseudoproblems of Philosophy* (London: Routledge & Kegan Paul, 1967).

¹⁰⁰ Victor Kraft, *Die Grundformen der wissenschaftlichen Methoden* (Vienna: Academy of Sciences, 1925).

¹⁰¹ See p. 641 of Herbert Feigl's charming and most informative essay, "The Wiener Kreis in America", in *Perspectives in American History* (The Charles Warren Center for Studies in American History, Harvard University, 1968), Vol. II, pp. 630-73; and also n. 106 below. [Upon inquiry Feigl suggests that Zilsel may have become a member after his—Feigl's—emigration to the United States.]

¹⁰² Herbert Feigl says (*ibid.*, p. 642) that it must have been in 1929, and no doubt he is right.

¹⁰³ My only published papers before I met Feigl—and for another four years after—were on educational topics. With the exception of the first [1925(a)] (published in an educational journal *Schulreform*) they were all ([1927(a)], [1931(a)], [1932(a)]) written at the invitation of Dr Eduard Burger, the editor of the educational journal *Die Quelle*.

¹⁰⁴ Feigl refers to the meeting in "Wiener Kreis in America". I have briefly described the opening move of our discussion in *C.& R.* [1963(a)], pp. 262 f.; see n. 27 on p. 263. See also "A Theorem on Truth-Content" [1966(g)], my contribution to the Feigl *Festschrift*.

¹⁰⁵ During that first long conversation, Feigl objected to my realism. (He was at that time in favour of a so-called "neutral monism", which I regarded as Berkeleyan idealism; I still do.) I am happy at the thought that Feigl too became a realist.

¹⁰⁶ Feigl writes, "Wiener Kreis in America", p. 641, that both Edgar Zilsel and I tried to preserve our independence "by remaining outside the Circle". But the fact is that I should have felt greatly honoured had I been invited, and it would never have occurred to me that membership in Schlick's seminar could endanger my independence in the slightest degree. (Incidentally, before reading this passage of Feigl's I did not realize that Zilsel was not a member of the Circle; Victor Kraft records him as one in *The Vienna Circle* [New York: Philosophical Library, 1953]; see p. 4.)

¹⁰⁷ See my publications listed on p. 44 of my paper "Quantum Mechanics Without 'The Observer' " [1967(k)].

¹⁰⁸ The manuscript of the first volume and parts of the manuscript of that version of *L.d.F.* which was cut by my uncle still exist. The manuscript of the second volume, with the possible exception of a few sections, seems to have been lost. (Added 1976.) The extant (German) material is at present being prepared by Troels Eggers Hansen for publication by J. C. B. Mohr in Tübingen.

¹⁰⁹ See in particular now my [1971(i)], reprinted with minor alterations as Chap. 1 of [1972(a)]; and also section 13 of my *Replies*.

¹⁰⁹a See sections 13 and 14 of my *Replies*.

¹¹⁰ See John Passmore's article "Logical Positivism" in *Encyclopedia of Philosophy*, ed. by Paul Edwards, Vol. V, p. 56 (see n. 7 above).

¹¹¹ This letter [1933(a)] was first published in *Erkenntnis*, 3, Nos. 4-6 (1933), 426 f. It is republished in translation in my *L.Sc.D.*, [1959(a)] and later editions, pp. 312-14, and in its orginal language in the second and later editions of *L.d.F.* [1966(e)], [1969(e)], etc., pp. 254-56.

¹¹² J. R. Weinberg, *An Examination of Logical Positivism* (London: Kegan Paul, Trench, Trubner & Co., 1936).

¹¹³ For a much fuller discussion of this legend, see sections 2 and 3 of my *Replies*.

¹¹³a (Added 1975.) I suppose that this phrase was an echo of John Laird, *Recent Philosophy* (London: Thornton Butterworth, 1936), who describes me as "a critic although also an ally" of the Vienna Circle (see p. 187; also pp. 187-90).

¹¹⁴ Cp. Arne Naess, *Moderne filosofer* (Stockholm: Almqvist & Wiksell/Gebers Förlag AB, (1965); English translation as *Four Modern Philosophers* (Chicago and London: University of Chicago Press, 1968). Naess writes in n. 13 on pp. 13 f. of the translation: "My own experience was rather similar to Popper's. . . . The polemic [in an unpublished book of Naess's] . . . written . . . between 1937

and 1939 was *intended* to be directed against *fundamental* theses and trends in the Circle, but was understood by Neurath as a proposal for modifications which were already accepted in principle and were to be made official in future publications. Upon this assurance I gave up plans to publish the work."

[114a] For the impact of all these discussions, see nn. 115 to 120.

[115] Cp. *C.&R.* [1963(a)], pp. 253 f.

[116] Rudolf Carnap, "Über Protokollsätze", *Erkenntnis*, **3** (1932), 215-28; see esp. 223-28.

[117] Cp. Rudolf Carnap, *Philosophy and Logical Syntax*, Psyche Miniatures (London: Kegan Paul, 1935), pp. 10-13, which correspond to *Erkenntnis*, **3** (1932), 224 ff. Carnap speaks here of "verification" where before he (correctly) reported me as speaking of "testing".

[118] Cp. C. G. Hempel, *Erkenntnis*, **5** (1935), esp. 249-54, where Hempel describes (with reference to Carnap's article "Über Protokollsätze") my procedure very much as Carnap had reported it.

[119] Rudolf Carnap, *Erkenntnis*, **5** (1935), 290-94 (with a reply to Reichenbach's criticism of *L.d.F.*). C. G. Hempel, *Deutsche Literaturzeitung*, **58** (1937), 309-14. (There was also a second review by Hempel.) I mention here only the more important reviews and criticisms from members of the Circle.

[120] Hans Reichenbach, *Erkenntnis*, **5** (1935), 367-84 (with a reply to Carnap's review of *L.d.F.*, to which Carnap in turn briefly replied). Otto Neurath, *Erkenntnis*, **5** (1935), 353-65.

[121] Werner Heisenberg, "Über quantentheoretische Umdeutung kinematischer und mechanischer Beziehungen", *Zeitschrift für Physik*, **33** (1925), 879-93; Max Born and Pascual Jordan, "Zur Quantenmechanik", *ibid.*, **34** (1925), 858-88; Max Born, Werner Heisenberg, and Pascual Jordan, "Zur Quantenmechanik II", *ibid.*, **35** (1926), 557-615. All three papers are translated in *Sources of Quantum Mechanics*, ed. by B. L. van der Waerden (Amsterdam: North-Holland Publishing Co., 1967).

[122] For a report of the debate see Niels Bohr, "Discussion with Einstein on Epistemological Problems in Atomic Physics", in *Albert Einstein: Philosopher-Scientist*, ed. by Paul Arthur Schilpp (Evanston, Ill.: Library of Living Philosophers, Inc., 1949); 3d ed. (La Salle, Ill.: Open Court Publishing Co., 1970), pp. 201-41. For a criticism of Bohr's contentions in this debate, see my *L.Sc.D.* [1959(a)], new Appendix * xi, pp. 444-56, *L.d.F.* [1966(e)] and [1969(e)], pp. 399-411, and [1967(k)].

[123] James L. Park and Henry Margenau, "Simultaneous Measurability in Quantum Theory", *International Journal of Theoretical*

Physics, **1** (1968), 211-83.

[124] See [1957(e)] and [1959(e)].

[125] See [1934(b)], pp. 171 f., [1959(a)], pp. 235 f., [1966(e)], pp. 184 f.; [1967(k)], pp. 34-38.

[126] *Albert Einstein: Philosopher-Scientist,* pp. 201-41 (see n. 122 above).

[127] See esp. [1957(i)], [1969(k)], now Chap. 5 of [1972(a)]; [1963 (h)]; [1966(f)], now Chap. 6 of [1972(a)]; [1967(k)]; and [1968(s)], now Chap. 3 of [1972(a)], in which also is reprinted, as Chap. 4, [1968(r)], where a fuller treatment can be found.

[128] Arthur March, *Die Grundlagen der Quantenmechanik* (Leipzig: Barth, 1931); cp. the Index of [1934(b)], [1959(a)], or [1966(e)].

[129] The results given here are partly of a later and partly of an earlier date. For my latest views see my contribution to the Landé *Festschrift,* "Particle Annihilation and the Argument of Einstein, Podolsky, and Rosen" [1971(n)].

[130] Cp. John von Neumann, *Mathematische Grundlagen der Quantenmechanik* (Berlin: Springer-Verlag, 1931), p. 170; or the translation, *Mathematical Foundations of Quantum Mechanics* (Princeton: Princeton University Press, 1955), p. 323. Thus even if von Neumann's argument were valid, it would not disprove determinism. Moreover, his assumed "rules" I and II on pp. 313 f. (cp. p. 225 f.) —German edition p. 167 (cp. p. 118)—are inconsistent with the commutation relations, as was first shown by G. Temple, "The Fundamental Paradox of the Quantum Theory", *Nature,* **135** (1935), 957. (That von Neumann's rules I and II are inconsistent with quantum mechanics was clearly implied by R. E. Peierls, "The Fundamental Paradox of the Quantum Theory", *Nature,* **136** [1935], 395. See also Park and Margenau, "Simultaneous Measurability in Quantum Theory" [see n. 123 above].) John S. Bell's paper is "On the Problem of Hidden Variables in Quantum Mechanics", *Reviews of Modern Physics,* **38** (1966), 447-52.

[131] C. S. Peirce, *Collected Papers of Charles Sanders Peirce,* ed. by Charles Hartshorne and Paul Weiss (Cambridge, Mass.: Harvard University Press, 1935), Vol. VI; see item 6.47 (first published 1892), p. 37.

[132] According to Schrödinger, Franz Exner made the suggestion in 1918: see Erwin Schrödinger, *Science, Theory, and Man* (New York: Dover Publications, 1957), pp. 71, 133, 142 f. (originally published as *Science and the Human Temperament* [London: Allen and Unwin, 1935]; see pp. 57 f., 107, 114); and *Die Naturwissenschaften,* **17** (1929), 732.

[133] von Neumann, *Mathematical Foundations of Quantum Mechanics*, pp. 326 f. (German edition p. 172): ". . . the apparent causal order of the world in the large (. . . [of the] objects visible to the naked eye) has certainly no other cause than the 'law of large numbers' and it *is completely independent of whether the natural laws governing the elementary processes are causal or not*". (Italics mine; von Neumann refers to Schrödinger.) Obviously this situation has no direct connection with quantum mechanics.

[134] See also my [1934(b)], [1959(a)], and later editions, section 78 (and also 67-70); [1950(b) and (c)]; [1957(g)], Preface; [1957(e)], [1959(e)]; [1966(f)], esp. section iv ([1972(a)], Chap. 6); [1967(k)].

[135] This is the view which I have upheld consistently. It can be found, I believe, in Richard von Mises.

[136] Alfred Landé, "Determinism versus Continuity in Modern Science", *Mind*, n.s. 67 (1958), 174-81, and *From Dualism to Unity in Quantum Physics* (Cambridge: Cambridge University Press, 1960), pp. 5-8. (I have called this argument "Landé's blade".) Added 1975: See now also John Watkins's paper "The Unity of Popper's Thought", in *The Philosophy of Karl Popper*, ed. by Paul Arthur Schilpp, pp. 371-412.

[137] Cp. [1957(e)], [1959(e)], and [1967(k)].

[138] Why should particles not be particles, at least to a first approximation, to be explained perhaps by a field theory? (A unified field theory of the type, say, of Mendel Sachs.) The only objection known to me derives from the "smear" interpretation of the Heisenberg indeterminacy formulae; if the "particles" are always "smeared", they are not real particles. But this objection does not seem to hold water: there is a statistical interpretation of quantum mechanics.
(Since writing the above I have written a contribution to the Landé *Festschrift* [1971(n)] referred to in n. 129 above. And since then, I have read two outstanding works defending the statistical interpretation of quantum mechanics: Edward Nelson, *Dynamical Theories of Brownian Motion* [Princeton: Princeton University Press, 1967], and L. E. Ballentine, "The Statistical Interpretation of Quantum Mechanics", *Reviews of Modern Physics*, 42 [1970], 358-81. It is most encouraging to find some support after a lone fight of thirty-seven years.)

[139] See esp. [1967(k)].

[139]a This sentence was added in 1975.

[140] W. Duane, "The Transfer in Quanta of Radiation Momentum to Matter", *Proceedings of the National Academy of Sciences* (Washington), 9 (1923), 158-64. The rule may be written:
$$\Delta p_x = nh/\Delta x \qquad \text{(n an integer).}$$

216 *Notes 141–9 to pp. 96–8.*

See Werner Heisenberg, *The Physical Principles of the Quantum Theory* (New York: Dover, 1930), p. 77.

141 Landé, *Dualism to Unity in Quantum Physics*, pp. 69, 102 (see n. 136 above), and *New Foundations of Quantum Mechanics* (Cambridge: Cambridge University Press, 1965), p. 5-9.

142 See esp. [1959(a)], [1966(e)], new Appendix * xi; and [1967(k)]

143 Albert Einstein, "Zur Elektrodynamik bewegter Körper", *Annalen der Physik*, 4th ser. **17**, 891-921; translated as "On the Electrodynamics of Moving Bodies" in Albert Einstein et. al., *The Principle of Relativity*, trans. by W. Pennett and G. B. Jeffrey (New York: Dover, 1923), pp. 35-65.

144 Einstein, *Relativity: Special and General Theory* (1920 and later editions). The German original is *Über die spezielle und die allgemeine Relativitätstheorie* (Brunswick: Vieweg & Sohn, 1916) (See nn. 32 and 33 above.)

144a (Added 1975.) This positivist and operationalist interpretation of Einstein's definition of simultaneity was rejected by me in my *O.S.* [1945(c)], p. 18, and more strongly in [1957(h)] and later editions, p. 20.

145 See Einstein's paper of 1905, section 1; in *Principle of Relativity*, pp. 38-40 (see n. 143 above).

146 By wrongly applying the very intuitive transitivity principle (*Tr*) to events beyond one system one can easily prove that *any* two events are simultaneous. But this contradicts the axiomatic assumption that within any inertial system there is a temporal order; that is, that for any two events within one system *one and only one* of the three relations holds: *a* and *b* are simultaneous; *a* comes before *b*; *b* comes before *a*. This is overlooked in an article by C. W. Rietdijk, "A Rigorous Proof of Determinism Derived from the Special Theory of Relativity", *Philosophy of Science*, **33** (1966), 341-44.

147 Cp. Marja Kokoszyńska, "Über den absoluten Wahrheitsbegriff und einige andere semantische Begriffe", *Erkenntnis*, **6** (1936), 143-65; cp. Carnap, *Introduction to Semantics*, pp. 240, 255 (see n. 15 above).

148 [1934(b)], section 84, "Wahrheit und Bewährung"; cp. Rudolf Carnap, "Wahrheit und Bewährung", *Proceedings of the IVth International Congress for Scientific Philosophy, Paris, 1935* (Paris: Hermann, 1936), Vol. IV, pp. 18-23; an adaptation appears in translation as "Truth and Confirmation", in *Readings in Philosophical Analysis*, ed. by Herbert Feigl and Wilfrid Sellars (New York: Appleton-Century-Crofts, Inc., 1949), pp. 119-27.

149 Many members of the Circle refused at first to operate with

the notion of truth: cp. Kokoszyńska, "Über den absoluten Wahr-heitsbegriff" (see n. 147 above).

[149a] (Added 1975.) See especially *L.Sc.D.* [1959(a)] and later edi-tions, points 4 to 6 on pp. 396 ff. (= *L.d.F.* [1966(e)], points 4 to 6 on pp. 349 f.).

[150] Cp. Appendix iv of [1934(b)] and [1959(a)]. After the war, a proof of the validity of the construction was given by L. R. B. Elton and myself. (It is, I am afraid, my fault that our paper was never published.) In his review of *L.Sc.D.* (*Mathematical Reviews*, **21** [1960], Review 6318) I. J. Good mentions a paper of his own, "Normal recurring Decimals", *Journal of the London Mathematical Society*, **21** (1946), 167-69. That my construction is valid follows easily—as David Miller has pointed out to me—from the consider-ations of this paper.

[151] Karl Menger, "The Formative Years of Abraham Wald and His Work in Geometry", *The Annals of Mathematical Statistics*, **23** (1952), 14-20; see esp. p. 18.

[152] Karl Menger, *ibid.*, p. 19.

[153] Abraham Wald, "Die Widerspruchsfreiheit des Kollektivs-begriffes der Wahrscheinlichkeitsrechnung", *Ergebnisse eines math-ematischen Kolloquiums*, **8** (1937), 38-72.

[154] Jean Ville, however, who read a paper in Menger's Colloquium at about the same time as Wald, produced a solution similar to my "ideal random sequence": he constructed a mathematical se-quence which from the very start was Bernoullian, that is, random. (It was a somewhat "longer" sequence than mine; in other words, it did not become as quickly insensitive to predecessor selection as mine did.) Cp. Jean A. Ville, *Étude critique de la notion de collec-tif, Monographies des Probabilités: calcul des probabilités et ses applications*, ed. by Émile Borel (Paris: Gauthier-Villars, 1939).

[155] For the various interpretations of probability, see esp. [1934 (b)], [1959(a)], and [1966(e)], section 48; and [1967(k)], pp. 28-34.

[156] See the Introduction before section 79 of [1934(b)], [1959(a)], [1966(e)].

[157] Compare to all this n. 243 to section 33, below, and text; see also section 16, text to n. 98.

[158] See [1959(a)], p. 401, n. 7; [1966(e)], p. 354.

[159] Some of this work is incorporated in the new appendices to *L.Sc.D.*, [1959(a)], [1966(e)], and later editions.

[160] I have read only two or three (very interesting) books about life in the Ghetto, especially Leopold Infeld, *Quest. The Evolution*

218   *Notes* 161–72 to pp. 107–15.

of a Scientist (London: Victor Gollancz, 1941).

161 Cp. [1945(c)] and later editions, Chap. 18, n. 22; Chap. 19, nn. 35-40 and text, Chap. 20, n. 44 and text.

162 See John R. Gregg and F. T. C. Harris, eds., *Form and Strategy in Science. Studies Dedicated to Joseph Henry Woodger* (Dordrecht: D. Reidel, 1964), p. 4.

163 Many years later Hayek told me that it was Gottfried von Haberler (later of Harvard) who in 1935 had drawn his attention to *L.d.F.*

164 Cp. Bertrand Russell, "The Limits of Empiricism", *Proceedings of the Aristotelian Society*, **36** (1936), 131-50. My remarks here allude especially to pp. 146 ff.

165 At the Copenhagen Congress—a congress for scientific philosophy—a very charming American gentleman took great interest in me. He said that he was the representative of the Rockefeller Foundation and gave me his card: "Warren Weaver, The European of the Rockefeller Foundation" (*sic*). This meant nothing to me; I had never heard about the foundations and their work. (Apparently I was very naive.) It was only years later that I realized that if I had understood the meaning of this encounter it might have led to my going to America instead of to New Zealand.

166 My opening talk to my first seminar in New Zealand was later published in *Mind* [1940(a)], and is now Chap. 15 of *C.&R.*, [1963 (a)] and later editions.

167 Cp. [1938(a)]; [1959(a)], [1966(e)], Appendix * ii.

168 Cp. H. von Halban, Jr, F. Joliot, and L. Kowarski, "Liberation of Neutrons in the Nuclear Explosion of Uranium", *Nature,* **143** (1939), 470 f.

169 Karl K. Darrow, "Nuclear Fission", *Annual Report of the Board of Regents of the Smithsonian Institution* (Washington, D.C.: Government Printing Office, 1941), pp. 155-59.

170 See the historical note in *The Poverty of Historicism* [1957(g)], p. iv; American ed. [1964(a)], p. v.

171 This connection is briefly described in my British Academy lecture [1960(d)], now the Introduction to *C.&R.* [1963(a)]; see sections II and III.

172 See *L.d.F.* [1934(b)], pp. 227 f.; [1959(a)], p. 55, n. 3 to section 11; [1966(e)], p. 27. See also [1940(a)], p. 404, [1963(a)], p. 313, where the method of testing is described as an essentially critical, that is, faultfinding method.

¹⁷³ Quite unnecessarily I used more often than not the ugly word "rationalist" (as in "rationalist attitude") where "rational" would have been better, and clearer. The (bad) reason for this was, I suppose, that I was arguing in defence of "rationalism".

¹⁷⁴ See *O.S.*, Vol. II, [1945(c)] and later editions, Chap. 24 (Chap. 14 of the German ed. [1958(i)]).

¹⁷⁵ Adrienne Koch used "Critical Rationalism" as the title of the excerpts from *O.S.* that she selected for her book *Philosophy for a Time of Crisis, An Interpretation with Key Writings by Fifteen Great Modern Thinkers* (New York: Dutton & Co., 1959) [1959(k)].

¹⁷⁶ Hans Albert, "Der kritische Rationalismus Karl Raimund Poppers", *Archiv für Rechts- und Sozialphilosophie*, **46** (1960), 391-415. Hans Albert, *Traktat über kritische Vernunft* (Tübingen: Mohr, 1968; and later editions).

¹⁷⁷ In the 4th ed. of *O.S.* [1962(c)], [1963(l) and (m)], and in later editions, there is an important *Addendum* to the second volume: "Facts, Standards, and Truth: A Further Criticism of Relativism" (pp. 369-96) which has been, so far as I know, overlooked by almost everybody.

¹⁷⁸ I now regard the analysis of causal explanation in section 12 of *L.d.F.* (and therefore also the remarks in *The Poverty* and other places) as superseded by an analysis based on my propensity interpretation of probability [1957(e)], [1959(e)], [1967(k)]. This interpretation, which presupposes my axiomatization of the probability calculus (see, for example, [1959(e)], p. 40; [1959(a)], [1966(e)], Appendices *iv and *v), allows us to discard the formal mode of speaking and to put things in a more realistic way. We interpret
(1) $p(a,b) = r$
to mean: "The propensity of the state of affairs (or the conditions) b to produce a equals r." (r is some real number.) A statement like (1) may be a conjecture, or deducible from some conjecture; for example, a conjecture about laws of nature.

We can then causally explain (in a generalized and weaker sense of "explain") a as due to the presence of b, even if r does not equal 1. That b is a classical or complete or deterministic cause of a can be stated by a conjecture like
(2) $p(a,bx) = 1$ for every x,
where x ranges over *all* possible states of affairs, including states incompatible with a or b. (We need not even exclude "impossible" states of affairs.) This shows the advantages of an axiomatization like mine, in which the second argument may be inconsistent.

This way of putting things is, clearly, a generalization of my analysis of causal explanation. In addition, it allows us to state *"nomic conditionals"* of various types—of type (1) with $r<1$, of type (1) with $r = 1$, and of type (2). (Thus it offers a solution of the so-called problem of counterfactual conditionals.) It allows us to solve Kneale's problem (see [1959(a)], [1966(e)], Appendix *x) of distinguishing between *accidentally* universal statements and naturally or physically *necessary* connections, as stated by (2). Notice however that there may be physically nonnecessary connections, which nevertheless are not accidental, like (1) with an *r* not far from unity. See also the reply to Suppes in my *Replies*.

[179] See also *The Poverty* [1957(g)], p. 125. Reference should be made to J. S. Mill, *A System of Logic*, 8th ed., Book III, Chap. XII, section 1.

[180] See Karl Hilferding, "Le fondement empirique de la science", *Revue des questions scientifiques*, 110 (1936), 85-116. In this paper Hilferding (a physical chemist) explains at considerable length my views, from which he deviates in allowing inductive probabilities in the sense of Reichenbach.

[181] See also Hilferding, "Le fondement empirique de la science", p. 111, with a reference to p. 27 (that is, section 12) of the 1st ed. of *L.d.F.* [1934(b)].

[182] See *The Poverty* [1957(g)], pp. 140 f. and 149 f., further developed in Chap. 14 of *O.S.* [1962(c) and (d)], [1963(l) and (m)]; [1966(i)]; [1967(d)]; [1968(r)] (now [1972(a)], Chap. 4); [1969(j)]; and in many unpublished lectures given at the London School of Economics and elsewhere.

[183] See [1957(g)], sections 31 and 32, esp. pp. 149 and 154 f.

[184] See Vol. II of [1962(c)], [1963(l) and (m)], pp. 93-99, and esp. pp. 97 f.

[185] See [1950(a)], pp. 170 f.; [1952(a)], Vol. I, pp. 174-76.

[186] See [1957(g)], sections 30-32; [1962(c)]; and more recently [1968 (r)] and [1969(j)].

[187] It was this situation which in 1945 led to the publication of a pamphlet *Research and the University* [1945(e)], drafted by me in co-operation with Robin S. Allan and Hugh Parton, and signed, after some minor changes, by Henry Forder and others. The situation changed in New Zealand very soon, but meanwhile I had left for England. (Added 1975: The story of this pamphlet is told by E. T. Beardsley in *A History of the University of Canterbury, 1873-1973*, by W. J. Gardner et al. [Christchurch, N.Z.: University of Canterbury, 1973].)

[188] See esp. [1947(a)] and [1947(b)]. I was led to this work, partly, by problems of probability theory: the rules of "natural deduction" are very closely related to the usual definitions in Boolean algebra.

See also Alfred Tarski's papers of 1935 and 1936, which now form Chaps. XI and XII of his book *Logic, Semantics, Metamathematics*, trans. by J. H. Woodger (London and New York: Oxford University Press, 1956).

[189] [1950(b) and (c)].

[190] [1946(b)]; Chap. 9 of [1963(a)] and later editions.

[191] The minutes of the meeting are not quite reliable. For example the title of my paper is given there (and it was so given on the printed list of meetings) as "Methods in Philosophy" instead of "Are there Philosophical Problems?", which was the title ultimately chosen by me. Furthermore, the Secretary thought I was complaining that his invitation was for a *brief* paper, to introduce a *discussion*—which in fact suited me very well. He completely missed my point (puzzle versus problem).

[192] See *C.&R.* [1963(a)], p. 55.

[193] See p. 167 of Ryle's review of *O.S.* in *Mind*, **56** (1947), 167–72.

[194] At a very early stage of the course he formulated, and showed the validity of, the metalinguistic rule of *indirect proof*:
    If *a* logically follows from non-*a*, then *a* is demonstrable.

[195] Now in Tarski, *Logic, Semantics, Metamathematics*, pp. 409–20 (see n. 188 above).

[196] *Ibid.*, pp. 419 f.

[197] See [1947(a)], [1947(b)], [1947(c)], [1948(b)], [1948(c)], [1948(e)], [1948(f)]. The subject has now been advanced by Lejewski. See his paper "Popper's Theory of Formal or Deductive Interference", in *The Philosophy of Karl Popper*, ed. by Paul Arthur Schilpp, pp. 632–70.

[198] The mistake was connected with the rules of substitution or replacement of expressions: I had mistakenly thought that it was sufficient to formulate these rules in terms of *interdeducibility*, while in fact what was needed was *identity* (of expressions). To explain this remark: I postulated, for example, that if in a statement *a*, two (disjoint) subexpressions *x* and *y* are both, wherever they occur, replaced by an expression *z*, then the resulting expression (provided it is a statement) is *interdeducible* with the result of replacing first *x* wherever it occurs by *y* and then *y* wherever it occurs by *z*. What I should have postulated was that the first result is *identical* with the second result. I realized that this was stronger, but I mistakenly thought that the weaker rule would suffice. The interesting (and so far unpublished) conclusion to which I was led later by repairing this mistake was that there was an essential difference between propositional and functional logic: while pro-

positional logic can be constructed as a theory of sets of statements, whose elements are partially ordered by the relation of deducibility, functional logic needs in addition a specifically morphological approach since it must refer to the subexpression of an expression, using a concept like *identity* (with respect to expressions). But no more is needed than the ideas of identity and subexpression; no further description especially of the shape of the expressions.

199 [1950(d)].

200 [1950(b) and c)].

201 See Kurt Gödel, "A Remark About the Relationship Between Relativity Theory and Idealistic Philosophy", in *Albert Einstein: Philosopher-Scientist*, pp. 555-62 (see n. 122 above). Gödel's arguments were (a) philosophical, (b) based on the special theory (see esp. his n. 5), and (c) based on his new cosmological solutions of Einstein's field equations, that is, on the possibility of closed four-dimensional orbits in a (rotating) Gödel universe, as described by him in "An Example of a New Type of Cosmological Solutions of Einstein's Field Equations of Gravitation", *Reviews of Modern Physics*, 21 (1949), 447-50. (The results (c) were challenged by S. Chandrasekhar and James P. Wright, "The Geodesics in Gödel's Universe", *Proceedings of the National Academy of Sciences*, 47 [1961], 341-47. Note however that even if Gödel's closed orbits are not geodesics, this does not in itself constitute a refutation of Gödel's views; for a Gödel orbit was never meant to be fully ballistic or gravitational: even that of a moon rocket is only partially so.)

202 Cp. Schilpp, ed., *Albert Einstein: Philosopher-Scientist*, p. 688 (see n. 122 above). Not only do I agree with Einstein, but I would even go so far as to say this. Were the existence (in the physical sense) of Gödel's orbits a *consequence* of Einstein's theory (which it is not), then this fact should be held against the theory. It would not, to be sure, be a conclusive argument: there is no such thing; and we may have to accept Gödel orbits. I think, however, that in such a case we ought to look for some alternative.

203 Harald Høffding wrote (in *Den menneskelige Tanke* [Copenhagen: Nordisk Forlag, 1910], p. 303; in the German translation *Der menschliche Gedanke* [Leipzig: O. Riesland, 1911], p. 333): "Knowledge, which is to describe and explain the world for us, always itself forms part of the existing world; for this reason new entities may always emerge to be dealt with by it. . . . We have no knowledge going beyond experience; but at no stage are we entitled to look upon experience as complete. Thus knowledge, even at its highest, provides us with nothing more than a segment of the existing world. Every reality, we may find, is itself again a part of

a wider reality." (I owe this passage to Arne Petersen.) The best intuitive idea of this incompleteness is that of a map showing the table on which the map is being drawn, and the map as it is drawn. (See also the reply to Watkins in my *Replies*.)

²⁰⁴ See my paper [1948(d)], now [1963(a)], Chap. 16 and, more fully, [1957(i)] and [1969(k)], now [1972(a)], Chap. 5.

²⁰⁴a (Added 1975: See now my [1974(z₂)].)

²⁰⁵ There is an interesting and hard-hitting article by William Kneale, "Scientific Revolution for Ever?", *The British Journal for the Philosophy of Science*, 19 (1968), 27-42, in which he seems to sense something of the position outlined above, and to criticize it. (In many points of detail, however, he misunderstands me; for example, on p. 36: "For if there is no truth, there cannot be any approximation to truth. . . ." This is true. But where did I ever suggest that there is no truth? The set of true theoretical statements of physics may not be [finitely] axiomatizable; in view of Gödel's theorem, it almost certainly is not. But the sequence of our attempts to produce better and better finite axiomatizations may well be a revolutionary sequence in which we constantly create new theoretical and mathematical means for more nearly approaching this unattainable end.

²⁰⁶ See *C.&R.* [1963(a)], p. 114 (n. 30 to Chap. 3 and text), and the third paragraph of section 19 of the present *Autobiography*.

²⁰⁷ In a letter to me of June 15, 1935, Einstein approved of my views concerning "falsifiability as the decisive property of any theory about reality".

²⁰⁸ See *Albert Einstein: Philosopher-Scientist*, p. 674 (see n. 122 above); also relevant is Einstein's letter on p. 29 of Schrödinger et al., *Briefe zur Wellenmechanik*, ed. by K. Przibram (Vienna: Springer-Verlag, 1963); in the English translation, *Letters on Wave Mechanics* (London: Vision, 1967), the letter appears on pp. 31 f.

²⁰⁹ See my paper "What is Dialectic?", now Chap. 15 of *C.&R.* [1963(a)]. This is a stylistically revised form of [1940(a)], with several additional footnotes. The passage summarized here in the text is from *C.&R.*, p. 313, first new paragraph. As shown by n. 3 of this chapter (n. 1 of [1940(a)]), I regarded this description (in which I stressed that testing a theory is part of its criticism; that is, of *EE*) as summarizing the scientific procedure described in *L.d.F.*

²¹⁰ Compare with this the problems "which comes first, the hen (*H*) or the egg (*O*)?", and "Which comes first, the Hypothesis (*H*) or the Observation (*O*)?", discussed on p. 47 of *C.&R.* [1963(a)].

See also [1949(d)], now in English as the Appendix to [1972(a)]; esp. pp. 345 f.

²¹¹ See, for example, [1968(r)], esp. pp. 36-39; [1972(a)], pp. 170-78.

²¹² Schrödinger defends this view as a form of idealism or pan-psychism in the second part of his posthumous book, *Mein Welt-bild* (Vienna: Zsolnay, 1961, Chap. 1, pp. 105-14); English trans-lation, *My View of the World* (Cambridge: Cambridge University Press, 1964, pp. 61-67).

²¹³ I am alluding to Winston Churchill, *My Early Life* (London, 1930). The arguments can be found in Chap. IX ("Education at Bangalore"), that is, on pp. 131 f. of the Keystone Library edition (1934), or the Macmillan edition (1944). I have quoted from the passage at length in section 5 of Chap. 2 of [1972(a)]; see pp. 42-43.

²¹⁴ The quotation is not from memory but from the first para-graph of Chap. 6 of Erwin Schrödinger, *Mind and Matter* (Cam-bridge: Cambridge University Press, 1958), p. 88; and of Erwin Schrödinger, *What Is Life?* & *Mind and Matter* (Cambridge: Cam-bridge University Press, 1967; two books issued in one paperback volume), p. 166. The views which Schrödinger defended in our conversations were very similar.

²¹⁵ [1956(b)].

²¹⁶ Incidentally, the replacement here of "impossible" by "infinitely improbable" (perhaps a dubious replacement) would not affect the main point of these considerations; for though entropy is connected with probability, not every reference to probability brings in entropy.

²¹⁷ See *Mind and Matter*, p. 86; or *What is Life?* & *Mind and Matter*, p. 164.

²¹⁸ See *Mind and Matter*, or *What is Life?* & *Mind and Matter*, loc. cit. He used the wording "methodology of the physicist", prob-ably to dissociate himself from a methodology of physics emanating from a philosopher.

²¹⁹ *What is Life?*, pp. 74 f.

²²⁰ *Ibid.*, p. 78.

²²¹ *Ibid.*, p. 79.

²²² See my [1967(b) and (h)].

²²³ See, for example, "Quantum Mechanics without 'The Obser-ver'" [1967(k)]; "Of Clouds and Clocks" [1966(f)] ([1972(a)], Chap. 6); "Is there an Epistemological Problem of Perception?" [1968(e)];

"On the Theory of the Objective Mind" [1968(r)], "Epistemology Without a Knowing Subject" [1968(s)] (respectively Chaps. 4 and 3 of *Obj. Kn.* [1972(a)]; and "A Pluralist Approach to the Philosophy of History" [1969(j)].

[224] Tarski has often been criticized for attributing truth to *sentences*: a sentence, it is said, is a mere string of words without meaning; thus it cannot be true. But Tarski speaks of *"meaningful sentences"*, and so this criticism, like so much philosophical criticism, is not only invalid but simply irresponsible. See *Logic, Semantics, Metamathematics,* p. 178 (Definition 12) and p. 156, n. 1 (see n. 188 above); and, for comments, my [1955(d)] (now an addendum to Chap. 9 of my [1972(a)] and [1959(a)], [1966(e)], and later editions, n. *1 to section 84.

[225] This holds even for the validity of some very simple rules, rules whose validity has been denied on intuitive grounds by some philosophers (esp. G. E. Moore); the simplest of all these rules is: from any statement *a*, we may validly deduce *a* itself. Here the impossibility of constructing a counterexample can be shown very easily. Whether or not anybody accepts this argument is his private affair. If he does not, he is simply mistaken. See also my [1947(a)].

[226] I have said things like this many times since [1934(b)], sections 27 and 29, and [1947(a)]—see [1968(s)]; ([1972(a)], Chap. 3), for example; and I have suggested that what I have called the "degree of corroboration of a hypothesis *h* in the light of the tests or of the evidence *e*", may be interpreted as a condensed report of the past critical discussions of the hypothesis *h* in the light of the tests *e*. (Cp. nn. 156-58 to section 20 above, and text.) Thus, I wrote, for example, in *L.Sc.D.* [1959(a)], p. 414: " . . . $C(h,e)$ can be adequately interpreted as degree of corroboration of *h*—or of the rationality of our belief in *h*, in the light of tests—only if *e* consists of reports of the outcome of sincere attempts to refute *h*. . .". In other words, only a report of a discussion which is sincerely critical can be said to determine, even partially, the *degree of rationality* (of our belief in *h*). In the quoted passage (as opposed to my terminology here in the text) I used the words "degree of rationality of our belief", which should be even clearer than "rational belief"; see also *ibid.*, p. 407, where I explain this, and make my objectivist attitude sufficiently clear, I think (as I have done *ad nauseam* elsewhere). Nevertheless the quoted passage has been construed (by Professor Lakatos, "Changes in the Problem of Inductive Logic", in *Problem of Inductive Logic*, ed. by Lakatos, n. 6 on pp. 412 f. [see n. 41 above]) as a symptom of the shakiness of my objectivism; and an indication that I am prone to subjectivist lapses. It is, I think, impossible to avoid all misunderstandings. I wonder how my present remarks about the insignificance of belief will be construed.

²²⁷ See esp. my [1971(i)], now Chap. 1 of [1972(a)].

²²⁸ What I have called the "fashionable view" may be traced back to J. S. Mill. For modern formulations see P. F. Strawson, *Introduction to Logical Theory* (London: Methuen & Co., 1952; New York: John Wiley & Sons, 1952), pp. 249 f.; Nelson Goodman, *Fact, Fiction, and Forecast* (Cambridge, Mass.: Harvard University Press, 1955), pp. 63-66; and Rudolf Carnap, "Inductive Logic and Inductive Intuition", in *Problem of Inductive Logic*, ed. by Lakatos, pp. 258-67, particularly p. 265 (see n. 41 above).

²²⁹ This seems to me a more carefully worded form of one of Carnap's arguments; see Carnap, "Inductive Logic and Inductive Intuition", p. 265, the passage beginning: "I think that it is not only legitimate to appeal to inductive reasoning in defending inductive reasoning, but that it is indispensable."

²³⁰ *Ibid.*, p. 311.

²³¹ For Carnap's "instance confirmation" see my *C.&R.* [1963(a)], pp. 282 f. What Carnap calls the "instance confirmation" of a law (a universal hypothesis) is equal in fact to the degree of confirmation (or the probability) of the next instance of the law; and this approaches 1/2 or 0.99, provided the relative frequency of the observed favourable instances approaches 1/2, or 0.99, respectively. As a consequence, a law that is refuted by every second instance (or by every hundredth instance) has an instance confirmation that approaches 1/2 (or 0.99); which is absurd. I explained this first in [1934(b)], p. 191, that is [1959(a)], p. 257, long before Carnap thought of instance confirmation, in a discussion of various possibilities of attributing "probability" to a hypothesis; and I then said that this consequence was "devastating" for this idea of probability. I am puzzled by Carnap's reply to this in Lakatos, ed., *Problem of Inductive Logic*, pp. 309 f. (see n. 41 above). There Carnap says about instance confirmation that its numerical value "is . . . an important characteristic of the law. In Popper's example, the law which is in the average satisfied by one half of the instances, has, on the basis of my definition, not the probability 1/2, as Popper erroneously believes, but 0." But although it does have what Carnap (and I) both call "probability 0", it also has what Carnap calls "instance confirmation 1/2"; and this was the issue under discussion (even though I used in 1934 the term "probability" in my criticism of the function which Carnap much later called "instance confirmation").

²³² I am grateful to David Miller for pointing out to me this characteristic of all Hintikka's systems. Jaakko Hintikka's first paper on the subject was "Towards a Theory of Inductive Generalization", in *Logic, Methodology and Philosophy of Science*, ed. by

Yehoshua Bar-Hillel (Amsterdam: North-Holland Publishing Co., 1964), Vol. II, pp. 274-88. Full references can be found in Risto Hilpinen, "Rules of Acceptance and Inductive Logic", *Acta Philosophica Fennica*, **21** (1968).

[233] According to Carnap's position of approximately 1949-56 (at least), inductive logic is analytically true. But if so, I cannot see how the allegedly rational degree of belief could undergo such radical changes as from 0 (strongest disbelief) to 0.7 (mild belief). According to Carnap's latest theories "inductive intuition" operates as a court of appeal. I have given reasons to show how irresponsible and biased this court of appeal is; see my [1968(i)], esp. pp. 297-303.

[234] Cp. *Fact, Fiction, and Forecast*, p. 65 (see n. 228 above).

[235] See [1968(i)]. For my positive theory of corroboration, see the end of section 20 above, and also the end of section 33, esp. n. 243 and text.

[236] See [1957(i)] and [1969(k)], now reprinted as Chap. 5 of [1972 (a)]; and [1957(l)].

[237] See [1959(a)], end of section 29, and p. 315 of the translation of [1935(a)], there in Appendix *i, 2, pp. 315-17; or [1963(a)], Introduction; and see below, n. 243 and text.

[238] I gave a course of lectures on this particular problem—criticism without justification—in the Institute of Advanced Studies in Vienna in 1964.

[239] See esp. [1957(i)] and [1969(k)], now Chap. 5 of [1972(a)]; Chap. 10 of [1963(a)]; and Chap. 2 of [1972(a)]. See n. 165a to my *Replies*.

[240] See [1934(b)], p. 186; [1959(a)], p. 252 (section 79).

[241] Cp. [1958(c)], [1958(f)], [1958(g)]; now Chap. 8 of [1963(a)].

[242] The term "metaphysical research programme" was used in my lectures from about 1949 on, if not earlier; but it did not get into print until 1958, though it is the main topic of the last chapter of the *Postscript* (in galley proofs since 1957). I made the *Postscript* available to my colleagues, and Professor Lakatos acknowledges that what he calls "scientific research programmes" are in the tradition of what I described as "metaphysical research programmes" ("metaphysical" because nonfalsifiable). See p. 183 of his paper "Falsification and the Methodology of Scientific Research Programmes", in *Criticism and the Growth of Knowledge*, ed. by Imre Lakatos and Alan Musgrave (Cambridge: Cambridge University Press, 1970).

243 Incidentally, realists believe, of course, in truth (and believers in truth believe in reality; see [1963(a)], p. 116)—they even know that there are "as many" true statements as there are false ones. (For what follows here, see also the end of section 20, above.) Since the purpose of this volume is to further the discussion between my critics and myself, I may here perhaps refer briefly to G. J. Warnock's review of my *L.Sc.D.* in *Mind*, 59 (1960), 99-101 (see also n. 25 to section 7 above). Here we read, on p. 100, about my views on the problem of induction: "Now Popper says emphatically that this venerable problem is insoluble. . . ". I am sure I have never said so, least of all emphatically, for I always flattered myself that I actually solved this problem in the book under review. Later we read, on the same page: "[Popper] wishes to claim for his own views, not that they offer a solution of Hume's problem, but that they do not permit it to arise." This clashes with the suggestion at the beginning of my book (esp. sections 1 and 4) that what I have called Hume's problem of induction is one of the two fundamental problems of the theory of knowledge. Later we get quite a good version of my formulation of that problem: "how. . . can [we] be justified in regarding as true, or even probably true, the general statements of. . . a scientific theory". My straight answer to this question was: *we cannot be justified*. (But we can sometimes be justified in *preferring* one competing theory to another; see the text to which the present note is appended.) Yet the review continues: "There is, Popper holds, no hope of answering this question, since it requires that we should solve the insoluble problem of induction. But, he says, it is needless and misguided to ask this question at all." None of the passages I have quoted are meant to be *critical*; rather, they claim to *report* what I "say emphatically"; "wish to claim"; "hold"; and "say". A little later in the review the criticism begins with the words: "Now does this eliminate the 'insoluble' problem of induction?".

Since I am at it, I may as well mention that this reviewer concentrates his criticism of my book upon the following thesis which I am putting here in italics (p. 101; the word "rely" here means, as the context shows, "rely for the future"): "Popper evidently assumes, what of course his language implies, that *we are entitled to rely* [for the future] *upon a well-corroborated theory*". But I have never assumed anything like this. What I assert is that a well-corroborated theory (which has been critically discussed and compared with its competitors, and which has *so far* "survived") is rationally *preferable* to a less well-corroborated theory; and that (short of proposing a new competing theory) we have no better way open to us than to prefer it, and act upon it, *even though we know very well that it may let us down badly in some future cases*. Thus I have to reject the reviewer's criticism as based on a complete misunderstanding of my text, caused by his substitution of his own problem of induction (the traditional problem) for mine (which is very different). See now also [1971(i)], reprinted as Chap. 1 of [1972(a)].

²⁴⁴ See Ernst Mach, *Die Prinzipien der Wärmelehre* (Leipzig: Barth, 1896), p. 240; on p. 239 the term "general philosophical" is equated with "metaphysical"; and Mach hints that Mayer (whom he greatly admired) was inspired by "metaphysical" intuitions.

²⁴⁵ See "A Note on Berkeley as Precursor of Mach" [1953(d)]; now Chap. 6 of [1963(a)].

²⁴⁶ See Schrödinger et al., *Briefe zur Wellenmechanik*, p. 32; I have used my own translations, but the letter can be found in English in the English ed., *Letters on Wave Mechanics*, pp. 35 f. (see n. 208 above). Einstein's letter is dated August 9, 1939.

²⁴⁷ Cp. Erwin Schrödinger, "Die gegenwärtige Situation in der Quantenmechanik", *Die Naturwissenschaften*, **23** (1935), 807-12, 823-28, 844-49.

²⁴⁸ (Italics mine.) See Einstein's letter referred to in n. 246 above, and also his very similar letter of December 22, 1950, in the same book, pp. 36 f. (translation, pp. 39 f.). (Note that Einstein takes it for granted that a probabilistic theory must be interpreted subjectively if it refers to a single case; this is an issue on which he and I disagreed from 1935 on. See [1959(a)], p. 459, and my footnote.)

²⁴⁹ See especially the references to Franz Exner's views in Schrödinger, *Science, Theory and Man*, pp. 71, 133, 142 f. (see n. 132 above).

²⁵⁰ Cp. my paper "Quantum Mechanics without 'The Observer'" [1967(k)], where references to my other writings in this field will be found (especially [1957(e)] and [1959(e)]).

²⁵¹ Van der Waerden's letter is dated October 19, 1968. (It is a letter in which he also criticizes me for a mistaken historical reference to Jacob Bernoulli, on p. 29 of [1967(k)].)

²⁵² Since this is an autobiography, I might perhaps mention that in 1947 or 1948 I received a letter from Victor Kraft, writing in the name of the Faculty of Philosophy of the University of Vienna, asking whether I would be prepared to take up Schlick's chair. I replied that I would not leave England.

²⁵³ Max Planck questioned Mach's competence as a physicist even within Mach's favourite field, the phenomenological theory of heat. See Max Planck, "Zur Machschen Theorie der physikalischen Erkenntnis", *Physikalische Zeitschrift*, **11** (1910), 1186-90. (See also Planck's preceding paper, "Die Einheit des physikalischen Weltbildes", *Physikalische Zeitschrift*, **10** [1909], 62-75; and Mach's

reply, "Die Leitgedanken meiner wissenschaftlichen Erkenntnislehre und ihre Aufnahme durch die Zeitgenossen", *Physikalische
Zeitschrift*, **11** [1910], 599-606.)

[254] See Josef Mayerhöfer, "Ernst Machs Berufung an die Wiener
Universität, 1895", in *Symposium aus Anlass des 50. Todestages
von Ernst Mach* (Ernst Mach Institut, Freiburg im Breisgau, 1966),
pp. 12-25. A charming (German) biography of Boltzmann is E.
Broda, *Ludwig Boltzmann* (Vienna: Franz Deuticke, 1955).

[255] See n. 256 and n. 261 below.

[256] See E. Zermelo, "Über einen Satz der Dynamik und die mechanische Wärmetheorie", *Wiedemannsche Annalen (Annalen der
Physik)*, **57** (1896), 485-94. Twenty years before Zermelo, Boltzmann's friend Loschmidt had pointed out that by reversing all
velocities in a gas the gas can be made to run backward and thus
to revert to the ordered state from which it is supposed to have
lapsed into disorder. This objection of Loschmidt's is called the
"reversibility objection", while Zermelo's is called the "recurrence
objection".

[257] Paul and Tatiana Ehrenfest, "Über zwei bekannte Einwände
gegen das Boltzmannsche *H*-Theorem", *Physikalische Zeitschrift*, **8**
(1907), 311-14.

[258] See, for example, Max Born, *Natural Philosophy of Cause
and Chance* (Oxford: Oxford University Press, 1949), who writes
on p. 58: "Zermelo, a German mathematician, who worked on
abstract problems like the theory of Cantor's sets and transfinite
numbers, ventured into physics by translating Gibbs's work on
statistical mechanics into German." But note the dates: Zermelo
criticized Boltzmann in 1896; published the translation of Gibbs
whom he greatly admired in 1905; wrote his first paper on set
theory in 1904, and his second only in 1908. Thus he was a
physicist before he became an "abstract" mathematician.

[259] Cp. Erwin Schrödinger, "Irreversibility", *Proceedings of the
Royal Irish Academy*, **53A** (1950), 189-95.

[260] See Ludwig Boltzmann, "Zu Hrn. Zermelo's Abhandlung:
'Über die mechanische Erklärung irreversibler Vorgänge'", *Wiedemannsche Annalen (Annalen der Physik)*, **60** (1897), 392-98. The
gist of the passage is repeated in his *Vorlesungen über Gastheorie*
(Leipzig: J. A. Barth, 1898), Vol. II, pp. 257 f.; again I have used my
own translation, but the corresponding passage can be found in L.
Boltzmann, *Lectures on Gas Theory*, trans. by Stephen G. Brush
(Berkeley and Los Angeles: University of California Press, 1964),
pp. 446 f.

[261] Boltzmann's best proof of $dS/dt \geq 0$ was based upon his so-

called collision integral. This represents the *average* effect upon a single molecule of *the system of all the other molecules of the gas.* My suggestion is that (a) it is not the collisions which lead to Boltzmann's results, but the *averaging* as such; the time coordinate plays a part because there was no averaging before the collision, and so entropy increase *seems* to be the result of physical collisions. My suggestion is further that, quite apart from Boltzmann's derivation, (b) collisions *between the molecules of the gas* are not decisive for an entropy increase, though the assumption of molecular disorder (which enters through the averaging) is. For assume that a gas takes up at one time one half of a box: soon it will "fill" the whole box —even if it is so rare that (practically) *the only collisions are with the walls.* (The walls are essential; see point (3) of [1956(g)].) I further suggest that (c) we may interpret Boltzmann's derivation to mean that an ordered system *X* becomes almost certainly (that is, with probability 1) disordered *upon collision with any system Y* (say, the walls) which is in a state chosen at random, or more precisely, in a state not matched in every detail to the state of *X*. In this interpretation the theorem is of course valid. For the "reversibility objection" (see n. 256 above) would only show that for systems such as *X* in its disordered state *there exists at least one* other ("matched") system *Y* which by (reverse) collision would return the system *X* to its ordered state. The mere mathematical existence (even in a constructive sense) of such a system *Y* which is "matched" to *X* creates no difficulty, since the probability that *X* should collide with a system matched to itself will be equal to zero. Thus the *H*-theorem, $dS/dt \geq 0$, holds *almost certainly for all colliding systems.* (This explains why the second law holds for all *closed* systems.) The "recurrence objection" (see n. 256 above) is valid, but it does not mean that the probability of a recurrence— of the system's taking up a state in which it was before—will be appreciably greater than zero for a system of any degree of complexity. Still, there are open problems. (See my series of notes in *Nature*, [1956(b)], [1956(g)], [1957(d)], [1958(b)], [1965(f)], [1967(b) and (h)], and my note [1957(f)] in *The British Journal for the Philosophy of Science*.)

[262] See [1956(b)] and section 30 (on Schrödinger) above, esp. the text to nn. 215 and 216.

[263] See above, section 30. I lectured on these matters to the Oxford University Science Society on October 20, 1967. In this lecture I also gave a brief criticism of Schrödinger's influential paper "Irreversibility" (see n. 259 above); he writes there on p. 191: "I wish to reformulate the laws of. . . irreversibility. . . in such a way, that the logical contradiction [which] *any* derivation of those laws from reversible models seems to involve is removed once and for ever." Schrödinger's reformulation consists in an ingenious way (a method

later called the "method of branch systems") of introducing Boltz-
mannian arrows of time by a kind of operational definition; the
result is Boltzmann's. And the method, like Boltzmann's, is too
strong: it does not (as Schrödinger thinks) save Boltzmann's derivation—that is, his physical explanation of the *H*-theorem; instead, it
provides, rather, a (tautological) definition from which the second
law follows immediately. So it makes any physical explanation of
the second law redundant.

²⁶⁴ *Die Prinzipien der Wärmelehre*, p. 363 (see n. 244 above). Boltzmann is not mentioned there by name (his name appears, with a
modicum of praise, on the next page) but the description of the
"move" ("*Zug*") is unmistakable: it really describes Boltzmann's
wavering. Mach's attack in this chapter ("The Opposition between
Mechanistic and Phenomenological Physics"), if read between
the lines, is severe; and it is combined with a hint of self-congrat-
ulation and with a confident belief that the judgement of history
will be on his side; as indeed it was.

²⁶⁵ The present section has been added here because it is, I believe,
significant for an understanding of my intellectual development, or
more especially, for my more recent fight against subjectivism in
physics.

²⁶⁶ See Leo Szilard, "Über die Ausdehnung der phänomenolo-
gischen Thermodynamik auf die Schwankungserscheinungen", *Zeitschrift für Physik*, **32** (1925), 753-88 and "Über die Entropiever-
minderung in einem thermodynamischen System bei Eingriffen
intelligenter Wesen", *ibid.*, **53** (1929), 840-56; this second paper has
been translated as "On the Decrease of Entropy in a Thermo-
dynamic System by the Intervention of Intelligent Beings", *Behavioural Science*, **9** (1964), 301-10. Szilard's views were refined by L.
Brillouin, *Scientific Uncertainty and Information* (New York: Academic Press, 1964). But I believe that all these views have been
clearly and decisively criticized by J. D. Fast, *Entropy*, revised and
enlarged reprint of 2d ed. (London: Macmillan, 1970), Appendix 5.
I owe this reference to Troels Eggers Hansen.

²⁶⁷ Norbert Wiener, *Cybernetics: Or Control & Communication in
the Animal & the Machine* (Cambridge, Mass.: M.I.T. Press, 1948),
pp. 44 f., tried to marry this theory to Boltzmann's theory; but I
do not think that the spouses actually met in logical space—not
even in that of Wiener's book, where they are confined to strictly
different contexts. (They could meet through the postulate that
what is called consciousness is *essentially* growth of knowledge,
that is, information increase; but I really do not wish to encourage
idealistic speculation, and I greatly fear the fertility of such a mar-
riage.) However, the subjective theory of entropy is closely connected
both with Maxwell's famous demon and with Boltzmann's *H*-

theorem. Max Born, for example, who believes in the original interpretation of the *H*-theorem, attributes to it a (partially?) subjective meaning, interpreting the collision integral and the "averaging" (both discussed in n. 261 to section 35, above) as "mixing mechanical knowledge with ignorance of detail"; this mixing of knowledge and ignorance, he says, "leads to irreversibility". Cp. Born, *Natural Philosophy of Cause and Chance,* p. 59 (see n. 258 above).

[268] See, for example, sections 34-39 and 43 of *L.d.F.* [1934(b)], [1966(e)], and of *L.Sc.D.* [1959(a)].

[269] See esp. [1959(a)], new Appendix *xi (2), p. 444; [1966(e)], p. 399.

[270] For measurement and its content-increasing (or information-increasing) function see section 34 of [1934(b)] and [1959(a)].

[271] For a general criticism of thought experiments see the new Appendix *xi of my *L.Sc.D.* [1959(a)], esp. pp. 443 f.

[272] Like the assumption that the gas consists of *one* molecule *M*, the assumption that, without expenditure of energy or negentropy, we can slide a piston from the side into the cylinder, is freely used by my opponents in their proofs of the convertibility of knowledge and negentropy. It is harmless here, and it is not really needed: See n. 274 below.

[273] David Bohm, *Quantum Theory* (New York: Prentice-Hall, 1951), p. 608, refers to Szilard, but operates with many molecules. He does not, however, rely on Szilard's arguments but rather on the general idea that Maxwell's demon is incompatible with the law of entropy increase.

[274] See my paper, "Irreversibility; or Entropy since 1905" [1957 (f)], a paper in which I referred especially to Einstein's famous paper of 1905 on Brownian movement. In that paper I also criticized, among others, Szilard, though not via the thought experiment used here. I had first developed this thought experiment some time before 1957, and I lectured about it, on the same lines as in the text here, in 1962, on Professor E. L. Hill's invitation, in the physics department of the University of Minnesota.

[275] See P. K. Feyerabend, "On the Possibility of a Perpetuum Mobile of the Second Kind", in *Mind, Matter, and Method, Essays in Honor of Herbert Feigl,* ed. by P. K. Feyerabend and G. Maxwell (Minneapolis: University of Minnesota Press, 1966), pp. 409-12. I should mention that the idea of building a flap into the piston (see Fig. 3 above), to avoid the awkwardness of having to slide it in from the side, is a refinement that Feyerabend made to my original analysis of Szilard's thought experiment.

[276] Samuel Butler has suffered many wrongs from the evolutionists, including a serious wrong from Charles Darwin himself who, though greatly upset by it, never put things right. They were put right, as far as possible, by Charles's son Francis, after Butler's death. The story, which is a bit involved, deserves to be retold. See pp. 167-219 of Nora Barlow, ed., *The Autobiography of Charles Darwin* (London: Collins, 1958), esp. p. 219, where references to most of the other relevant material will be found.

[277] See [1945(a)], section 27; cp. [1957(g)] and later editions, esp. pp. 106-8.

[278] I am alluding to Schrödinger's remarks on evolutionary theory in *Mind and Matter*, especially those indicated by his phrase "Feigned Lamarckism"; see *Mind and Matter*, p. 26; and p. 118 of the combined reprint cited in n. 214 above.

[279] The lecture [1961(j)] was delivered on October 31, 1961, and the manuscript was deposited on the same day in the Bodleian Library. It now appears in a revised version, with an addendum, as Chap. 7 of my [1972(a)].

[280] See [1966(f)]; now Chap. 6 of [1972(a)].

[280]a See [1966(f)].

[281] See section 33 above, esp. n. 242.

[282] See *L.Sc.D.*, section 67.

[283] For the problem of "degrees of prediction" see F. A. Hayek, "Degrees of Explanation", first published in 1955 and now Chap. 1 of his *Studies in Philosophy, Politics and Economics* (London: Routledge & Kegan Paul, 1967); see esp. n. 4 on p. 9. For Darwinism and the production of "a great variety of structures", and for its irrefutability, see esp. p. 32.

[284] Darwin's theory of sexual selection is partly an attempt to explain falsifying instances of this theory; such things, for example, as the peacock's tail, or the stag's antlers. See the text before n. 286.

[285] For the problem of "explanation in principle" (or "of the principle") in contrast to "explanation in detail", see Hayek, *Philosophy, Politics and Economics*, Chap. 1, esp. section VI, pp. 11-14.

[286] David Lack makes this point in his fascinating book, *Darwin's Finches* (Cambridge: Cambridge University Press, 1947), p. 72: "... in Darwin's finches all the main beak differences between the species may be regarded as adaptations to difference in diet." (Footnote references to the behaviour of birds I owe to Arne Petersen.)

[287] As Lack so vividly describes it, *ibid.*, pp. 58 f., the *absence* of

a long tongue in the beak of a woodpeckerlike species of Darwin's finches does not prevent this bird from excavating in trunks and branches for insects—that is, it sticks to its taste; however, due to its particular anatomical disability it has developed a skill to meet this difficulty: "Having excavated, it picks up a cactus spine or twig, one or two inches long, and holding it lengthwise in its beak, pokes it up the crack, dropping the twig to seize the insect as it emerges." This striking behavioural trend may be a nongenetical "tradition" which has developed in that species with or without teaching among its members; it may also be a genetically entrenched behaviour pattern. That is to say, a genuine behavioural invention can take the place of an anatomic change. However this may be, this example shows how the behaviour of organisms can be a "spearhead" of evolution: a type of biological problem solving which may lead to the emergence of new forms and species.

[288] See now my 1971 Addendum, "A Hopeful Behavioural Monster", to my Spencer Lecture, Chap. 7 of [1972(a)], and Alister Hardy, *The Living Stream: A Restatement of Evolution Theory and Its Relation to the Spirit of Man* (London: Collins, 1965), Lecture VI.

[289] This is one of the main ideas of my Spencer Lecture, now Chap. 7 of [1972(a)].

[290] The theory of geographic separation or geographic speciation was first developed by Moritz Wagner in *Die Darwin'sche Theorie und das Migrationsgesetz der Organismen* (Leipzig: Duncker und Humblot, 1868); English translation by J. L. Laird, *The Darwinian Theory and the Law of Migration of Organisms* (London: Edward Stanford, 1873). See also Theodosius Dobzhansky, *Genetics and the Origin of Species*, 3d rev. ed. (New York: Columbia University Press, 1951), pp. 179-211.

[291] See [1966(f)], pp. 20-26, esp. pp. 24 f., point (11). Now [1972 (a)], p. 244.

[292] See [1970(l)], esp. pp. 5-10; [1972(a)], pp. 289-95.

[292a] The present and the next paragraphs of the text (and the corresponding notes) were inserted in 1975.

[292b] See Sir Alister Hardy, *The Living Stream* (cp. n. 288 above), esp. Lectures VI and VII. See also W. H. Thorpe, "The Evolutionary Significance of Habitat Selection", *The Journal of Animal Ecology*, 14 (1945), 67-70.

[293] Since I completed my *Autobiography* I have taken up a suggestion of John Eccles to call the third world "world 3"; see J. C. Eccles, *Facing Reality* (New York, Heidelberg and Berlin: Springer-Verlag, 1970). See also n. 7a above.

[294] This argument for some thing's reality—that we can take "cross bearings" which agree—is, I think, due to Winston Churchhill. See p. 43 of Chap. 2 of my *Obj. Kn.* [1972(a)].

[295] Cp. p. 15 of [1967(k)]: ". . . by and large I regard as excellent Landé's suggestion to call physically real what is 'kickable' (and able to kick back if kicked)."

[296] Take, for example, Einstein's misunderstanding of his own requirement of covariance (first challenged by Kretschmann), which had a long history before it was finally cleared up, mainly (I think) due to the efforts of Fock and Peter Havas. The relevant papers are Erich Kretschmann, "Über den physikalischen Sinn der Relativitätspostulate, A. Einsteins neue und seine ursprüngliche Relativitätstheorie", *Annalen der Physik*, 4th ser. **53** (1917), 575-614; and Einstein's reply, "Prinzipielles zur allgemeinen Relativitätstheorie", *ibid.*, **55** (1918), 241-44. See also V. A. Fock, *The Theory of Space, Time and Gravitation* (London: Pergamon Press, 1959; 2d rev. ed., Oxford, 1964); and Havas, "Four-Dimensional Formulations of Newtonian Mechanics and Their Relation to Relativity", (see n. 32 above).

[297] See [1968(r)], [1968(s)]; see also "A Realist View of Logic, Physics, and History" [1970(l)], and [1966(f)]. (These papers are now respectively Chaps. 4, 3, 8, 6 of [1972(a)].)

[298] The talk of "substances" arises from the problem of change ("What remains constant in change?") and from the attempt to answer *what-is?* questions. The old witticism that Bertrand Russell's grandmother plagued him with—"What is mind? No matter! What is matter? Never mind!"—seems to me not only to the point but perfectly adequate. Better ask: "What does mind?"

[299] The last two sentences may be regarded as containing an argument against panpsychism. The argument is, of course, inconclusive (since panpsychism is irrefutable), and it remains so even if it is strengthened by the following observation: even if we attribute conscious states to (say) all atoms, the problem of explaining the states of consciousness (such as recollection or anticipation) of higher animals remains as difficult as it was before, without this attribution.

[300] See my papers "Language and the Body-Mind Problem" [1953(a)] and "A Note on the Body-Mind Problem" [1955(c)]; now Chaps. 12 and 13 of [1963(a)].

[301] Wittgenstein ("The riddle does not exist": *Tractatus*, 6.5) exaggerated the gulf between the world of describable ("sayable") facts and the world of that which is deep and which cannot be said. There are gradations; moreover, the world of the sayable does not always lack depth. And if we think of depth, there is a gulf within

those things that can be said—between a cookery book and Copernicus's *De revolutionibus*—and there is a gulf within those things that cannot be said—between some piece of artistic tastelessness and a portrait by Holbein; and these gulfs may be far deeper than that between something that is sayable and something that is not. It is his facile solution of the problem of depth—the thesis "the deep is the unsayable"—which unites Wittgenstein the positivist with Wittgenstein the mystic. Incidentally, this thesis had long been traditional, especially in Vienna (and not merely among philosophers). See the quotation from Robert Reininger in *L.Sc.D.*, n. 4 to section 30. Many positivists agreed; for example, Richard von Mises, who was a great admirer of the mystic poet Rilke.

³⁰² David Miller suggests that I called in world 3 in order to redress the balance between worlds 1 and 2.

³⁰³ See sections 10 and 15 above.

³⁰⁴ After writing this I became acquainted with the second volume of Konrad Lorenz's collected papers (*Über tierisches und menschliches Verhalten,* Gesammelte Abhandlungen [Munich: R. Piper & Co. Verlag, 1967], Vol. II; see esp. pp. 361 f.). In these papers Lorenz criticizes, with a reference to Erich von Holst, the view that the delimitation between the mental and the physical is also one between the higher and the lower functions of control: some comparatively primitive processes (such as a bad toothache) are intensely conscious, while some highly controlled processes (such as the elaborate interpretation of sense stimuli) are unconscious, so that their result—perception—appears to us (wrongly) as just "given". This seems to me an important insight not to be overlooked in any theory of the body-mind problem. (On the other hand, I cannot imagine that the all-absorbing character of a bad toothache caused by a dying nerve has any biological value as a control function; and we are here interested in the hierarchical character of *controls*.)

³⁰⁵ R. W. Sperry ("The Great Cerebral Commissure", *Scientific American,* **210** [1964], 42-52; and "Brain Bisection and Mechanisms of Consciousness", in *Brain and Conscious Experience,* ed. by J. C. Eccles [Berlin, Heidelberg and New York: Springer-Verlag, 1966], pp. 298-313) warns us that we must not think that the separation is absolute: there is a certain amount of overspill to the other side of the brain. Nevertheless he writes, in the second paper mentioned, p. 300: "The same kind of right-left mental separation [reported about patients manipulating objects] is seen in tests involving vision. Recall that the right half of the visual field, along with the right hand, is represented together in the left hemisphere, and vice versa. Visual stimuli such as pictures, words, numbers, and geometric forms flashed on a screen directly in front of the subject and to the right

side of a central fixation point, so that they are projected to the dominant speech hemispheres, are all described and reported correctly with no special difficulty. On the other hand, similar material flashed to the left half of the visual field and hence into the minor hemisphere are completely lost to the talking hemisphere. Stimuli flashed to one half field seem to have no influence whatever, in tests to date, on the perception and interpretation of stimuli presented to the other half field."

[305]a (Added 1975.) See the most interesting book by A. D. De Groot, *Thought and Choice in Chess* (The Hague: Mouton, 1965; New York: Basic Books, 1966).

[306] Wolfgang Köhler, *The Place of Value in a World of Fact* (New York: Liveright, 1938). I have substituted "Values" and "Facts" for "Value" and "Fact", to indicate my stress on pluralism.

[307] See for this the end of the reply to Ernst Gombrich in my *Replies*.

[308] Schiller says something like this:
> Friends, what a pleasure to serve you! But I do so from fond inclination.
> Thus no virtue is mine, and I feel greatly aggrieved.
> What can I do about it? I must teach myself to abhor you,
> And, with disgust in my heart, serve you as duty commands.

[309] See the *Addendum* "Facts, Standards, and Truth" in *O.S.*, 4th ed. [1962(c)] and later editions, Vol. II.

Main Publications and Abbreviations of Titles

In the *Notes* the following abbreviations are used to refer to the Author's main publications. References in square brackets are to the *Select Bibliography*.

L.d.F.=*Logik der Forschung* 1934; 6th edn. (based on *L.Sc.D.*) 1976. See [1934(b)] and [1976(a)]; see also *L.Sc.D.*

O.S.=*The Open Society and Its Enemies*, vol. 1, *The Spell of Plato;* vol. 2, *The High Tide of Prophecy: Hegel, Marx, and The Aftermath* 1945; 10th impression 1974.
See [1945(b), (c)], [1950(a)], [1974(z_8)]. Translations into Dutch, Finnish, German, Italian, Japanese, Portuguese, Spanish, Turkish; forthcoming: French.

The Poverty=*The Poverty of Historicism* 1944/45; 1957, 8th impression 1974. See [1944(a), (b)], [1945(a)], [1957(g)], [1974(z_7)].
Translations into Arabic, Dutch, French, German, Italian, Japanese, Norwegian, Spanish.

L.Sc.D.=*The Logic of Scientific Discovery* 1959; 8th impression 1975. (Incorporating an English translation of *L.d.F.* [1934 (b)].) See [1959(a)], [1975(u)]. Translations into French, German, Italian, Japanese, Portuguese, Serbo-Croat, Spanish; forthcoming: Polish and Romanian.

C.&R.=*Conjectures and Refutations: The Growth of Scientific Knowledge* 1963; 5th impression 1974.
See [1963(a)], [1974(z_4)]. Translations into Italian and Spanish; forthcoming: German and Japanese.

Obj.Kn.=*Objective Knowledge: An Evolutionary Approach* 1972; 4th impression 1975.
See [1972(a)], [1975(r)]. Translations into German, Italian, Portuguese, Spanish, Japanese.

Replies=Replies to my Critics, in Paul A. Schilpp (ed.), *The Philosophy of Karl Popper*, vols, 14/I and 14/II in *The Library of Living Philosophers* (La Salle, Ill.: Open Court Publishing Co., 1974), pp. 961 to 1197.

Select Bibliography

This Bibliography follows in its numbering (such as "[1945(a)]") the "Bibliography of the Writings of Karl Popper", compiled by Troels Eggers Hansen for *The Philosophy of Karl Popper*, vols. 14/I and 14/II of *The Library of Living Philosophers,* ed. by Paul A. Schilpp (La Salle, Ill.: Open Court Publishing Co., 1974), pp. 1199-1287. Some items have been omitted and new items added.

1925 (a) "Über die Stellung des Lehrers zu Schule und Schüler. *Schulreform* (Vienna), 4, pp. 204-208.
Gesellschaftliche oder individualistische Erziehung?",

1927 (a) "Zur Philosophie des Heimatgedankens", *Die Quelle* (Vienna), 77, pp. 899-908.
(b) " *'Gewohnheit' und 'Gesetzerlebnis' in der Erziehung*", unpublished, a thesis presented (unfinished) to the Pedagogic Institute of the City of Vienna.

1928 (a) *Zur Methodenfrage der Denkpsychologie,* unpublished; dissertation submitted for a doctorate of the Philosophical Faculty of the University of Vienna.

1931 (a) "Die Gedächtnispflege unter dem Gesichtspunkt der Selbsttätigkeit", *Die Quelle* (Vienna), 81, pp. 607-619.

1932 (a) "Pädagogische Zeitschriftenschau", *Die Quelle* (Vienna), 82, pp. 301-303; 580-582; 646-647; 712-713; 778-781; 846-849; 930-931.

1933 (a) "Ein Kriterium des empirischen Charakters theoretischer Systeme", a letter to the editor, *Erkenntnis*, 3, pp. 426-427.

1934 (b) *Logik der Forschung*, Julius Springer Verlag, Vienna (with the imprint "1935").

1935 (a) " 'Induktionslogik' und 'Hypothesenwahrscheinlichkeit' ", *Erkenntnis*, 5, pp. 170-172.

1938 (a) "A Set of Independent Axioms for Probability", *Mind*, 47, pp. 275-277.

1940 (a) "What is Dialectic?", *Mind*, 49, pp. 403-426.

1944 (a) "The Poverty of Historicism, I", *Economica*, 11, pp. 86-103.
(b) "The Poverty of Historicism, II. A Criticism of Historicist Methods", *Economica*, 11, pp. 119-137.

1945 (a) "The Poverty of Historicism, III", *Economica*, **12**, pp. 69-89.
    (b) *The Open Society and Its Enemies*, volume I, *The Spell of Plato*, George Routledge & Sons, Ltd., London.
    (c) *The Open Society and Its Enemies*, volume II, *The High Tide of Prophecy: Hegel, Marx, and The Aftermath*, George Routledge & Sons Ltd., London.
    (e) "Research and the University: A Statement by a Group of Teachers in the University of New Zealand", *The Caxton Press* (Christchurch, New Zealand); written in co-operation with R. S. Allan, J. C. Eccles, H. G. Forder, J. Packer, and H. N. Parton.

1946 (b) "Why are the Calculuses of Logic and Arithmetic Applicable to Reality?", *Aristotelian Society, Supplementary Volume XX: Logic and Reality*, Harrison and Sons Ltd., London, pp. 40-60.

1947 (a) "New Foundations for Logic", *Mind*, **56**, pp. 193-235.
    (b) "Logic Without Assumptions", *Proceedings of the Aristotelian Society*, XLVII, pp. 251-292.
    (c) "Functional Logic without Axioms or Primitive Rules of Inference", *Koninklijke Nederlandsche Akademie van Wetenschappen, Proceedings of the Section of Sciences* (Amsterdam), **50**, pp. 1214-1224, and *Indagationes Mathematicae*, **9**, pp. 561-571.

1948 (b) "On the Theory of Deduction, Part I, Derivation and its Generalizations." *Koninklijke Nederlandsche Akademie van Wetenschappen, Proceedings of the Section of Sciences* (Amsterdam), **51**, pp. 173-183, and *Indagationes Mathematicae*, **10**, pp. 44-54.
    (c) "On the Theory of Deduction, Part II. The Definitions of Classical and Intuitionist Negation", *Koninklijke Nederlandsche Akademie van Wetenschappen, Proceedings of the Section of Sciences* (Amsterdam), **51**, pp. 322-331, and *Indigationes Mathematicae*, **10**, pp. 111-120.
    (d) "Prediction and Prophecy and their Significance for Social Theory", *Library of the Tenth International Congress of Philosophy*, **1**: *Proceedings of the Tenth International Congress of Philosophy*, edited by E. W. Beth, H. J. Pos, and J. H. A. Hollak, North-Holland Publishing Company, Amsterdam, pp. 82-91.
    (e) "The Trivialization of Mathematical Logic", *ibid.*, pp. 722-727.
    (f) "What can Logic do for Philosophy?" *Aristotelian Society, Supplementary Volume XXII: Logical Positivism and Ethics*, Harrison and Sons Ltd., London, pp. 141-154.

1949 (d) "Naturgesetze und theoretische Systeme", *Gesetz und Wirklichkeit*, edited by Simon Moser, Tyrolia Verlag, Innsbruck and Vienna, pp. 43-60.

1950 (a) *The Open Society and Its Enemies*, Princeton University Press.
     (b) "Indeterminism in Quantum Physics and in Classical Physics, Part I", *The British Journal for the Philosophy of Science*, 1, pp. 117-133.
     (c) "Indeterminism in Quantum Physics and in Classical Physics, Part II", *The British Journal for the Philosophy of Science*, 1, pp. 173-195.
     (d) *De Vrije Samenleving en Haar Vijanden*, F. G. Kroonder, Bussum, Holland.

1952 (a) *The Open Society and Its Enemies*, second English edition, Routledge & Kegan Paul, London.

1953 (a) "Language and the Body-Mind Problem", *Proceedings of the XIth International Congress of Philosophy*, 7, North-Holland Publishing Company, Amsterdam, pp. 101-107.
     (d) "A Note on Berkeley as Precursor of Mach", *The British Journal for the Philosophy of Science*, 4, pp. 26-36.

1954 (c) "Self-Reference and Meaning in Ordinary Language", *Mind*, 63, pp. 162-169.

1955 (c) "A Note on the Body-Mind Problem. Reply to Professor Wilfrid Sellars", *Analysis*, 15, pp. 131-135.
     (d) "A Note on Tarski's Definition of Truth", *Mind*, 64, pp. 388-391.

1956 (b) "The Arrow of Time", *Nature*, 177, p. 538.
     (g) "Irreversibility and Mechanics", *Nature*, 178, p. 382.

1957 (a) "Philosophy of Science: A Personal Report", *British Philosophy in the Mid-Century: A Cambridge Symposium*, edited by C. A. Mace, George Allen and Unwin, London, pp. 155-191.
     (d) "Irreversible Processes in Physical Theory", *Nature*, 179, p. 1297.
     (e) "The Propensity Interpretation of the Calculus of Probability, and the Quantum Theory", *Observation and Interpretation; A Symposium of Philosophers and Physicists: Proceedings of the Ninth Symposium of the Colston Research Society held in the University of Bristol, April 1st-April 4th, 1957*, edited by S. Körner in collaboration with M. H. L. Pryce, Butterworths Scientific Publications, London, pp. 65-70, 88-89.

(f) "Irreversibility; or Entropy since 1905", *The British Journal for the Philosophy of Science*, **8**, pp. 151-155.

(g) *The Poverty of Historicism*, Routledge & Kegan Paul, London, and The Beacon Press, Boston, Mass.

(h) *The Open Society and Its Enemies*, third edition, Routledge & Kegan Paul, London.

(i) "The Aim of Science", *Ratio*: (Oxford), **1**, pp. 24-35.

(j) "Über die Zielsetzung der Erfahrungswissenchaft", *Ratio* (Frankfurt a.M.), **1**, pp. 21-31.

(k) *Der Zauber Platons: Die offene Gesellschaft und ihre Feinde*, Band I, Francke Verlag, Bern.

(l) "Probability Magic or Knowledge out of Ignorance", *Dialectica*, **11**, pp. 354-372.

1958 (b) "Irreversible Processes in Physical Theory", *Nature*, **181**, pp. 402-403.

(c) "Das Problem der Nichtwiderlegbarkeit von Philosophien", *Deutsche Universitätszeitung (Göttingen)*, **13**, pp. 7-13.

(f) "On the Status of Science and of Metaphysics. Two Radio Talks: (i) Kant and the Logic of Experience. (ii) The Problem of the Irrefutability of Philosophical Theories", *Ratio* (Oxford), **1**, pp. 97-115.

(g) "Über die Möglichkeit der Erfahrungswissenschaft und der Metaphysik, Zwei Rundfunkvorträge: (i) Kant und die Möglichkeit der Erfahrungswissenschaft. (ii) Über die Nichtwiderlegbarkeit philosophischer Theorien", *Ratio* (Frankfurt a.M.), **2**, pp. 1-16.

(i) *Falsche Propheten: Hegel Marx und die Folgen, Die offene Gesellschaft und ihre Feinde*, Band II, Francke Verlag, Bern.

1959 (a) *The Logic of Scientific Discovery*, Hutchinson & Co., London; Basic Books Inc., New York.

(e) "The Propensity Interpretation of Probability", *The British Journal for the Philosophy of Science*, **10**, pp. 25-42.

(g) "Woran glaubt der Westen?", in *Erziehung zur Freiheit*, edited by Albert Hunold, Eugen Rentsch Verlag, Stuttgart, pp. 237-262.

(k) "Critical Rationalism", in *Philosophy for a Time of Crisis: An Interpretation with Key Writings by Fifteen Great Modern Thinkers*, edited by Adrienne Koch, Dutton & Co., New York, pp. 262-275.

1960 (d) "On the Sources of Knowledge and of Ignorance", *Proceedings of The British Academy*, **46**, pp. 39-71.

1961 (d) "Selbstbefreiung durch das Wissen", in *Der Sinn der Geschichte*, edited by Leonhard Reinisch, C. H. Beck Verlag, Munich, 1961, pp. 100-116. (English translation [1968 (t)].)

(f) *On the Sources of Knowledge and of Ignorance*, Annual Philosophical Lecture, Henriette Hertz Trust, British Academy, Oxford University Press, London.

(h) "Philosophy and Physics", *Atti del XII Congresso Internazionale di Filosofia*, **2**, G. C. Sansoni Editore, Florence, pp. 367-374.

(j) *Evolution and the Tree of Knowledge*, Herbert Spencer Lecture, delivered on October 30th, 1961, in Oxford. (Now Chapter 7 of [1972(a)].)

1962 (c) *The Open Society and Its Enemies*, fourth English edition, Routledge & Kegan Paul, London.

(d) *The Open Society and Its Enemies*, Routledge Paperbacks, Routledge & Kegan Paul, London.

(f) "Julius Kraft 1898-1960", *Ratio* (Oxford), **4**, pp. 2-10.

(k) "Die Logik der Sozialwissenschaften", in *Kölner Zeitschrift für Soziologie und Sozialpsychologie*, Heft, **2**, pp. 233-248. (See also [1969(m)] and [1976(b)].)

1963 (a) *Conjectures and Refutations: The Growth of Scientific Knowledge*, Routledge & Kegan Paul, London; Basic Books Inc., New York.

(h) "Science: Problems, Aims, Responsibilities", *Federation Proceedings* (Baltimore), **22**, pp. 961-972.

(l) *The Open Society and Its Enemies*, Princeton University Press, Princeton, N.J.

(m) *The Open Society and Its Enemies*, The Academy Library, Harper & Row, New York and Evanston.

1964 (a) *The Poverty of Historicism*, The Academy Library, Harper & Row, New York and Evanston.

1965 (f) "Time's Arrow and Entropy", *Nature*, **207**, pp. 233-234.

1966 (a) *The Open Society and Its Enemies*, fifth English edition, Routledge Paperbacks, Routledge & Kegan Paul, London.

(e) *Logik der Forschung*, second edition, J. C. B. Mohr (Paul Siebeck), Tübingen.

(f) *Of Clouds and Clocks: An Approach to the Problem of Rationality and the Freedom of Man*, Washington University Press, St. Louis, Missouri. (Now in [1972(a)].)

(g) "A Theorem on Truth-Content", *Mind, Matter and Method: Essays in Philosophy and Science in Honor of Herbert Feigl*, edited by Paul K. Feyerabend and Grover Maxwell, University of Minnesota Press, Minneapolis, Minnesota, pp. 343-353.

(i) "Historical Explanation: An Interview with Sir Karl Popper", *University of Denver Magazine*, **3**, pp. 4-7.

1967 (b) "Time's Arrow and Feeding on Negentropy", *Nature*, **213**, p. 320.

(d) "La rationalité et le statut du principe de rationalité", *Les Fondements Philosophiques des Systemes Economiques: Textes de Jaques Rueff et assais rédigés en son honneur 23 août 1966*, edited by Emil M. Classen, Payot, Paris, pp. 142-150.

(e) "Zum Thema Freiheit", in *Die Philosophie und die Wissenschaften: Simon Moser zum 65. Geburtstag*, edited by Ernst Oldemeyer, Anton Hain, Meisenheim am Glan, pp. 1-12.

(h) "Structural Information and the Arrow of Time", *Nature*, **214**, p. 322.

(k) "Quantum Mechanics without 'The Observer'", *Quantum Theory and Reality*, edited by Mario Bunge, Springer-Verlag, Berlin, Heidelberg, New York, pp. 7-44.

(t) "Einstein's Influence on My View of Science: An Interview", in *Einstein: The Man and his Achievement*, edited by G. J. Whitrow, B.B.C., London, pp. 23-28.

1968 (e) "Is there an Epistemological Problem of Perception?", *Proceedings of the International Colloquium in the Philosophy of Science*, **3**: *Problems in the Philosophy of Science*, edited by Imre Lakatos and Alan Musgrave, North-Holland Publishing Company (Amsterdam), pp. 163-164.

(i) "Theories, Experience, and Probabilistic Intuitions", *Proceedings of the International Colloquium in the Philosophy of Science*, **2**: *The Problem of Inductive Logic*, edited by Imre Lakatos, North-Holland Publishing Company (Amsterdam), pp. 285-303.

(r) "On the Theory of the Objective Mind", *Akten des XIV Internationalen Kongresses für Philosophie*, **1**, University of Vienna, Verlag Herder, Vienna, pp. 25-53.

(s) "Epistemology Without a Knowing Subject", *Proceedings of the Third International Congress for Logic, Methodology and Philosophy of Science: Logic, Methodology and Philosophy of Science III*, edited by B. van Rootselaar and J. F. Staal, North-Holland Publishing Company, Amsterdam, pp. 333-373.

(t) "Emancipation through Knowledge", in *The Humanist Outlook*, edited by A. J. Ayer, Pemberton Publishing Company, London, pp. 281-296.

1969 (e) *Logik der Forschung*, third edition, J. C. B. Mohr (Paul Siebeck), Tübingen.

(h) *Conjectures and Refutations, The Growth of Scientific Knowledge*, third edition, Routledge & Kegan Paul, London.

(j) "A Pluralist Approach to the Philosophy of History", *Roads to Freedom: Essays in Honour of Friedrich A. von Hayek*, edited by Erich Streissler, Gottfried Haberler, Friedrich A. Lutz and Fritz Machlup, Routledge & Kegan Paul, London, pp. 181-200.

(k) "The Aim of Science", *Contemporary Philosophy*: *A Survey*, edited by Raymond Klibansky, III: *Metaphysics, Phenomenology, Language and Structure*, La Nuova Italia Editrice, Florence, pp. 129-142.

(m) "Die Logik der Sozialwissenschaften", in *Der Positivismusstreit in der deutschen Soziologie*, edited by H. Maus and F. Fürstenberg, Hermann Luchterhand Verlag, Neuwied and Berlin, pp. 103-123. (See also [1976(b)].)

1970 (d) "Plato, *Timaeus* 54E-55A", *The Classical Review*, XX, pp. 4-5.

(l) "A Realist View of Logic, Physics, and History", *Physics, Logic and History*, edited by Wolfgang Yourgrau and Allen D. Breck, Plenum Press, New York and London, pp. 1-30, and 35-37.

1971 (g) "Revolution oder Reform?", in *Revolution oder Reform? Herbert Marcuse und Karl Popper — Eine Konfrontation*, edited by Franz Stark, Kösel-Verlag, Munich, pp. 3, 9-10, 22-29, 34-39, 41. (English translation [1972(f)].)

(i) "Conjectural Knowledge: My Solution of the Problem of Induction", *Revue Internationale de Philosophie*, No. 95-96, **25** fasc. 1-2, pp. 167-197.

(l) "Conversation with Karl Popper", in *Modern British Philosophy* by Bryan Magee, Secker & Warburg, London, pp. 66-82.

(n) "Particle Annihilation and the Argument of Einstein, Podolsky, and Rosen", *Perspectives in Quantum Theory: Essays in Honor of Alfred Landé*, edited by Wolfgang Yourgrau and Alwyn van der Merwe, M.I.T. Press, Cambridge, Mass., and London, pp. 182-198.

1972 (a) *Objective Knowledge: An Evolutionary Approach*, Clarendon Press, Oxford.

(f) "On Reason & the Open Society: A Conversation", *Encounter*, **38**, No. 5, pp. 13-18.

1973 (a) "Indeterminism is Not Enough", *Encounter*, **40**, No. 4, pp. 20-26.

(n) *Die offene Gesellschaft und ihre Feinde*, volumes I and II, third edition, Francke Verlag, Bern and Munich.

1974 (b) "Autobiography of Karl Popper", in *The Philosophy of Karl Popper*, in *The Library of Living Philosophers*, edited by P. A. Schilpp, volume I, Open Court Publishing Co., La Salle, pp. 3-181.

(c) "Replies to my Critics", in *The Philosophy of Karl Popper*, in *The Library of Living Philosophers*, edited by P. A. Schilpp, volume II, Open Court Publishing Co., La Salle, pp. 961-1197.

(z_2) "Scientific Reduction and the Essential Incompleteness of All Science", in *Studies in the Philosophy of Biology*, edited by F. J. Ayala and T. Dobzhansky, Macmillan, London, pp. 259-284.

(z_4) *Conjectures and Refutations*, fifth edition, Routledge & Kegan Paul, London.

(z_7) *The Poverty of Historicism*, eighth impression, Routledge & Kegan Paul, London.

(z_8) *The Open Society and Its Enemies*, tenth impression, Routledge & Kegan Paul, London.

1975 (o) "How I See Philosophy", in *The Owl of Minerva. Philosophers on Philosophy*, edited by C. T. Bontempo and S. J. Odell, McGraw-Hill, New York, pp. 41-55.

(p) "The Rationality of Scientific Revolutions", in *Problems of Scientific Revolution. Scientific Progress and Obstacles to Progress in the Sciences, The Herbert Spencer Lectures 1973*, edited by Rom Harré, Clarendon Press, Oxford, pp. 72-101.

(r) *Objective Knowledge: An Evolutionary Approach.* Fourth impression, Clarendon Press, Oxford.

(t) "Wissenschaft und Kritik", in *Idee und Wirklichkeit: 30 Jahre Europäisches Forum Alpbach*, Springer-Verlag, Vienna and New York, pp. 65-75.

(u) *The Logic of Scientific Discovery*, eighth impression, Hutchinson, London.

1976 (a) *Logik der Forschung*, sixth revised impression, J. C. B. Mohr (Paul Siebeck), Tübingen.

(b) "The Logic of the Social Sciences", in *The Positivist Dispute in German Sociology*, Heinemann Educational, London, pp. 87-104.

(c) "Reason or Revolution?", in *The Positivist Dispute in German Sociology*, Heinemann Educational, London, pp. 288-300.

Index

COMPILED BY J. SHËARMUR

For reasons of space, entries for related terms are usually conflated. Thus for falsifiability see falsification, for materialism see matter, for Marxism see Marx, etc. References to discussions of Popper's publications will be found under the (shortened) title, e.g. under "Open Society". Nn introduces references to note numbers.